FIELDING'S
BURLESQUE DRAMA

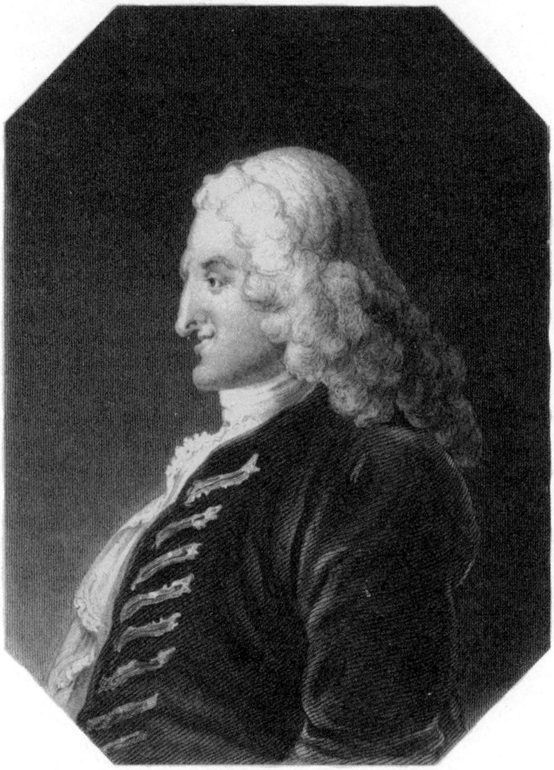

FIELDING'S BURLESQUE DRAMA

ITS PLACE IN THE TRADITION

BY PETER LEWIS

FOR THE UNIVERSITY OF DURHAM
Edinburgh University Press

© Peter Lewis 1987

Edinburgh University Press
22 George Square, Edinburgh

Printed in Great Britain by
Redwood Burn Limited,
Trowbridge, Wilts

British Library Cataloguing
  in Publication Data
Lewis, Peter
Fielding's burlesque drama—
  (University of Durham series)
1. Fielding, Henry—
  Dramatic works
I. Title   II. Series
822.5   PR3458.D7
ISBN 0 85224 542 4

Contents

	Preface	vi
	List of Plates	vii
1.	Introduction	1
2.	The Importance of *The Rehearsal*	11
3.	After Buckingham: Thomas Duffett and other Minor Writers	24
4.	The Contribution of John Gay	36
5.	*The Author's Farce*	86
6.	*Tom Thumb* and *The Tragedy of Tragedies*	111
7.	*The Covent-Garden Tragedy*	135
8.	*Pasquin* and *Tumble-Down Dick*	150
9.	*Eurydice, The Historical Register for the Year 1736,* and *Eurydice Hiss'd*	181
10.	Conclusion	203
	Index	215

Preface

I owe a considerable debt of gratitude to all those who stimulated my interest in the drama and literature of the Restoration and the eighteenth century and who encouraged my research, especially the late Professor Douglas Grant, Professor A. Norman Jeffares, Professor Cecil Price, and Professor Roger Sharrock. In a different way, I am greatly indebted to the various inhabitants and frequenters of the old Research Room in the School of English at the University of Leeds where I began work on the drama of the period, particularly Margaret Clayton, Lloyd Fernando, Geoffrey Hill, Jack Healy, Brendan Kennelly, and Jon Silkin. I should like to thank Professor T. W. Craik and Professor J. R. Watson for their interest in this book when I was preparing the final draft and for reading the typescript with an eye for improvements. The financial assistance I have received from the Staff Travel and Research Fund of the University of Durham to enable me to work in London has been an enormous help, and publication of the book in its present form would not have been possible without the support of the University's Publication Board; I am deeply grateful for this support. In assisting me to find suitable contemporary prints for inclusion in this book, the staff of the Department of Prints and Drawings in the British Museum were most obliging, and the prints are reproduced by courtesy of the Trustees of the British Museum, the British Library and the Mansell Collection. In order to avoid a deluge of endnotes, I have refrained from providing detailed page and line references for every quotation from the dramatic texts mentioned in this book. Except where otherwise noted, as in the case of plays by the principal authors under discussion, quotations from Restoration and Augustan plays are normally taken from the first, and often only, edition.

List of Plates

Frontispiece: Henry Fielding (Mansell Collection)

1. Scene from Buckingham's *The Rehearsal* (British Library)
2. Scene from Settle's *The Empress of Morocco* (British Library)
3. Scene from Handel's *Flavio* (British Museum)
4. (a) Scene from Gay's *The Beggar's Opera* by Hogarth
   (b) Key identifying figures in the scene (Mansell Collection)
5. 'The Beggar's Opera Burlesqued' (British Museum)
6. New Haymarket Theatre or Little Theatre in the Haymarket (Mansell Collection)
7. Scene from Johnson's *The Blazing Comet* (British Museum)
8. 'Masquerade Ticket' by Hogarth (Mansell Collection)
9. Scene from Theobald's *Perseus and Andromeda* (British Library)
10. Scene from Fielding's *The Tragedy of Tragedies* by Hogarth (Mansell Collection)
11. 'A Harlot's Progress' (pl.1) by Hogarth (Mansell Collection)
12. 'Author's Benefit Ticket' for Fielding's *Pasquin* (Mansell Collection)
13. 'The Judgment of the Queen o' Common Sense Address'd to Henry Fielding' (British Museum)
14. 'Rich's Glory, or His Triumphant Entry into Covent Garden' (Mansell Collection)
15. 'Punch Kicking Apollo' (British Museum)
16. 'A Just View of the British Stage, or Three Heads Are Better than None' by Hogarth (British Museum)
17. 'The Stage Mutiny' by John Laguerre (British Museum)
18. Farinelli (British Museum)

List of Plates   viii

19. 'R-b-n's Progress in Eight Scenes' (pl.8) (British Museum)
20. 'The Festival of the Golden Rump' (British Museum)
21. Scene from Carey's *Chrononhotonthologos* (British Museum)

Plates 1–9 *follow p.* 104 *and Plates* 10–21 *follow p.* 168

Introduction

In English theatre history, the dates 1660 and 1737 stand out as prominent landmarks. One immediate consequence of the restoration of the monarchy in 1660 was the reopening of the theatres and the revitalizing of the English dramatic tradition after the mid-century period of closure and prohibition. Just over three-quarters of a century later, the Licensing Act of 1737, brought in by Sir Robert Walpole's Government, imposed a strict censorship on the stage and closed the non-patent theatres in London. The effect was to stifle some of the most innovative developments in English drama of the previous ten years and to bring to an end Henry Fielding's short but prolific and enterprising career as a playwright and a man of the theatre.

Fielding's subsequent achievement as a novelist so overshadows his work for the stage that his plays have suffered neglect in comparison with his fiction. Only his *Tom Thumb* plays (including *The Tragedy of Tragedies*) are at all well known today, and productions of his plays are very rare indeed. Yet during the 1730s prior to the Licensing Act, Fielding became one of the most important figures in London theatrical life, and in any history of eighteenth-century English drama he must loom large as an outstanding playwright.

Despite his considerable dramatic output, Fielding never attempted tragedy, preferring to burlesque contemporary versions of the genre except for the new 'bourgeois' tragedy associated with George Lillo, whom Fielding admired and championed. The nearest approach to the tragic in his theatrical oeuvre is in such plays as *The Modern Husband*, ostensibly comedies but more accurately described as *drames* or 'problem plays', which explains why they appealed to George Bernard Shaw. As Fielding's novels indicate, his literary gifts were those of a writer much more at home serving the Comic rather than the Tragic Muse, and led him naturally to comedy, farce, satire, parody, and burlesque. He wrote orthodox comedies, some more satirical than others, as well as 'serious' comedies approximating to the *drame*. He translated and adapted French comic drama, both comedy and farce, and wrote farces, ballad farces, and ballad operas of his own. But he also wrote a number of irregular plays that are not adequately described as 'comedy', 'farce', or 'ballad opera'. These are his dramatic burlesques and satires: *The Author's Farce, The Tragedy of Tragedies (Tom Thumb), The Covent-Garden Tragedy, Pasquin, Tumble-Down Dick, The Historical Register for the Year 1736, Eurydice,* and *Eurydice Hiss'd*. Although these form a decidedly amorphous group, the differences between them often being more evident than the resemblances, they all owe something to the tradition of burlesque drama Fielding inherited from his Restoration predecessors and Augustan contemporaries. It is the aim of this study to examine Fielding's debt to the burlesque tradition and his individual treatment and transformation of it in this group of plays.[1]

Only one play written before the closing of the theatres in 1642, Beaumont's *The Knight of the Burning Pestle* (1607), can properly be called a dramatic burlesque. Traces of burlesque can, of course, be found in a number of pre-1642 plays, including *A Midsummer Night's Dream* and *Hamlet*, and the device of a play within a play, often the mainstay of post-1660 burlesque plays, was used extensively by Shakespeare and his contemporaries. Yet only in Beaumont's play is burlesque central rather than peripheral or incidental. Examples of burlesque poetry and prose in Elizabethan and Jacobean literature are rare too, although not as few and far between as in the case of drama.[2]

The period between 1660 and 1737, which corresponds more or less exactly to the greatest age of English satirical writing, is particularly rich in burlesque drama. This is not surprising since burlesque, like parody, has affinities with satire even though it is not necessarily satirical. Like literary parody, dramatic burlesque can range from gentle playfulness to uncompromising ridicule; the attitude of the burlesquer or the parodist to what he is burlesquing or parodying may be hostile, but at the other extreme it can be wryly affectionate. During the Restoration and Augustan periods, burlesque was often but by no means invariably applied as a critical corrective. All literary and dramatic forms and works, whether good, bad, or indifferent, are capable of being parodied and burlesqued by determined exponents of these methods; masterpieces, no less than trash, can be grist to their mill. But for burlesque drama to have flourished so successfully at this time, one essential requirement was the existence of a greater variety of theatrical forms than had been the case in the first half of the seventeenth century. The proliferation of dramatic genres towards the end of this century and especially at the beginning of the following one presented far more potential targets to the burlesquer than ever before, and furthermore a number of these invited burlesque in a way that the comedies and tragedies of Shakespeare and his contemporaries did not.

Tragedy, for example, laid itself increasingly open to attack as it became more elevated, heroic, and neoclassical, and burlesque was the most effective instrument of humorous and deflationary criticism available.

The upsurge of burlesque writing that followed the Restoration was mainly due to the Continental (particularly French) influence which crossed the Channel with Charles II. On the Continent the development of burlesque poetry in the seventeenth century was a comically irreverent response to the domination of neoclassicism, and at first took the form of travesties of classical literature, especially the *Aeneid*. In the middle of the century Scarron published his influential burlesque of Virgil's epic, *Le Virgile travesti*, in which the characters and events of the *Aeneid* are transformed into low comedy. Scarron's purpose was two-fold. He provided an amusing criticism of his immediate target, the *Aeneid*, but by using racy octosyllabics as opposed to the sedate alexandrines of French neoclassical poetry he also cocked a snook at the self-conscious solemnity and pretentious high-mindedness of some of his contemporaries by the oblique method of attacking Virgil. Scarron's success quickly led to a cult of burlesque poetry in France, some of it being classical travesty like *Le Virgile travesti* itself, and some of it being social, political, and personal satire employing Scarron's methods. The popularity of this kind of burlesque, in which a low style is applied to elevated subject matter, led neoclassical critics such as Boileau to condemn it for its flippancy and its disrespect for the classics, and to recommend mock-heroic, in which a high style is applied to unworthy subject matter, as a more dignified alternative for comic poetry.

Soon after the Restoration, such English poets as Samuel Butler and Charles Cotton naturalized the French burlesque idiom, using it for both classical travesty and topical satire. Butler wrote his anti-Puritan satire, *Hudibras*, in octosyllabic couplets with comic rhymes, a verse form subsequently called 'burlesque' in Restoration and Augustan England.[3] Identical in method and style although otherwise different are the numerous classical travesties in which such poets as Homer, Ovid, and Virgil are subjected to burlesque treatment, the most popular being Cotton's imitation of Scarron, *Scarronides; or, Virgile travestie*. The real difference between Scarron and Cotton lies in the difference between France and England. Although neoclassicism was very influential in England after 1660, it had less of a cultural stranglehold than it did in France, and consequently classical travesty was not as much an assault on critical and theoretical orthodoxy in England as it was in France. Cotton's English burlesque of Virgil therefore lacked some of the contemporary significance that Scarron's French burlesque possessed.

Burlesque reached the Restoration stage not long after the reopening of the theatres and before the publication of *Scarronides* (1664–65) in Sir William Davenant's *The Playhouse To Be Let* (1663). During the first act of this play, the Poet advocates burlesque as a new kind of comic drama likely to appeal to audiences because of its novelty, and the final act is devoted to a burlesque playlet featuring Caesar, Ptolemy, Antony and Cleopatra. Davenant employs a longer line than Butler (octosyllabics were very rarely used in burlesque plays); hendecasyllabic couplets with double rhymes, as in the Eunuch's expository speech near the opening, is his chosen verse form:

> A cruel wight, whose name is Mark Anthony,
> So hard of heart that it is held all boney,
> Is here arriv'd for love of our black Gypsy,
> On Cleopatra he has cast a sheep's-eye.
> And Caesar too, with many a stout tarpauling,
> Landed with him and comes a caterwawling.   (v)

As in *Scarronides* the humour derives from the debasement of characters usually rendered as noble and magnificent to farcical stereotypes, but although a classical travesty Davenant's playlet is not based on a classical work. Its immediate source was the central part of Katherine Phillips' contemporaneous neoclassical tragedy *Pompey* (1663), a version of Corneille's *Pompée*. This does not mean, however, that Davenant was attempting to ridicule contemporary drama by burlesque imitation or that his caricatures of great Romans and Egyptians have a satirical purpose. He follows a couple of scenes in *Pompey* quite closely, but he also introduces completely extraneous material and characters such as Antony and Cleopatra. The satirical potential of Davenant's method is obvious, but he himself is exploiting burlesque principally for light-hearted entertainment and sheer fun. Like most English writers of classical travesty at the time, he is not criticizing another work but transforming it into a novel and fashionable form of comic writing.

In considering the subsequent development of burlesque drama, it is important to distinguish between those, such as Davenant's, which are harmless comic extravaganzas based on classical works or stories, and those, including the next English burlesque play, *The Rehearsal* (1671) by George Villiers, Second Duke of Buckingham, that apply the same method to contemporary dramatic forms and specific plays but with a manifestly satirical purpose. John Wright's unperformed *Mock-Thyestes* (1674), written as a scholarly diversion and without any satirical intention after he had made a serious translation of Seneca's *Thyestes*, is a good example of a classical travesty in dramatic form having no reference to the contemporary stage. The burlesque play in Hudibrastic couplets follows the original closely, but both the characters and the action are vulgar versions of those in Seneca's tragedy, these lines spoken by Megaera to

Tantalus being not untypical:

> Allons; and stand not thus hum drum:
> Or Faith I'le run this Pin i' your bum.
> . . .
> Well, since I can't this way prevail,
> I'le try now to perswade your *Tail*.
> Your *Toby* I'le so feaze with this
> Rod that has lain three weeks in piss,
> That you shall begg the thing to do,
> Before we part, and thank me too. (1)

Less crude and written in decasyllabics but otherwise similar is the considerably later fragment of burlesque tragedy called *Andromeda* in the last act of John Durant Breval's comedy *The Play is the Plot* (1718), which he later converted into a highly successful afterpiece, *The Strolers*, by isolating the scenes dealing with the travelling actors who perform *Andromeda*. The inner play itself, based on the love story of Perseus and Andromeda, is a witty and accomplished piece of non-satirical burlesque writing particularly notable for its double and triple rhymes; this speech by Cepheus to Perseus illustrates its flavour:

> Most Valiant Sir, we beg your further stay
> At this our Court of *Æth-i-o-pi-a*,
> Where you have gain'd such Fame, and charm'd us all
> By your high Worth, and Feats Heroicall;
> We have not us'd you quite so ill, I trow,
> Tho' you have kept your self Incognito;
> Nor shew'd so little Complaisance, I hope,
> That you shou'd thus uncourteously elope;
> Just when my Daughter's Wedding too is near;
> *En Verité*, 'twould not be Cavalier:
> Then pray pull off your Boots, and *Beauveroy*,
> For, gentle Knight, you shall not go, *ma foy*. (v, i)

However, since contemporary tragedies, operas, and pantomimes often used classical subject matter, a classical travesty could easily be a satirical burlesque as well. An obvious example is Fielding's burlesque of pantomime, *Tumble-Down Dick* (1736), in which the travesty of the Phaethon story is simultaneously a parodic satire of a popular pantomime, *The Fall of Phaeton*, incorporating a solemn dramatization of the myth. In other cases, such as John Gay's *Achilles* (1733), a comic version of the Greek warrior's stay on Scyros while disguised as a female, classical travesty is less fully integrated with satirical burlesque so that the criticism directed against a dramatic form, in this instance Italian opera, is intermittent rather than systematically sustained. In parts of *Achilles* the travesty exists for its own humorous sake and not for any other purpose, something even more true of Breval's *The Rape of Helen* (1733).

The burlesque drama of the Restoration and Augustan periods clearly exhibits an extraordinary variety, and this is true even if one sets aside the pure classical travesties such as Wright's *Mock-Thyestes*. Some satirical burlesques, especially *The Rehearsal*, are single-minded and relentlessly hard-hitting. Others, including Gay's *The What D'Ye Call It* (1715) and Fielding's *The Tragedy of Tragedies* (1731), are milder in tone. And some, notably Henry Carey's *Chrononhotonthologos* (1734), are so indulgently playful that the satirical point is in danger of being lost in good-natured exuberance, as in Bombardinion's burlesque speech of anguished guilt and psychological derangement after killing the eponymous King:

> Ha! What have I done?
> Go, call a Coach, and let a Coach be call'd;
> And let the Man that calls it be the Caller;
> And, in his Calling, let him nothing call,
> But Coach! Coach! Coach! Oh! for a Coach, ye Gods!

The degree of hostility on the part of the burlesque dramatist varies considerably from play to play, even by the same author, as indeed do the techniques. Some plays, such as *Tumble-Down Dick*, employ the methods (though not the octosyllabics) of contemporary burlesque poetry, the use of a low style for supposedly elevated subject matter. Others, including Fielding's *The Covent-Garden Tragedy* (1732), employ the methods of mock-heroic poetry, the use of a high style for low subject matter. And some use extreme exaggeration (*Chrononhotonthologos*) or a very individual technique (Fielding's *The Author's Farce* (1730)) or a mixture of methods (*The Rehearsal*).

Burlesque can be verbal, situational, visual, or any combination of these elements; it can involve close parody of particular speeches, scenes, and theatrical devices, or be much more general. The device of a play within a play is an important feature of many satirical burlesques, following the example of *The Rehearsal*, in which the inner burlesque play is supposedly being rehearsed and is surrounded by a framework of comment and discussion by those attending or participating in the rehearsal. However, some burlesques, like *The Tragedy of Tragedies* and *The Covent-Garden Tragedy*, are completely self-contained and without any framing device, while others, like *The What D'Ye Call It* and *The Author's Farce*, retain a framing device but one substantially different from Buckingham's. In Fielding's dramatic satires of 1736–37, on the other hand, the rehearsal form is adopted but made to serve the purpose of political and social satire with burlesque reduced to secondary importance if it is present at all. Although some satirical burlesques of the period are concerned only with drama and closely related topics such as playwrights and theatre managers, others combine burlesque with other types of satire. In *The Rehearsal* and *The What D'Ye Call It*, there are traces of social and political satire, but in Gay, Arbuthnot, and Pope's *Three Hours after Marriage* (1717), Gay's *The Beggar's Opera* (1728), and Fielding's *Pasquin* (1736) and *Eurydice Hiss'd* (1737) burlesque is only one of a number of coexisting elements and by no means the most important. Burlesque drama obviously took a considerable number of forms between 1660 and 1737, but what most of these plays do have in common is that the weapon of burlesque is turned against contemporary drama.

Heroic drama and tragedy bore the brunt of the burlesque, although Italian opera came in for an increasing share of raillery in the later part of this period. The Restoration heroic play and its close musical relative, English dramatic opera, were the first targets, being ridiculed in the 1670s by Buckingham in *The Rehearsal* and by Thomas Duffett in his three burlesque plays, *The Empress of Morocco* (1673), *The Mock-Tempest* (1674), and *Psyche Debauch'd* (1675). Subsequently, most of the various kinds of tragic drama which critics have tried to identify – 'heroic', 'pathetic', and 'pseudo-classical' – took their turn in the pillory, especially at the hands of Gay and Fielding.[4] Only so-called 'bourgeois' tragedy escaped unscathed, an exemption that is easy to understand considering its concern with more ordinary, domestic, and 'novelistic' subjects than usual in Restoration and Augustan tragedy, which often merited burlesque of its pretensions.

Orthodox comedy, on the other hand, did not attract the attention of burlesque dramatists. Because comedy aims lower than tragedy, it is much less exposed to mockery, and the prose medium of most comedies after 1660, unlike the high-flown verse of many tragedies, presented few rhetorical and stylistic possibilities for burlesque. Only when comedy degenerated into farcical intrigue comedy or when it moved in the direction of 'exemplary' or 'sentimental' comedy, as it increasingly did in the early eighteenth century, did it invite burlesque, and even then on a much smaller scale than contemporary tragedy.

The establishment of the afterpiece as a normal part of an evening's theatrical entertainment at the turn of the century led directly to more diversity of dramatic types and therefore more opportunities for burlesque. In the early eighteenth century, especially in the ten years preceding the Licensing Act of 1737, more theatres were functioning and more productions were staged than during the later seventeenth century, so that Fielding was presented with far more potential targets than Buckingham had been over half a century earlier.

Italian influence became particularly strong after 1700, and this led to the immense success of two forms new to the English stage, Italian opera and pantomime, both of which soon attracted the attention of burlesque dramatists. Italian opera was imported in the first decade of the century, and rapidly became and subsequently remained a major attraction, displacing the English dramatic opera of the Restoration. The lasting popularity of Italian opera is an indication of one of the most significant tendencies after 1660, the increasing part played by music, from entr'actes to full-scale operas. For neoclassical critics, this development, along with the closely related proliferation of spectacle and 'machinery', was symptomatic of the degeneration of the theatre into a place where mindless rather than profitable entertainment was what audiences really wanted. Pantomime, which established itself as one of the main types of afterpiece after 1720, was particularly vulnerable to such criticism. While taking a great deal from the *commedia dell'arte*, which a few Restoration comic dramatists had previously exploited, pantomime fused the Italian harlequinade with such diverse ingredients as operatic spectacle and music, dancing, and farce. As a result, pantomime was intensely theatrical, depending to a great extent for its impact on fast-moving action, scenic devices, exotic sets, magical transformations, *commedia dell'arte* masks, and a *deus ex machina* to ensure the triumph of love between the hero, Harlequin, and the heroine, Colombine. The demand for pantomime reached the point where pantomimic afterpieces had long runs while mainpieces changed frequently. It was pantomime that many members of the theatregoing public went to see.

A totally different new form, since it could be a vehicle for burlesque and satire, was ballad opera, which achieved widespread popularity following the extraordinarily favourable reception of the prototype, *The Beggar's Opera*, in 1728. Gay's work is a play with an unusually high musical content rather than an opera in the Italian (and modern) sense, but it was partly conceived as an antidote to Italian opera, which it burlesques. Gay's answer to Italian music was to set his own words to well-loved English melodies, mainly ballad tunes. *The Beggar's Opera* itself is not an afterpiece, but many of the numerous ballad operas that followed in its wake were shorter and appeared as afterpieces, thus competing with pantomime in the 1730s. Although many ballad operas are no more than farcical, the form, unlike Italian opera, permitted considerable variety, from classical travesty to pastoral to social and political satire (as in the case of *The Beggar's Opera*). Especially during the 1730s, there was a close link between dramatic satire and ballad opera.

The advent of the afterpiece as a staple feature of theatrical presentation was a great boost for burlesque drama. If brevity is a virtue, it is doubly so for burlesque and parody, which almost always work best in concentrated doses. To labour a joke is to destroy it. One reason for the relative paucity of dramatic burlesques before 1700 is the enormous difficulty in sustaining burlesque for the duration of a full-length play. Significantly, Davenant's seminal classical travesty occupies only one act of *The Playhouse To Be Let*. Buckingham succeeds in *The Rehearsal*, but only by generating a good deal of comedy from the rehearsal framework surrounding the burlesque episodes themselves. Duffett, on the other hand, who in the 1670s wrote full-length burlesque plays without rehearsal structures, soon becomes tedious, and not only because his literary talent was slight. In the twenty-five years before the Licensing Act, however, most burlesques were afterpieces. Exceptions include *The Beggar's Opera*, but Gay's burlesque of Italian opera is only one of a number of interwoven strands in this complex play. Although not all of Fielding's dramatic burlesques and satires are afterpieces, it was he, more than any other dramatist, who exploited the afterpiece as a burlesque and satirical weapon.

NOTES
1. Despite the quantity of scholarly energy that Fielding has engendered in the twentieth century, comparatively little attempt has been made to examine this aspect of his work. His three principal modern biographers, Wilbur L. Cross (*The History of Henry Fielding*, New Haven, 1918), F. Homes Dudden (*Henry Fielding: His Life, Works, and Times*, Oxford, 1952) and Pat Rogers (*Henry Fielding: A Biography*, London, 1979), do trace his dramatic development and provide important information without going into this particular topic in depth. Recent editors of individual plays have shed a great deal of light on these, but have not been concerned with Fielding's burlesque and satirical drama as a whole. The most comprehensive treatment of Fielding's years as a playwright and man of the theatre is by the French scholar Jean Ducrocq, *Le Théâtre de Fielding: 1728-1737 et ses prolongements dans l'oeuvre romanesque* (Paris, 1975), but the most valuable suggestions about how Fielding's dramatic burlesques and satires might be approached have come from two Americans, Jean B. Kern ('Fielding's Dramatic Satire', *Philological Quarterly* 54 (1975) 239-57) and J. Paul Hunter (*Occasional Form*, Baltimore, 1975, chs 2-3). Although less centrally concerned with this aspect of Fielding's work, other scholars, including Ian Donaldson in *The World Upside-Down: Comedy from Jonson to Fielding* (Oxford, 1970) and C. J. Rawson in *Henry Fielding and the Augustan Ideal under Stress* (London, 1972), have opened up new perspectives in Fielding studies that are invaluable to any student of his dramatic and literary achievement. The much-debated problem of Fielding's shifting political position and its relevance to his literary and dramatic work has recently received careful historical analysis by both Bertrand A. Goldgar in *Walpole and the Wits* (Lincoln, Nebraska, 1976) and Brian McCrea in *Henry Fielding*

and the Politics of Mid-Eighteenth-Century England (Athens, Georgia, 1981).

Regarding the period as a whole, the two major twentieth-century histories of English drama, Allardyce Nicoll's *A History of English Drama 1600-1900* (vols 1 and 2) and *The Revels History of Drama in English* (vol. 5), include some coverage of the burlesque tradition, as does Robert D. Hume's authoritative *The Development of English Drama in the Late Seventeenth Century* (Oxford, 1976), although his cut-off date is 1710. Hume's subsequent *The Rakish Stage: Studies in English Drama, 1660-1800* (Carbondale and Edwardsville, Illinois, 1983) does, however, contain an extremely informative essay covering the years of Fielding's involvement in the theatre, 'The London Theatre from *The Beggar's Opera* to the Licensing Act'. The appropriate volumes of *The London Stage 1660-1800* are as indispensable as always for historical information, as is *The London Theatre World, 1660-1800*, ed. Robert D. Hume (Carbondale and Edwardsville, 1980), but the three most important studies for the student of Restoration and Augustan dramatic burlesque and satire are: Dane Farnsworth Smith, *Plays about the Theatre in England from The Rehearsal in 1671 to the Licensing Act in 1737* (New York, 1936); V. C. Clinton-Baddeley, *The Burlesque Tradition in the English Theatre after 1660* (London, 1952); and Jean B. Kern, *Dramatic Satire in the Age of Walpole 1720-1750* (Ames, Iowa, 1976).

2. See George Kitchin, *A Survey of Burlesque and Parody in English* (Edinburgh, 1931), ch. 2.

3. For a good survey of the usage of 'burlesque', 'parody', 'travesty', 'mock-heroic', and 'Hudibrastic' in the late seventeenth and early eighteenth centuries, see Richmond P. Bond, *English Burlesque Poetry 1700-1750* (Cambridge, Mass., 1932) ch. 2. The problem of definition in a specifically dramatic context is an important theme in Leo Hughes, *A Century of English Farce* (Princeton, 1956), especially ch. 1. John D. Jump's book in the 'Critical Idiom' series, *Burlesque* (London, 1972), offers a more general analysis of this and related terms.

4. While it is possible, even easy, to question the validity of these and similar labels, including 'comedy of manners', 'genteel comedy', and 'sentimental comedy', they have entered the critical vocabulary and stubbornly resist attempts to excise them. As convenient ways of indicating tendencies they remain useful, as long as they are not interpreted as rigidly defining genres and sub-genres, or as indicating historical uniformity. It is therefore preferable to deconstruct than to eschew them. Scholars inevitably resort to some form of critical terminology: throughout *The Rakish Stage* Robert D. Hume perceptively analyses the ways in which critical terminology applied to drama between 1660 and 1800 has falsified historical actuality, sometimes grossly, but he himself cannot avoid labels and categories. Indeed, he has added a number to the existing battery. What Hume demonstrates is that considerable care is needed in handling inherited critical vocabulary.

CHAPTER TWO

The Importance of *The Rehearsal*

By the time Fielding began his literary career at the end of the 1720s, a considerable body of burlesque writing had accumulated since 1660. Much of this output was in the form of poetry rather than drama, but a significant number of theatrical works had been staged and published. It is impossible to tell how familiar Fielding was with this dramatic writing, but some of the plays now identified by the historian of drama as belonging to or having an affinity with the burlesque tradition were probably unknown to him. Burlesque was often an ephemeral form of writing, very much of the moment, and few burlesque plays transcended the immediate situation that prompted them, to achieve more universal appeal. Consequently, regular productions or even occasional revivals of burlesque plays were rare, though not unknown. Whether Fielding knew Davenant's *The Playhouse To Be Let* is uncertain, but one play from the Restoration that he must have known well is the first major burlesque play after 1660, Buckingham's immensely successful *The Rehearsal*. This therefore merits more detailed consideration here than many subsequent dramatic burlesques.

The Rehearsal, first produced by the King's Company at their theatre in Bridges Street, Drury Lane on 7 December 1671 after a long, complicated gestation period, is the foundation stone on which the tradition of Restoration and Augustan dramatic burlesque is built. Even those subsequent burlesque plays that depart from *The Rehearsal* in their methods, such as Gay's *The What D'Ye Call It* and Fielding's *The Tragedy of Tragedies*, are considerably indebted to it. Just as *The Rehearsal* is not the first play in the history of English drama to burlesque dramatic forms, scurrilous caricature on the stage did not begin with Buckingham's presentation of Dryden as Bayes – a number of Elizabethan and Jacobean plays contain satirical portraits of contemporary poets and dramatists. Yet in its total organization, *The Rehearsal* undoubtedly made a highly original contribution to English drama, its structure and methods being derived from Molière's *L'Impromptu de Versailles* (1663) rather than from any previous English play.

After its initial success, Buckingham revised and expanded *The*

Rehearsal, which was to remain popular for more than a hundred years. Performances were given fairly frequently and new editions published regularly until the end of the eighteenth century. One of Garrick's favourite roles was Bayes, and he consequently gave the play a considerable fillip in the middle of the eighteenth century. Its influence was correspondingly great. It initiated the flow of Restoration and Augustan dramatic satires and burlesques, and the titles of some of these proclaim their link with *The Rehearsal,* in which the play by Bayes that is rehearsed features two Kings of Brentford: examples include the anonymous *The Female Wits; or, The Triumvirate of Poets at Rehearsal* (1696), Charles Gildon's *A New Rehearsal; or, Bays the Younger* (1714), and Thomas D'Urfey's *The Two Queens of Brentford; or, Bayes No Poetaster* (1721). Even orthodox comedy was not unaffected by it; Joseph Arrowsmith's *The Reformation* (1673), for instance, exhibits features plainly adopted from *The Rehearsal,* notably a Bayes-like English Tutor.[1]

Although Sheridan's *The Critic* (1779) is often seen as the culmination of the Restoration and eighteenth-century tradition of burlesque drama, it closely follows the pattern of *The Rehearsal,* which it refurbishes in order to bring Buckingham's dramatic and personal satire up to date. In *The Critic,* pseudo-Shakespearean historical tragedy such as Richard Cumberland's *The Battle of Hastings* (1778), not Restoration heroic drama as in *The Rehearsal,* is the primary target; and Cumberland, in the form of Sir Fretful Plagiary, replaces Dryden as the dramatist abused. Nevertheless, Sheridan's methods of burlesquing contemporary tragedy and many of his satirical jibes are almost identical to Buckingham's. The conversations of the Puff, Sneer, Dangle trio in *The Critic* recall those of the Bayes, Smith, Johnson trio in *The Rehearsal,* and Puff's interjections during the rehearsal of his tragedy, *The Spanish Armada,* echo those of Bayes. Buckingham's example moulded the pattern of much subsequent dramatic burlesque and remained powerful for over a century.

The Rehearsal has attracted the attention of many scholars, editors, and critics since the eighteenth century, when two Keys to the play were prepared, attempting to identify all its personal and literary allusions and the passages from contemporary drama parodied by Buckingham. During the twentieth century, two notable editions have appeared,[2] as have several important analyses, including Dane Farnsworth Smith's comprehensive catalogue of forty-four different ways in which Bayes is ridiculed and of fifty-nine aspects of Restoration drama and stage presentation burlesqued by Buckingham.[3] By far the most original (and the most controversial) of recent studies is George McFadden's speculative investigation of the political satire in the play.[4] Some of his observations and identifications are invaluable, but he overstates his case when he suggests that *The Rehearsal* is essentially a topical political satire veiled as a dramatic burlesque. Because of Buckingham's deep involvement in politics, it is tempting to translate the play into a kind of political allegory, especially as in 1668 he did contribute an outrageous scene of personal and political satire to *The Country Gentleman,* the suppressed and recently rediscovered comedy he wrote with Sir Robert Howard. Yet if political satire were the primary aim of *The Rehearsal,* it is difficult to believe that Buckingham would have developed the dramatic burlesque so comprehensively, since this would obviously have the effect of largely masking any other intention. There are political allusions in the play, as McFadden shows, but these are secondary. The real importance of McFadden's essay lies in his revelation that the most influential burlesque play of the Restoration and eighteenth century, coming virtually at the outset of the post-1660 burlesque tradition, is by no means innocent of political satire, concealed though this may be.

Buckingham's main dramatic target is the rhymed heroic play of the early Restoration period, although contemporary tragicomedy and dramatic opera also attract his burlesque attention. As a result of modern research into the origins, theory, and history of the heroic play, the casually dismissive attitude towards the entire genre that used to be common is giving way to a more understanding response to its aims and its variety. Even so, few scholars would make considerable claims for its artistic achievement, except perhaps in the hands of Dryden, and the heroic play not only laid itself wide open to burlesque attack by critics unwilling to accept it on its own flamboyant and ultra-royalist terms, but for the most part thoroughly deserved it. The best case for the heroic play is put by its leading dramatist, Dryden, especially in *Of Heroique Plays,* the prefatory essay he wrote for the publication of *The Conquest of Granada* (1672), where he defends the form as the dramatic equivalent of epic. Yet theory is one thing, practice another. The desire of Restoration dramatists to break away from the blank verse of their pre-Commonwealth predecessors and to create a distinctive idiom by using rhymed couplets is very understandable, especially as part of the pursuit of linguistic and literary propriety characterizing the second half of the seventeenth century. Yet ideal as the couplet was for didactic, philosophical, and satirical poetry, it proved to be too inflexible for the totally different medium of the stage, and much of the notorious inflation, as well as the emotional and intellectual shallowness, of heroic drama can certainly be accounted for by its poetic rigidity. The French alexandrine is remarkably different from the English pentameter, as the notorious failure of English verse translators to provide satisfactory versions of Corneille and Racine indicates. It is not the case, as used to be thought, that the immediate popularity of *The Rehearsal* made the rhymed rant of heroic plays unendurable to contemporary audiences and so brought an end to their flow, but by the end of the 1670s the dramatists themselves, including Dryden, were reverting to blank verse.

The structure of *The Rehearsal* is ideally suited to its burlesque function, allowing for ample satire and comment on the poetry, form, and characterization of heroic plays and Restoration tragicomedies as well as on their staging. Furthermore, by presenting the mock play within *The Rehearsal* as a serious example of heroic drama written by a typical Restoration dramatist (Bayes), Buckingham can attack not only the genre but also its authors. As the Preface of the anonymous *Complete Key* to Gay's *The What D'Ye Call It* puts it, Buckingham *'has laid his Finger on the proper Subjects of Ridicule, such as,* ill-contriv'd Plots, unnatural Connections, silly Peripetia's, unreasonable Machinery, affected Stile, extravagant Rants *and* Nonsense, *and in particular the* arbitrary Pedantry *of one over-grown Writer.*'[5] Apart from the direct parodies of heroic drama and the burlesques of its conventions that constitute Bayes' inchoate play about love, honour, and political intrigue, the rehearsal structure permits a commentary on the mock play by two representatives of practical common sense, Johnson and Smith; discussions between them and Bayes, who exposes himself to ridicule with almost every word he utters; occasional remarks by the actors; and a satirical display of theatrical devices and tricks, which are always much more in evidence during rehearsal than in actual performance.

Indeed, one great advantage of presenting the mock play in rehearsal, and therefore distancing it, is that Bayes' heroic play is deprived of the normal illusion that operates in the theatre, thus exposing its contrived artificiality as well as theatrical illusion to full glare. This does not mean that Restoration and Augustan frame plays such as *The Rehearsal* are precursors of Pirandello, Stoppard, and Absurdist playwrights who play philosophical and relativistic games with illusion and reality, and critics who make such a connection are imposing twentieth-century expectations on the earlier drama. The chief danger in using a rehearsal as the vehicle for satire is that the commonsense critics might dominate the play: criticism would then be too explicitly stated instead of being parodically enacted. Buckingham's success in avoiding this danger and in achieving an admirable balance between the mock play and the surrounding framework is particularly laudable when it is remembered that no tradition of dramatic burlesque existed to guide him when he was writing *The Rehearsal*.

The kernel of Buckingham's satire is undoubtedly the mock play. Effective as the surrounding framework is in furthering his attack, its success largely depends on the success of the mock play itself. Good burlesque comes primarily from imitations of the poetic style, stock situations, dramatic clichés, and methods of staging to be ridiculed that exaggerate or transform the originals just enough to elucidate their absurdities and banalities. If the imitations are insufficiently exaggerated, they will not be apprehended as burlesque. If they are crudely over-exaggerated, they will fall to the level of farcical extravaganza even if the burlesque intention is recognizable. Buckingham usually manages to achieve the necessary equilibrium, not an easy task when the form being burlesqued often teeters on the edge of self-parody.

Despite V. C. Clinton-Baddeley's protestations throughout *The Burlesque Tradition in the English Theatre after 1660* that 'unwinking nonsense, which owes nothing to direct parody, is the very marrow of burlesque',[6] direct parody is a vital ingredient of Restoration and Augustan burlesque drama, particularly of *The Rehearsal*; Clinton-Baddeley himself acknowledges that the play 'is laced with direct parody'.[7] Many of Drawcansir's lines in *The Rehearsal*, which define the self-righteous swagger and intense narcissism of the typical hero, are very closely modelled on some of Almanzor's most high-flown speeches in Dryden's *The Conquest of Granada* (Part I, 1670; Part II, 1671):

> ALMANZOR He who dares love; and for that love must dy,
> And, knowing this, dares yet love on, am I.   (Part II, IV, iii)
>
> DRAWCANSIR He that dares drink, and for that drink dares dye,
> And, knowing this, dares yet drink on, am I.   (IV, I)

Very similar to such direct parodies, though not based so closely on specific speeches, are Buckingham's non-parodic burlesques of the unendurable dilemmas, stock poses, and static debates of heroic drama. Drawcansir's final speech, delivered after he has joined in the battle and killed *'em all on both sides'*, amplifies the usual boasts of the semi-divine hero about his prowess and invulnerability:

> Others may boast a single man to kill;
> But I, the blood of thousands daily spill.
> Let petty Kings the names of Parties know:
> Where e'er I come, I slay both friend and foe.
> The swiftest Horsemen my swift rage controuls,
> And from their Bodies drives their trembling souls.
> If they had wings, and to the Gods could flie,
> I would pursue and beat 'em through the skie:
> And make proud *Jove*, with all his Thunder, see
> This single Arm more dreadful is, than he.   (V, i)

This articulates the absurdities inherent in the braggadocio of the hero, whose 'honour' is here implied to be an excuse for disdainful pride and bloodthirsty violence. In *The Conquest of Granada*, for example, Almanzor is very disappointed at the brevity of one of the battles:

> We have not fought enough; they fly too soon:
> And I am griev'd the noble sport is done. (Part I, III, i)

Indeed, Almanzor's conduct and boasts are not much less exaggerated than Drawcansir's. At one point, Almanzor, who regards himself as living on a superior plane of existence to the other characters and consequently believes that he is not subject to ordinary laws, even says that he will 'At once beat those without, and these within' (Part I, III, i).

Buckingham's verbal burlesques usually function by exaggeration and only occasionally involve genuinely mock-heroic metaphors or substitutions. Exaggeration is not the hallmark of mock-heroic satire, which substitutes the ordinary for the supposedly exotic and sublime in order to dispel the mirage of spurious wonder they evoke. Buckingham's mock-heroic substitution of London place names for the remote cities and romantic settings of heroic drama illustrates the method, as does the introduction into a potentially heroic passage of some trivial commonplace or unelevated object:

> PRETTY-MAN The blackest Ink of Fate, sure, was my Lot,
> And, when she writ my Name, she made a blot. (III, iv)

The incongruous linking of 'blot', a product of human clumsiness, with 'Fate', an ineluctable non-human force, is responsible for the mock-heroic debasement of the typical hero's contemplation of his destiny; 'fate' is conspicuous by its presence in most heroic plays. Buckingham employs the same mock-heroic method, a means of attack to which heroic drama is particularly vulnerable, in the most famous burlesque episode in the play, Volscius' dilemma when trying to choose between love and honour; such monologues are a regular feature of heroic drama. In this case, the mock-heroic disparity is between the idealistic debate, usually couched in sonorous abstractions, and the metaphorical terms in which it is conducted here – Volscius compares his mental struggles with the putting on and removing of his boots, and finally *'Goes out hopping with one Boot on, and the other off'* (III, v).

Closely linked with verbal burlesque is situational burlesque, usually achieved by satirical exaggeration of particular incidents and stock situations in heroic plays. Buckingham probably based his burlesque of the ease with which kings are deposed, governments overthrown, and peripeteia effected in Restoration drama on the changing fortunes of the opposing factions in *The Conquest of Granada* and on Leonidas' transformations from lost child to Crown Prince to condemned traitor to King in another of Dryden's plays, *Marriage A-la-Mode* (1671), but his satire is equally relevant to all similar 'topsie-turvy' scenes in heroic drama and tragicomedy:

> PHYSICIAN Let's then no more our selves in vain bemoan:
> We are not safe until we them unthrone.
> USHER 'Tis right:
> And, since occasion now seems debonair,
> I'll seize on this, and you shall take that Chair.
> *[They draw their swords, and sit down in the two great Chairs upon the Stage.]*
> BAYES There's now an odd surprize; the whole State's turn'd quite topsie-turvy, without any puther or stir in the whole world, I gad.
> JOHNSON A very silent change of a Government, truly, as ever I heard of.   (II, iv)

The final reversal that restores the rightful Kings of Brentford to their thrones and drives out the usurpers is also executed with the aplomb and straight-faced humour characteristic of Buckingham's best situational burlesques. This scene (in V, i) satirizes the tragicomic method of extricating heroes and heroines from apparently inescapable difficulties and of resolving seemingly irresolvable problems by unexpectedly introducing a *deus ex machina* in order to chastise the wicked, reward the good, reinstate order, and bring happiness to the deserving.

Often integrated with situational burlesque is visual burlesque, which cannot properly exist except in performance. Buckingham presumably intended the presentation of the entire mock play to be a visual burlesque of Restoration productions of heroic drama and tragicomedy, but the term 'visual burlesque' is used here with a more limited range of reference. Through the comments made by Johnson, Smith, and Bayes about the staging of the mock play they are witnessing, Buckingham is able to criticize explicitly certain aspects of Restoration stage presentation, but he employs visual burlesque to recreate in burlesque terms those scenic devices and theatrical effects he wished to censure. In the last two acts of *The Rehearsal*, a series of visual burlesques accompanies the situational burlesques. At the end of the funeral scene when Lardella's restoration to life is celebrated by a banquet, there is visual burlesque of ludicrous stage properties and costumes, based on the scene in Thomas Porter's tragedy *The Villain* (1662) in which the Host provides his guests with food and drink concealed in his clothes, such as cream stored in his scabbard. Pallas contributes to the banquet in a similar way:

> Lo, from this conquering Lance,
> Does flow the purest Wine of *France*:
> *[Fills the Boles out of her Lance.]*

And, to appease your hunger, I
Have, in my Helmet, brought a Pye:
Lastly, to bear a part with these,
Behold a Buckler made of Cheese.   (IV, i)

An equally fruitful integration of visual burlesque and situational burlesque occurs in the last act. When the genuine Kings of Brentford return to reclaim their thrones, they do not appear at the head of an army. Dressed in white and singing a close parody of a duet from Dryden's *Tyrannick Love* (1669) to an accompaniment by *'three Fidlers sitting before them, in green'* (V, i), the Kings descend from the heavens in a 'triumphant Carr', and eventually step out of the clouds onto their thrones; the action closely resembles that in Dryden's play, in which the two spirits who sing the duet, Nakar and Damilcar, descend in clouds. In addition to the verbal burlesque, this ridicules the arbitrary inclusion of dramatically irrelevant songs in many Restoration plays, the use of stage machines to obtain sensational effects at the cost of dramatic sense (visual burlesque), and those miraculous reversals in heroic drama and tragicomedy accomplished by a *deus ex machina* (situational burlesque).

Buckingham's visual burlesque is not always linked with verbal or situational burlesque. The various dances indicated in the mock play, such as the chaotic dance of the resurrected soldiers (II, v), the funeral-banquet dance (IV, i), and the *'grand Dance'* immediately following the unexpected return of the Kings of Brentford (V, i), are intended as visual burlesques of the many dances incorporated in Restoration plays, frequently without any dramatic justification. These dances are introduced in an extremely capricious way; Bayes justifies the funeral-banquet dance by a flimsy argument – 'we must first have a Dance, for joy that *Lardella* is not dead' (IV, i) – and the *'grand Dance'* begins even more unexpectedly:

FIRST KING Come, now to serious counsel we'l advance:
SECOND KING I do agree; but first, let's have a Dance.   (V, i)

In addition to ridiculing the many dances in contemporary plays, such as those in Dryden's *The Indian Emperour* (1665), *Tyrannick Love,* and *The Conquest of Granada,* Buckingham's burlesque dances make it clear that dramatic sense and artistic cohesion were being sacrificed for the sake of stupendous stage displays. The stage direction for the mock play at the beginning of the last act demands a sumptuous set piece that is obviously intended to burlesque by exaggeration those scenes in heroic drama (for which Roger Boyle, Earl of Orrery was famous) in which the stage is crowded with kings, princes, lords, ladies and guards. Bayes explains elsewhere that 'Heroic Verse, never sounds well, but when the Stage is full' (IV, i).

In the framework surrounding the mock play, the dialogue of Bayes, Johnson, Smith, and the actors serves to ridicule some eminent dramatists of the time, especially Dryden, to attack heroic drama and tragicomedy directly, and to heighten the passages of parody and burlesque. Despite George McFadden's ingenious suggestion that Bayes corresponds to Henry Bennet, Earl of Arlington, the obvious interpretation that Bayes points to the Poet Laureate of the day, Dryden, who succeeded Davenant in 1669, cannot be seriously questioned, although it is certainly possible that Arlington is implicated at a secondary level. The historical record is virtually unequivocal about the identification of Bayes with Dryden. The fact that Dryden was subsequently ridiculed as Bayes in Matthew Prior and Charles Montague's *The Hind and the Panther Transvers'd to the Story of The Country Mouse and the City-Mouse* (1687), their parody of Dryden's religious allegory, speaks for itself; as in *The Rehearsal* on which it is obviously modelled, a framework of conversation between Bayes, Johnson, and Smith surrounds the passages of parody.

Unfortunately for Dryden, a number of his personal characteristics made him a sitting duck for a satirist, and Buckingham did not fail to make the most of them. Because he employs the usual satirical methods of exaggeration and distortion, Buckingham is manifestly unfair to Dryden in many ways, but Bayes is nevertheless an extremely effective caricature and a brilliant stage creation. Dryden obtained his revenge by reserving an honoured place for Buckingham as Zimri in *Absalom and Achitophel*. Yet just as Zimri is a representative figure as well as being a satirical sketch of Buckingham, Bayes (even ignoring the political level outlined by McFadden) is more than a caricature of Dryden. Bayes too is a representative figure, as Sheridan Baker emphasizes in an important essay on the universal qualities of *The Rehearsal*, and unless this were the case it would be difficult to account for the sustained popularity of the play long after Dryden's death and the demise of the rhymed heroic play.[8] Dryden was the immediate model for Bayes, but Bayes expands beyond the specific to become 'an energetic display of the universal comedy of human vanity, particularly in that mode of vanity in which literature takes its being',[9] and his egotistical self-sufficiency marks him as a precursor of Swift's narrator, the Grub Street hack, in *A Tale of a Tub*.

Ridicule of Bayes is continuous throughout the play, but the first act, which leads up to the rehearsal of Bayes' play in the later acts, is a particularly relentless attack on him. At his first appearance, he is revoltingly sycophantic and also boastful about his new play, but unable to explain to Johnson the meaning, which he confuses with the plot, of his last play. He can, however, expatiate on his imbecile rules for play writing, including his 'Rule of Transversion' ('changing Verse into Prose, or Prose into verse') and his view of invention – a mixture of witty aphorisms overheard in coffee houses and sheer plagiarism:

> Why, Sir, when I have any thing to invent, I never trouble my head about it, as other men do; but presently turn over this Book, and there I have, at one view, all that *Perseus, Montaigne, Seneca's Tragedies, Horace, Juvenal, Claudian, Pliny, Plutarch's lives,* and the rest, have ever thought upon this subject: and so, in a trice, by leaving out a few words, or putting in others of my own, the business is done.   (I, i)

Bayes reveals himself as proud, contemptuous, and mentally blind in many other ways during the opening act. He mistakes his own silly puns (such as 'I make 'em call her *Armarillis*, because of her Armor') for wit, and confesses that he wrote a part just for his mistress; his words *'bel Esperansa de ma vie'* allude to Dryden's putative mistress, Anne Reeve, who as a member of Killigrew's company played Esperanza in *The Conquest of Granada* in 1670. He comments that his Prologue and Epilogue are interchangeable and just as appropriate for any other play as his own. He plans to ensure applause at the performance of his play by arranging for 'two or three dozen of my friends, to be ready in the Pit, who, I'm sure, will clap, and so the rest, you know, must follow'. He also launches into a diatribe against critics, which parades his lack of self-awareness until it virtually becomes an unintentional diatribe against himself.

In the other four acts, during which parody and burlesque assume increasing importance, the ridicule of Bayes is frequently integrated into the satire on Restoration drama. Several passages in the mock play exposing poetic and dramatic clichés are interrupted by self-congratulatory exclamations from Bayes at what he believes to be instances of his originality and artistic brilliance. Smith and Johnson do occasionally state directly what they think of Bayes, but the ridicule of Bayes is so successful because most of it comes from his own mouth. In his presentation of Bayes, Buckingham provides the qualities and characteristics he wished to mock with dramatic actuality and, like all good satirists, does not rely to any great extent on explicit comments about them.

In Bayes, Buckingham is in fact employing a standard Restoration and Augustan satirical device, later adopted by Swift for his personae. Buckingham makes Bayes put the case for the heroic play, but in a slightly exaggerated form that reduces the case to absurdity. While expounding the poetic 'merits' and dramatic 'subtleties' of his play, Bayes unwittingly reveals all the flaws of heroic drama as well as his own pompous inanity. Bayes' self-satisfied description of his interminable 'Conquest', which cannot 'be acted in less than a whole week', is simultaneously Buckingham's condemnation of the unwieldy structure of the play it alludes to, Dryden's two-part, ten-act *The Conquest of Granada*:

> And then, Sir, this contrivance of mine has something of the reason of a Play in it too; for as every one makes you five Acts to one Play, what do me I, but make five Plays to one Plot: by which means the Auditors have every day a new thing. (IV, i)

Similar speeches, in which Buckingham projects his satire through the 'mask' of Bayes, abound. When asked about Drawcansir, Bayes proudly outlines his hero's characteristics, but in such a way that Buckingham speaks through him to sum up the absurdities of Almanzor and his like:

> Why, Sir, a fierce *Hero*, that frights his Mistress, snubs up Kings, baffles Armies, and does what he will, without regard to numbers, good manners, or justice. . . . you shall see him, in the last Act, win above a dozen Battles, one after another, I gad, as fast as they can possibly come upon the Stage. (IV, i)

Johnson and Smith's persistent interrogation of Bayes about the absurdities of his play forces him to make numerous inane defences of his dramatic incompetence and at the same time mediates between the mock play and the audience to point up the burlesque. In the bustle of a Restoration theatre, the subtle burlesque of *The Rehearsal* cannot have been easy to apprehend without the attendant commentary of Johnson and Smith, whose main dramatic function is therefore to drive home Buckingham's satire. Their questions undoubtedly elicit some of Bayes' most damning speeches, such as his dismissal of Smith's intelligent curiosity about the totally unexplained meaning of Pretty-man's baffling declamation, 'It is resolv'd' (II, iii), as both ignorance of contemporary fashions and failure to appreciate original writing.

Johnson and Smith's frequent ironic praise of Bayes' verbal and formal peculiarities is another method of underscoring the satire, and they often undermine the pretensions of heroic drama by this oblique method; but when they do express their views explicitly, they reveal themselves as upholders of Good Sense and Reason who invoke the neoclassical yardstick of Nature as a measure of reproof. Johnson openly derides the current dramatic pursuit of novelty and specious originality at the expense of art and reason. Bayes, on the other hand, blandly deceives himself about the virtues of 'the new way of writing' – 'That's a general Rule, you must ever make a *simile*, when you are surpris'd; 'tis the new way of writing' (II, iii) – and unquestioningly equates 'new' with 'good' when trying to justify the irrationalities of his play:

> JOHNSON But why two Kings of the same place?
> BAYES Why? because it's new; and that's it I aim at. I despise your *Johnson* and *Beaumont*, that borrow'd all they writ from Nature: I am for fetching it purely out of my own fancy, I. (II, i)

Shortly after this confession, Johnson rightly censures what Bayes calls 'good language' as 'very fantastical, most abominably dull, and not one word to the purpose', and complains, again in the name of Nature, that no scene in Bayes' play is 'like any thing thou canst imagine has ever been the practice of the World'.

At the opening and again at the end of *The Rehearsal*, Buckingham uses the actors of the mock play to contribute to the cumulative satire of heroic drama and its authors. When discussing the play they have to perform, two of the actors are full of scornful incomprehension while another (the First Player) succeeds in clarifying Buckingham's objections to 'the new way of writing' (I, i) by ostensibly defending them. The actors' criticism in the concluding scene is less direct than at the opening but nonetheless valuable. After Johnson and Smith make their final protest against Bayes and his play by leaving the theatre before the rehearsal is over, the Third Player discovers and reads 'a foul piece of papyr' outlining the final act of Bayes' play. On reading this, he too decides that enough is enough: 'This will never do: 'tis just like the rest. Come, let's begone' (V, i). Like Johnson and Smith, the actors cannot endure unlimited nonsense and abandon Bayes' play with unanimous relief.

Although the criticism of heroic drama and other contemporary forms contained in *The Rehearsal* is essentially destructive, Buckingham's ridicule has a vital positive function. He attacked Restoration drama because it departed so far from the neoclassical aesthetic and ethical values of Nature and Sense that he wished to uphold. In the Epilogue to *The Rehearsal*, Buckingham makes a connection between art and life, arguing that a society producing such artistic perversions as heroic drama must itself be in danger of abandoning sanity for its opposite. The plea for an aesthetic revering classical lucidity and simplicity is also a plea for the establishment of social and moral standards based on Reason:

> *If it be true, that Monstrous births presage*
> *The following mischiefs that afflict the Age,*
> *And sad disasters to the State proclaim;*
> *Plays without head or tail, may do the same.*
> *Wherefore, for ours, and for the Kingdomes peace,*
> *May this prodigious way of writing cease.*

Let's have, at least, once in our lives, a time
When we may hear some reason, not all Rhyme:
We have these ten years felt its Influence;
Pray let this prove a year of Prose and Sence.

NOTES
1. Buckingham's play also gave its name to a number of the publications in the pamphlet war surrounding Andrew Marvell in 1672-73 that had nothing to do with drama. Marvell's *The Rehearsal Transpros'd* was answered by other satirical essays, including *Rosemary and Bayes, The Transproser Rehears'd*, and *S'too him Bayes*.
2. *The Rehearsal*, ed. Montague Summers (Stratford-upon-Avon, 1914); ed. D. E. L. Crane (Durham, 1976). All quotations are from the latter, which contains a helpful bibliography. Like several other plays discussed in this book, *The Rehearsal* is included in a most useful modern anthology, *Burlesque Plays of the Eighteenth Century*, ed. Simon Trussler (London, 1969).
3. *Plays about the Theatre in England*, ch. 2. See also my '*The Rehearsal*: A Study of its Satirical Methods', *Durham University Journal* 31 (1970) 96-113; reprinted in *Die englische Satire*, ed. Wolfgang Weiss (Darmstadt, 1982) 284-314.
4. 'Political Satire in *The Rehearsal*', *Yearbook of English Studies* 4 (1974) 120-8.
5. *A Complete Key to the Last New Farce The What D'Ye Call It* (London, 1715) [v-vi].
6. *The Burlesque Tradition*, 32.
7. *Ibid.*, 31.
8. 'Buckingham's Permanent *Rehearsal*', *Michigan Quarterly Review* 12 (1973) 160-71.
9. *Ibid.*, 161.

After Buckingham:
Thomas Duffett and other Minor Writers

The Rehearsal did what it did so well, immediately establishing itself as a theatrical favourite, that any play written in direct imitation of it, such as the anonymous *The Female Wits; or, The Triumvirate of Poets at Rehearsal*, was likely to be but a pale reflection of the original. *The Female Wits* was produced at Drury Lane in 1696 and published in 1704 as the work of 'W.M.', possibly William Mountfort.[1] The twin aims of its author were to ridicule three popular women writers of the 1690s, the 'triumvirate' of Delarivier (usually but incorrectly named Mary) Manley, Mary Pix, and Catherine Trotter, and to criticize their plays. The Bayes-figure is Marsilia, a portrait of Mrs Manley, and the inner play burlesques her spectacular tragedy *The Royal Mischief* (1696), staged only a few months before *The Female Wits*. By the 1690s tragic drama had become much more imbued with pathos and sentiment than it had been when Buckingham was writing, and the emotionalism of Mrs Manley's play is one of the targets of *The Female Wits*. Yet in spite of this difference as well as the change of sex of the Bayes-figure, the author follows too closely in the footsteps of *The Rehearsal* to add significantly to its methods and achievement, and rarely recaptures Buckingham's wit and inventiveness.

If this is true of *The Female Wits*, it is even more true of a later and better-known derivative of *The Rehearsal*, D'Urfey's *The Two Queens of Brentford; or, Bayes No Poetaster* (1721), which actually announces itself as 'The Sequel of the Famous Rehearsal' and even retains such characters as Bayes, Johnson, Smith and Prince Prettyman. D'Urfey's 'Musical Farce or Comical Opera' virtually demands to be compared with *The Rehearsal*, but considering the success of Buckingham's play the comparison is not flattering. Not surprisingly, D'Urfey's play never reached the stage because it proved disastrous in rehearsal. What does make *The Two Queens of Brentford* interesting are its satirical references to the current theatrical vogue, Italian opera. The singing lion that Bayes solemnly presents as an 'Opera Rarity' is aimed at the lion in Mancini's popular *Idaspe* (1710), an operatic beast that occasioned a great deal of amused comment, including one of Addison's *Spectator* papers (13).

Only Fielding in *Tumble-Down Dick* and Sheridan in *The Critic* managed to produce orthodox burlesques of the major stature of *The Rehearsal* using Buckingham's method, although Fielding did employ the technique most successfully in his rather different dramatic satires. Nevertheless, lesser writers could achieve impressive burlesque works when they followed Buckingham's example less slavishly than either the author of *The Female Wits* or D'Urfey. An admirable example is Richard Leveridge's afterpiece, *The Comick Masque of Pyramus and Thisbe* (1716), which has been undeservedly neglected by scholars.[2] The description 'Comick Masque' refers to the short Italian-style operas in one or two acts performed as afterpieces at this time. These were known as masques or musical masques, and the Prologue to the inner play alludes satirically to three of these, Colley Cibber's *Venus and Adonis* (1715), his *Myrtillo* (1715), and John Hughes' *Apollo and Daphne* (1716). As the title suggests, Leveridge's burlesque of Italianate opera is derived from *A Midsummer Night's Dream*, the play within a play being a sung version of the playlet about Pyramus and Thisbe performed by the 'mechanicals' in Shakespeare's comedy. The composer of this farcical 'tragic opera' is Semibreve, who corresponds to Bayes in *The Rehearsal*, and he is accompanied in the outer play by Crotchet and Gamut, the counterparts of Johnson and Smith in Buckingham's play. Leveridge saw that Shakespeare's burlesque of rhetorical bombast could easily be transformed into operatic burlesque by setting it to Italianate music, and the burlesque largely depended on the incongruity between the text and the serious music, which has not survived. Even when a singing Wall, a singing Moon, and a singing Lion perform, the appearance of operatic solemnity is maintained. Although derived from Shakespeare's talking Lion, Leveridge's gentle animal is another mockery of the ferocious lion in *Idaspe*.

The direct influence of Buckingham is not only to be seen in dramatic burlesques employing his rehearsal technique or at least incorporating an inner play. Despite its name, Gildon's *A New Rehearsal; or, Bays the Younger* (1714) is not a burlesque play but a piece of criticism in the form of a conversation, like Dryden's *Essay of Dramatick Poesie*. Nevertheless, it is heavily indebted to the framework surrounding the mock play in *The Rehearsal*, since Gildon's mouthpieces, Freeman and Truewit, are derived from Smith and Johnson, while his caricatures of Nicholas Rowe as Bays and of Alexander Pope as Sawny Dapper are modelled on Buckingham's Bayes. *A New Rehearsal* is also relevant to the burlesque tradition because its severe if somewhat crude attack on Rowe and his plays, including his so-called 'she-tragedies', amounts to a critique of aspects of contemporary tragedy, including the increasingly pathetic and sentimental tendencies. Gay's magnificent burlesque of pathetic tragedy, *The What D'Ye Call It*, appeared in the following year.

By no means all burlesque plays in the years after *The Rehearsal* follow its example. Some eschew the rehearsal method completely, being self-contained mock plays without any framing device. As in the cases of the burlesque playlet in Davenant's *The Playhouse To Be Let* and Wright's *Mock-Thyestes*, these conform much more closely to the current methods of literary travesty than to Buckingham's refined techniques. Thomas Duffett, the writer who made the most important contribution to the burlesque tradition in the theatre between *The Rehearsal* and the end of the seventeenth century, chose this alternative way. None of his three individual though artistically unsubtle burlesque plays, produced in quick succession not long after Buckingham's play, employs a rehearsal structure, and in each the elevated subject matter of his targets is grossly debased by being subjected to extremely vulgar treatment. Duffett also differs from Buckingham in that he was not attempting a general satire of heroic drama and dramatic opera by alluding to a wide range of plays, but was travestying specific theatrical productions. His three burlesques were staged by the King's Company at a time when it was trying to recover after the destruction by fire of its Bridges Street theatre in 1672; they were aimed at recent performances by the Duke's Company at the rival theatre, Dorset Garden, which was better equipped for providing spectacle and scenic effects, and therefore able to present heroic plays and dramatic operas more elaborately and sumptuously. *The Empress of Morocco* (1673) was directed at Settle's heroic play of the same name (1673); *The Mock-Tempest; or, The Enchanted Castle* (1674) at Shadwell's operatic version of Dryden and Davenant's adaptation of *The Tempest* (1674); and *Psyche Debauch'd* (1675) at Shadwell's dramatic opera *Psyche* (1675).

Duffett was certainly trying to win support for the King's Company just before and for a short time after it moved into its new Drury Lane theatre in 1674, but the main question about his burlesques is whether they are dramatizations of theatrical envy and sour grapes devised as anti-Dorset Garden propaganda, or whether they embody genuine critical perceptions about the works they burlesque and about theatrical spectacle itself, as is the case with *The Rehearsal*. Are they exercises in travesty, like the playlet in Davenant's *The Playhouse To Be Let* (also based on a contemporary play) and Wright's *Mock-Thyestes*, though with a different motive; or do they amount to satire of dramatic pretentiousness and absurdity? Is one of the driving forces behind his visual burlesque of the Dorset Garden productions a recognition that drama was becoming too sensational, that poetry was being sacrificed for scenic ingenuity? Is his deliberate coarseness of language and action a criticism of the inflated rhetoric and grandiose characters of the plays burlesqued? Because of his close parody of these plays and because of the example recently set by *The Rehearsal*, it is tempting to think so; but even the most enthusiastic of his few defenders, his recent editor Ronald Eugene DiLorenzo, does not claim this, arguing only that 'his effort was directed primarily toward winning over a part of the audience from Dorset Garden, and also to having a bit of intramural fun'.[3]

Settle's *The Empress of Morocco* was one of the most successful productions at Dorset Garden during the 1673-74 season and the plates included in the lavish first edition give a good idea of its extremely spectacular nature. To judge from these, the final horrific scene in which 'Crimalhaz *appears cast down on the Gaunches, being hung on a Wall set with spikes of Iron*' (v, i) was particularly sensational. Among the other theatrical thrills are the action-packed ambush scene with sword fights and guns being fired (IV, ii) and the elaborate masque set in Hell with Pluto, Proserpine, Orpheus, and assorted furies, including a dance performed *'by several infernal Spirits, who ascend from under the Stage'* (IV, iii). In his own very much shorter *Empress of Morocco*, Duffett turns Settle's conception upside down by substituting a low-life world (with characters such as a drayman and a chimney sweep) for the courtly milieu of Settle's heroic play. Duffett retains the names of Settle's characters, but otherwise transforms them into mockeries of the originals. Muly Labas, who is the son of the Emperor in Settle's play, appears as a corn cutter (in the sense of chiropodist, not agricultural worker) in Duffett's travesty, and the Empress herself, Laula, is reduced to a hostess. Vulgarity and buffoonery replace magniloquence and pomp at every level. Instead of acting with dignity like Settle's courtiers, Duffett's burlesque courtiers play Hot-Cockles, an uncouth rural game involving the beating of someone's bottom and the victim's subsequent attempt to identify his assailant. Instead of heroic couplets, Duffett uses nondescript doggerel couplets with feminine endings. Insult was added to injury in the production of Duffett's travesty by having the three leading female roles played by men.

Considering the visual impact of Settle's play in performance, it is not surprising to find an extended piece of visual burlesque at the very centre of Duffett's burlesque. One of the highly theatrical set pieces of Settle's play, incorporating music, song, dance, and spectacle, is the Moorish dance performed before the Court, which is the subject of one of the illustrative plates in the first edition. Duffett's parodic answer to this scene is an extended Heathen dance, at the end of which Muly Labas *'falls down, being dead drunk'* (I, ii); during the dance there is a song about alcohol and in praise of brandy. Duffett's stage direction indicates that he closely models his visual burlesque on Settle's ornate scene, even down to 'an artificial broad spreading broom' for the *'artificial Palm-tree'* of the original (II, i). There are some equally close correspondences between the two plays at the verbal as well as at the visual level, but Duffett's debasement of Settle's rhetoric is schoolboyish travesty without the critical dimension that gives Buckingham's parodies their incisiveness.

In the first and by far the longer of the two Epilogues to *The Empress of Morocco*, Duffett turns his attention to another recent and opulent production at Dorset Garden, Davenant's adaptation of *Macbeth*, with its 'emended' speeches, additional scenes (in couplets), extra characters, songs, dances, flying witches, and elaborate sets and scenic devices. In this case Duffett concentrates on only one aspect of the play, the operatic witch episodes, which Davenant had expanded considerably from Shakespeare's tragedy, especially by the use of music; Davenant's witches are primarily singing witches. Duffett's witches, all of whom were played by men, also sing, but their principal song is a celebration of prostitution. Heccate and the three witches, who are themselves presented as members of 'the Trade', each sing a toast to a well-known whore of the time before joining in a chorus of praise for yet another prostitute. The opening of Duffett's Epilogue parallels the entry of Davenant's flying witches, but the episode is ludicrous, not thrillingly spectacular as Davenant's was intended to be. Duffett's storm proceeds with no attempt at theatrical illusion; Thunder and Lightning appear as characters, and the effects are revealed for what they really are. This stripping down of spectacle to its mundane mechanics continues when the witches make their bizarre entrances, Heccate's supposedly 'Glorious Charriot' being exposed as 'a large Wicker Basket'. Although Duffett's visual burlesque pokes fun at the 'new' *Macbeth*, it is doing little more than making an obvious point about all dramatic illusion and hardly amounts to a perceptive criticism of Davenant's theatrical extravagance. Duffett's conception of travesty is too unsophisticated for that.

Duffett's two subsequent burlesques differ from *The Empress of Morocco* in being full-length five-act plays and in being mainly in prose, but in their basic method of vulgarizing as much as possible the characters, conduct, dialogue, and settings of his targets, with copious reference to sex, prostitution, venereal disease, and bodily functions, they are similar. Because of their larger scale, both *The Mock-Tempest* and *Psyche Debauch'd* expand beyond simple travesty so that some characters are not just antitypes but assume a dramatic existence not wholly dependent on their counterparts in Shadwell's operas. Yet this is not the unequivocal improvement that DiLorenzo claims it to be in the Introduction of his edition. Both plays do more than is strictly required of them as burlesques, but they are still first and foremost burlesques, and as burlesques they might well have been better if more concentrated and compact. Duffett's limitations as a writer would not be so obvious in shorter forms.

Shadwell's operatic *Tempest*, with its flying spirits, extended songs, and chorus of devils, was a most lavish production, making use of all the resources of Dorset Garden. Duffett follows the operatic *Tempest* closely, sometimes line by line, providing numerous songs and his own chorus of devils, but he transfers the action to the London underworld of brothels and prisons, filling his stage with prostitutes and rogues instead of princes and nobles. Included in the cast are three whores named Beantosser, Moustrappa, and Drinkallup. The opening storm scene is replaced by a riotous assault on a brothel by a mob in which chamber pots feature prominently. Prospero, the former Duke of Milan, is transformed into Prospero Whiffe, once 'a man of great power, Duke of my Lord Mayors Dogg-kennel' (I, ii) and now the head keeper of 'the enchanted castle' of Bridewell, the notorious house of correction in Blackfriars, which is the equivalent of the enchanted island. By winning the affection of the dogs in Prospero Whiffe's care, his brother, working in association with Alonzo, Duke of Newgate, not King of Naples as in *The Tempest*, has ousted him from his position, but has refrained from killing him because, as Prospero tells Miranda, 'Near the Kenell they dar'd not for the love my dogged Subject bore me' (I, ii). Such low situational and verbal parallels to the original are sustained throughout. Prospero's threat to trap Ariel inside an oak tree for twelve winters unless he stops complaining becomes Prospero Whiffe's 'If thou more murmur'st, in some small dimple of her Cheek I'le peg thee, where Twelve Sommers more thou shalt lye stewing like a Maggot in a *Holland* Cheese' (IV, i); Ariel's song 'Where the Bee sucks, there suck I' (V, ii) becomes '*Where good Ale is, there suck I*' (V, ii). Duffett converts Ferdinand into Quakero, a religious fanatic and also a hypocrite, whose lustful pursuit of Miranda Whiffe is a grotesque perversion of Ferdinand's attitude of reverence towards Miranda. Duffett's gift for deflationary burlesque is not contemptible although contempt is what he has usually received from critics, but his talent is over-stretched in such a large-scale work. Despite the wit of his best bawdy passages, unrelenting crudity becomes tiresome after a while and the joke wears thin.

Psyche Debauch'd is longer than *The Mock-Tempest* and more ambitious in that it shows Duffett trying harder to develop the characters and action of his play beyond the confines of strict travesty; he even includes some material not derived in any way from *Psyche*. Nevertheless, his burlesque of Shadwell's dramatic opera contains a great deal of very close parody – verbal, situational, and visual. The production of *Psyche* must have been more spectacular than that of the operatic *Tempest*. The text is full of lengthy stage directions for highly exotic settings and sensational effects so that the

Fielding's Burlesque Drama

work seems to have been designed as an eye-stunning showpiece for the capabilities of Dorset Garden. Duffett seized on this visual aspect of *Psyche*, but his own stage directions are often much less detailed than Shadwell's and simply provide the producer and designer with the basic information, leaving a lot to their imaginations to fill in. Shadwell's precise instructions for the scene in Hell at the opening of Act v, complete with the burning ruins of buildings, a lake of fire, numerous devils tormenting the damned, a vast crowd of the dead waiting to be ferried across the Styx by Charon, and Pluto on his throne rising from under the stage, become in Duffett's version:

> A common Prison confused.
> *A great noise heard – Singing, Shreeking, Groaning,*
> *Roaring, and Ratling of Chains.*   (v)

In his characteristic way, Duffett systematically debases the Psyche myth so grandiosely retold by Shadwell, substituting earthiness, bawdy, and nonsense for the high-flown. The Venus figure in *Psyche Debauch'd* is Woossat, who makes her first appearance in Act I *'in a Charriot drawn by two Brooms'* (not doves as in *Psyche*) to the accompaniment of *'Horrid Musick'* (not soft music as in *Psyche*). Furthermore, she was played by an actor, as were two other female parts, a farcical device also used in the staging of *The Empress of Morocco*. The equivalent of Psyche herself, Princess None-so-fair or Nonsy for short, was acted by the famous comedian Joe Haynes, whose appearance as the heroine must have been hilarious to audiences familiar with his usual performances. But in the production of *Psyche Debauch'd*, sex reversal was taken further than in the earlier play by having two of the male roles played by women. The action of *Psyche Debauch'd* is entirely in keeping with these absurd characters and reproduces that of *Psyche* in burlesque form. What might be called the element of exuberant pantomimic nonsense in Duffett's conception also infects the language of *Psyche Debauch'd*, freeing it at times from the vulgarity and coarse innuendo typical of his verbal burlesque. Duffett transforms a solemn ritual conducted by priests in Shadwell's opera into a mock-invocation of sheer nonsense:

> CHIEF PRIEST *Jupiter, Juno, Minerva, Saturn, Cibele.*
> RESPONSE Be propitious to our vows and prayers.
> CHIEF PRIEST *Mars, Bellona, Venus, Cupido, Vulcanus.*
> RESPONSE Be propitious to our vows and prayers.
> CHIEF PRIEST *Bacchus, Pan, Neptunus, Sylvanus, Fawnus, Vertumnus, Palemon.*
> RESPONSE Be propitious to our vows and prayers.
> CHIEF PRIEST All ye Gods, Goddesses, and all the powers.
> RESPONSE Be propitious to our vows and prayers. (*Psyche*, 11)

SECOND PRIEST *James Naylor, Pope Joan, Wat. Tyler, Mall. Cutpurs, Chocorelly.*
ALL-ANSWER Help our *Opera*, because 'tis very silly.
SECOND PRIEST *Massaniello, Mosely, Jack-straw, Jantredisco, Pimponelli.*
ALL-ANSWER Help our *Opera*, because 'tis very silly.
SECOND PRIEST *Hocus-pocus, Don-Quixot, Jack Adams, Mary Ambry, Frier Bungy, William Lilly.*
ALL-ANSWER Help our *Opera*, because 'tis very silly.
SECOND PRIEST *Carpentero, Paintero, Dancero, Musickero, Songstero, Punchanelly.*
ALL-ANSWER Help our *Opera*, because 'tis very silly.

(*Psyche Debauch'd*, II, i)

Duffett's brief career as a writer of dramatic burlesque belongs to a short period in which one of the two London companies was seriously disadvantaged after the burning down of its theatre and had to fight hard to recapture its audience, not only when working in temporary premises but even after it had moved into its new theatre. Travesty of popular productions by the other company was a way of trying to achieve this. Once the King's Company had fully established itself in Drury Lane, there was not the same pressure to continue with Duffett's kind of burlesque, and the amalgamation of the two companies in 1682 put an end to the possibility of travestying productions by a rival theatre. Warfare between London companies did recur intermittently, notably after Thomas Betterton's secession in 1695 and Theophilus Cibber's rebellion in 1733, and plays directly related to these skirmishes were performed, but the use of travesty as an inter-theatrical weapon was never revived. In this sense, Duffett is without successors. The theatres employed other weapons to win audiences, such as the farcical afterpiece from 1695 onwards. It is therefore unlikely that Duffett exerted any direct influence on subsequent writers of burlesque plays in the way that Buckingham did. Nevertheless, some of these, including Fielding, also found the method of travesty rewarding, even though their burlesque aims were different from his. Duffett's achievement is undoubtedly limited, but in ridiculing specific productions and in eschewing Buckingham's rehearsal method he made an original contribution to burlesque drama and deserves credit for this.

Some subsequent burlesques resemble Duffett's work much more than Buckingham's. Like each of Duffett's burlesques, Colley Cibber's 'Comical Tragedy' *The Rival Queans* is a self-contained travesty of a single play, Lee's popular tragedy *The Rival Queens; or, The Death of Alexander the Great*(1677).[4] Cibber follows Lee very closely indeed. His characters have the same names as Lee's but are debased to the level of contemporary low life, 'queans' replacing 'queens': the female rivals, Roxana and Statira, are presented as whores and Alexander as a city bully:

> ALEXANDER P'shaw! prithee dear *Rocky* now,
> Don't be troublesome, you see I'm busy.
> ROXANA Rejected then! sent Supperless away!
> ALEXANDER Get to the Rose, and call for what you please,
> Pullet with Eggs, Beef-stakes, or Sausages.
> Bid, *Rause*, send in the Bill to me, away;
> Sup any where without me, and I'll pay.   (III, i)

Although Cibber compresses a few scenes, his usual technique is a line-by-line parody of Lee, and he sometimes retains entire lines of the original, changing only a few words in a particular speech. Where *The Rival Queans* differs from Duffett's plays is in being more of a literary than a theatrical travesty. Burlesque stage directions abound in Duffett, whereas Cibber concentrates almost entirely on the text. A performance of the play would inevitably have produced some visual burlesque, but Cibber does not seem to have been concerned with this; his travesty, unlike Duffett's, was not conceived as a theatrical reply to another company's production. Duffett's plays followed their targets within a matter of months; Cibber probably wrote *The Rival Queans* in 1703, a quarter of a century after Lee's play reached the stage, and it was not performed until 1710.

Although Steele criticized Lee's tragedy on moral grounds and actually commended Cibber's burlesque in *The Tatler* (191), it is unlikely that Cibber's motive was to expose the immorality of Lee's heroic characters, since his own work depends so much on crudity and bawdy. *The Rival Queans* is not a satirical burlesque of a play exemplifying a genre that Cibber found worthy of ridicule. In this it differs significantly from two of Fielding's burlesques, *The Covent-Garden Tragedy* and *Tumble-Down Dick*, both of which are also based on a single play yet satirize in general pseudo-classical tragedy and pantomime respectively. Cibber travesties a well-known example of a kind of play, heroic tragedy, that was going out of fashion in the first decade of the eighteenth century because of the current emphasis on pathos in tragic drama. *The Rival Queans* is therefore a symptom of changes in taste rather than a Buckingham-like critical diagnosis of dramatic absurdity.

Two subsequent burlesques in the manner of Duffett resemble Leveridge's *The Comick Masque of Pyramus and Thisbe* in mocking the new theatrical craze of the early eighteenth century, Italian opera. The first Italianate opera to be staged in England, *Arsinoe*, appeared in 1705, with the even more successful *Camilla* and others following soon after, and within a few years a vogue for the form had developed. *Arsinoe* was sung in English and some subsequent operas were sung in a mixture of English and Italian, but the production of

Mancini's *Idaspe* in 1710, in which only Italian was used, set the pattern for the future. As early as 1708 Richard Estcourt incorporated a short burlesque of Italian opera, *Prunella*, as an Interlude in a production of *The Rehearsal* in which he himself played Bayes. Estcourt made fun of *Arsinoe* and *Camilla* by setting inane and trivial words to music from these operas and by substituting London grocers and tradesmen for the dignified figures of the operas. As a burlesque, *Prunella* is artistically crude and undistinguished, but its appearance so soon after the arrival of Italian opera is historically important.

The other Duffett-like burlesque of Italian opera is Mrs Aubert's *Harlequin-Hydaspes; or, The Greshamite* (1719), aimed specifically at Mancini's *Idaspe* (or *Hydaspes*), which she transforms into a kind of harlequinade by replacing the operatic characters with the usual figures of the *commedia dell'arte*. Scaramouch, Harlequin, Pierrot, and Colombine are substituted for Darius, Hydaspes, Arbaces, and Berenice respectively, while the Middle Eastern setting of *Idaspe* is changed to Gresham College, the educational institution founded in London at the end of the sixteenth century by Sir Thomas Gresham. However, Mrs Aubert concentrates her satire more on the malevolent Greshamite Doctor, who is the equivalent of Artaxerxes in *Idaspe* and the most important character in much of the mock opera, than on Italian opera. Her attempt to combine attacks on current medical practice and Gresham College with dramatic burlesque is not very satisfactory, and *Harlequin-Hydaspes*, although virtually a scene-by-scene travesty of *Idaspe*, finally seems more like a harlequinade derived from an operatic plot than an effective burlesque of Mancini's opera. The best burlesque episode, the killing of the lion by Harlequin in the final scene, refers to the notorious lion in *Idaspe*, also ridiculed by Leveridge.

If Italian opera soon became a target for the burlesquer, contemporary comedy remained largely unscathed until the Scriblerian mockery of *Three Hours after Marriage* in 1717 (discussed in the next chapter). *The Rehearsal* does contain a few passing allusions to Restoration comedies, but these are marginal to the main burlesque thrust. Nevertheless, two comic plays from around the turn of the century, George Farquhar's first comedy *Love and a Bottle* (1698) and the anonymous *The Roving Husband Reclaim'd* (1706), have been interpreted as satirical burlesques, and if this is the case they would be the first substantial burlesques of Restoration and eighteenth-century comic drama.

Love and a Bottle has usually been regarded as an immature work, an entertaining but overloaded ragbag of familiar comic devices and conventions, including mistaken identities, multiple disguises and a complex intrigue plot. However, Eugene Nelson James has suggested that this overloading serves a deliberate burlesque purpose, with Farquhar making fun of the conventions of contemporary comedy by exaggerating them.[5] Because there is no evidence to suggest that Farquhar's contemporaries took the play as a burlesque of the conventions rather than an individual reworking of them, this could be an example of something that strikes a critic today as burlesque but that was not intended or understood as such at the time. The unperformed play by the famous actor Joseph Haynes (or Hayns), *A Fatal Mistake* (1692), has been interpreted in the twentieth century as a burlesque of heroic tragedy since it is difficult to take seriously, but might it not simply be a genuine though feeble attempt at tragedy? When tragedy fails, the result is often unintentional bathos, which at a distance can look like the intentional bathos of burlesque. James nevertheless draws attention to unorthodox elements in Farquhar's play which can be interpreted as playfully mocking over-elaboration rather than original but serious handling of comic conventions. But even if there is some truth in James' speculations, *Love and a Bottle* cannot be described as a burlesque play because the principal impulse behind it is not burlesque. *Love and a Bottle* is primarily a comedy, and any burlesque is integrated into Farquhar's creation of his own comic world. Farquhar began his theatrical career in the year of Jeremy Collier's *A Short View of the Immorality and Profaneness of the English Stage* (1698), when drama was under severe attack from moralistic critics and when comedy was in a state of transition, with some of its conventions being challenged and questioned.

The unperformed *The Roving Husband Reclaim'd* is less problematical, though again the play as a whole does not register as a sustained burlesque. By listing *The Roving Husband Reclaim'd* as a burlesque, Allardyce Nicoll is implicitly claiming it as the first burlesque of sentimentalism in comedy,[6] and Robert D. Hume calls it 'a sardonic burlesque . . . providing all the elements of tearful didacticism in a deliciously flippant way'.[7] The description on the title page, 'Writ by a Club of Ladies, in Vindication of Virtuous Plays', is clearly ironic, but until the fifth act the play conforms in many ways to the typical intrigue comedy of the period, featuring upper-class rakes and the usual contrast between sophisticated city and unsophisticated country life. The one character who stands apart from the licentiousness surrounding her is Thoughtless' wife, Fidelia, an embodiment of womanly virtue. Burlesque is most conspicuous in the ostensibly serious dénouement, where virtue not only triumphs over vice but also reduces the wicked to remorseful penitence. Having failed to seduce Fidelia, Colonel Courtlove is about to rape her when she kneels and prays in an extremely histrionic way. Her appeal for divine intervention is immediately answered, Thoughtless arriving like a *deus ex machina* to take his wife in his arms.

Courtlove is converted from his immoral life on the spot, and the play ends with some fatuous moralizing by Thoughtless about the advantages of faithful wives. This ludicrously melodramatic conclusion is a palpable hit at similar scenes in the popular 'reforming' comedies of the time, such as Cibber's *Love's Last Shift* (1696) and *The Careless Husband* (1704), the first of which elicited Vanbrugh's critical but not actually burlesque reply in *The Relapse* (1696). Until comic dramatists presented emotional reformation scenes to satisfy the changing taste of the town at the turn of the century, comedy gave far fewer opportunities for burlesque than other genres and consequently escaped this form of attention.

NOTES
1. The text is available in the Augustan Reprint Society series, 124 (Los Angeles, 1967), with an extended introduction by Lucyle Hook. It is also included as an Appendix in an anthology of plays, *The Female Wits: Women Playwrights of the Restoration*, ed. Fidelis Morgan (London, 1981). The play is discussed by Smith in *Plays about the Theatre in England*, 71-8.
2. I have discussed this in detail in 'Richard Leveridge's *Comick Masque of Pyramus and Thisbe*', *Restoration and 18th Century Theatre Research* 15, 1 (1976) 33-41.
3. *Three Burlesque Plays of Thomas Duffett*, ed. DiLorenzo (Iowa City, 1972) xi. All quotations are from this edition.
4. Cibber's burlesque has been published in the Lake Erie College Studies series (Painesville, Ohio, 1965) with an introduction by William M. Peterson, who also discusses the play in 'Cibber's *Rival Queans*', *Notes and Queries 204* (1959) 164-8.
5. 'The Burlesque of Restoration Comedy in *Love and a Bottle*', *Studies in English Literature 1500-1900* 5 (1965) 469-90.
6. *Early Eighteenth Century Drama* (3rd ed., Cambridge, 1952) 182.
7. *The Rakish Stage*, 189.

The Contribution of John Gay

Fielding made his début as a playwright in 1728, the year of *The Beggar's Opera*, and until Gay's death four years later their theatrical careers overlapped. Fielding's most obvious debt to Gay is formal since he repeatedly used the genre of ballad opera, whether for comedy, farce, or satire, but he is also Gay's immediate successor in the fields of dramatic burlesque and dramatic satire. Like Dryden before him, but unlike the writers he is usually linked with (such as Swift and Pope) who had little to do with the theatre, Gay excelled as both poet and dramatist. He essayed the regular forms of comedy and tragedy, but he was decidedly more original as well as more successful in irregular forms, notably but not only in the genre he himself created, ballad opera.

Gay's first dramatic work, *The Mohocks* (1712), a short afterpiece which failed to reach the stage, is something of an oddity and gives an indication of the direction in which his talent would lead him not long afterwards in *The What D'Ye Call It* (1715) and *Three Hours after Marriage* (1717). Gay labelled *The Mohocks* a 'Tragi-Comical Farce' and provided the published version with a satirical preface in which he dedicates the play ironically to John Dennis, the major Augustan critic noted for his dogmatic pronouncements. This preface, with its attack on doctrinaire neoclassical rules of writing (especially the unities) which Dennis himself propounded, gives the impression that the play could be a burlesque of contemporary tragedy, in particular of Dennis' recent *Appius and Virginia* (1709) and similar pseudo-classical works. Gay seems to have begun the play with the intention of burlesquing Dennis by substituting the rough-and-tumble adventures of the contemporary aristocratic rakehells and bullies called Mohocks (after the North American Indian tribe) for the historical remoteness and elevated rhetoric of pseudo-classical tragedy. The play undoubtedly opens as burlesque, but after only one scene this gives way to a farcical comedy about an adventure of the Mohocks, who capture the city Watch and accuse them in front of magistrates of being Mohocks. The change of direction is clearly marked by the shift from the language of burlesque to the language of farce, from mock-heroic blank verse to brisk prose.

Gay's first attempt at mock-heroic poetry is the quasi-Miltonic *Wine* (1708), and in *The Mohocks* he again uses mock-heroic to deflate what he regarded as the pretentiousness of the high style, particularly in pseudo-classical tragedy. According to Thomas B. Stroup,[1] Gay's burlesque is at least partly aimed at the content and style of *Paradise Lost*, although the ironical dedication contains no hint of this anti-Miltonic element. Milton's reputation was very much in the ascendant at this time, thanks to the enthusiastic appraisals of such influential critics as Dennis and Addison, and Gay may have been cocking a snook at the current cult of Milton. The names of the Mohocks, such as Abaddon, Moloch, and Mirmidon, are undoubtedly suggestive of the fallen angels in Milton's epic. It would have been easy for Gay to burlesque simultaneously *Paradise Lost* and the poetry of contemporary tragedy since the latter frequently aspires to the epic style, like that of the Restoration heroic play. Nevertheless, Gay's burlesque has more immediate sources in Restoration and Augustan drama than in Milton. By incongruously putting low subject matter, the activities and aspirations of hoodlums, into an elevated heroic idiom, thus generating a mock-heroic discrepancy between content and style, Gay exposes the stilted, inflated rhetoric of Dennis and his contemporaries to ridicule, as in Abaddon's description of a fray with the Watch:

> Thus far our Riots with Success are crown'd,
> Have found no stop, or what they found o'ercame;
> In vain th'embattell'd Watch in deep array,
> Against our Rage oppose their lifted Poles;
> Through Poles we rush triumphant, Watchman rolls
> On Watchman; while their Lanthorns kick'd aloft
> Like blazing Stars, illumine all the Air.   (Scene 1)[2]

The first two lines of this speech closely imitate in a parodic way the opening couplet of Dryden's tragedy *Tyrannick Love*, spoken by Maximin:

> Thus far my Arms have with success been crown'd;
> And found no stop, or vanquish'd what they found.

But it is an episode at the end of the first act of Dennis' *Appius and Virginia*, in which Lucius Icilius and the conspirators solemnly vow to kill Appius, that provides Gay with his principal burlesque target. In Gay's mock-heroic equivalent to Dennis' oath-taking ceremony (by no means the only one in contemporary tragedy), the Mohocks form a circle, kneel, and swear allegiance to their 'most High and Mighty Emperor', before promising:

> That we'll to Virtue bear invet'rate Hate,
> Renounce Humanity, defie Religion;

That Villany, and all outragious Crimes
Shall ever be our Glory and our Pleasure.   (Scene 1)

Probably the most interesting aspect of *The Mohocks* is that it shows Gay experimenting as early as 1712 with the ironical method of satire he brought to perfection in *The Beggar's Opera*, staged sixteen years later. The band of Mohocks, presented as a courtly assembly with its own emperor, strict protocol, and standards of conduct, foreshadows in some respects Macheath's gang of criminals. The New Mohock's respectful greeting to the Mohock Emperor, 'Great Potentate!', is especially anticipatory of the ironic inversions in *The Beggar's Opera*, but in *The Mohocks* Gay does not exploit the potential of mock-heroic for political satire as he does in the later work.

In his next irregular play, *The What D'Ye Call It*, first produced on 23 February 1715 at Drury Lane as an afterpiece to one of its targets, Rowe's tragedy *Jane Shore* (1714), Gay sustains his burlesque intention without the abrupt shift into farcical comedy that characterizes *The Mohocks*. The description of the play on the title-page as 'A Tragi-Comi-Pastoral Farce', which recalls Polonius' cataloguing of dramatic kinds in *Hamlet*, is profoundly ironic. *The What D'Ye Call It* proved to be extremely popular during the first half of the eighteenth century, and its success did much to encourage the growth of the burlesque afterpiece. It was certainly the most important dramatic burlesque since *The Rehearsal*, although it is also more than a burlesque, as several scholars, including the recent editor of Gay's *Dramatic Works* (1983), John Fuller, have noted.[3] In the present context, the emphasis is on the play as burlesque.

Before Gay, no one had attempted an extensive burlesque of the drama exhibiting the influence of sentimentalism, especially pathetic tragedy, which had emerged after *The Rehearsal* and Duffett's three burlesques. Gildon's *A New Rehearsal* is an onslaught against the best-known writer of pathetic tragedy, Nicholas Rowe, but it is not a burlesque. As the phrase 'Tragi-Comi-Pastoral Farce' suggests, Gay's burlesque is directed against several dramatic and poetic modes, but his principal targets are the main tragic dramatists of the previous forty years: Dryden, Otway, Lee, Banks, Southerne, Rowe, Philips, and Addison. The tragedies that Gay selects in particular for burlesque treatment are Otway's *Venice Preserv'd* (1682), Banks' *The Unhappy Favourite* (1681), Philips' *The Distrest Mother* (1712), and Rowe's *Jane Shore* (1714), although he also had Southerne's *Oroonoko* (1695), Congreve's *The Mourning Bride* (1697), Rowe's *The Ambitious Stepmother* (1700) and *The Fair Penitent* (1703), Banks' *The Albion Queens* (1704) and Addison's *Cato* (1713) very much in mind. Thomas Wilkes records that an anonymous burlesque version of *Cato* was produced shortly after its target in 1713, but this work is not extant.⁴ Several of these tragedies were subsequently burlesqued by Fielding in *The Tragedy of Tragedies*, and *The Distrest Mother* is the chief victim of his bawdy burlesque play, *The Covent-Garden Tragedy*.

The Preface to *The What D'Ye Call It* is much more elaborate and even more ironical than the dedication of *The Mohocks*. For the purpose of ridicule, Gay assumes the persona of a modern playwright, who presents the 'Tragi-Comi-Pastoral Farce' as an extremely serious contribution to dramatic art, and indeed as an important step forward because no previous writer has attempted to interweave *'the several Kinds of the Drama with each other, so that they cannot be distinguish'd or separated'*. Gay ironically defends the play against accusations that it is neither tragedy, comedy, pastoral, nor farce according to Augustan definitions by a succession of specious arguments, culminating in the following evasions:

> *After all I have said, I would have these Criticks only consider, when they object against it as a Tragedy, that I design'd it something of a Comedy; when they cavil at it as a Comedy, that I had partly a View to Pastoral; when they attack it as a Pastoral, that my Endeavours were in some degree to write a Farce; and when they would destroy its Character as a Farce, that my Design was a Tragi-Comi-Pastoral: I believe when they consider this, they will all agree, that I have happily enough executed what I purpos'd, which is all I contend for. Yet that I might avoid the Cavils and Misinterpretations of severe Criticks, I have not call'd it a Tragedy, Comedy, Pastoral, or Farce, but left the Name entirely undetermin'd in the doubtful Appellation of* the What d'ye call it, *which Name I thought unexceptionable; but I added to it a* Tragi-Comi-Pastoral Farce, *as it comprized all those several Kinds of the* Drama.

By labelling his play as 'Tragi-Comi-Pastoral Farce', Gay's 'mask' can answer any possible objections to the play by claiming that what has been criticized has been misunderstood. The entire argument of the Preface is deliberately confused and contradictory. It appears to be a solemn exposition of a 'serious' play, but is Gay's own criticism of the 'mask', who represents the typical modern dramatist. For example, Gay's 'mask', who resembles Swift's 'mask' of the modern author in *A Tale of a Tub*, first justifies the presence of an embryo's ghost as integral to the tragedy, then defends the ghosts as part of the comic design, and finally dismisses the ghost scene as an inconsequential farcical incident *'without any Coherence with the rest of the Piece'*. Having unwittingly established the complete absurdity of his play, the 'mask' concludes with a comment that voices Gay's own censure of contemporary plays:

> the Success this Piece has met with upon the Stage, gives encouragement to our Dramatick Writers to follow its Model; and evidently demonstrates that this sort of Drama is no less fit for the Theatre than those they have succeeded in.

The supreme irony is that *The What D'Ye Call It* was at first taken seriously by some people. Pope records that

> The common people of the pit and gallery received it at first with great gravity and sedateness, some few with tears; but after the third day they also took the hint, and have ever since been very loud in their clapps.[5]

The pretence of seriousness is essential to good mock-heroic writing; the artistic success of the almost exactly contemporary *The Rape of the Lock* and the acuteness of its social criticism depend to a great extent on the apparently earnest way in which trivia are discussed in epic terms. The mock play in *The What D'Ye Call It* is offered as a genuine example of modern drama, an appearance intensified in eighteenth-century performances by the actors' gravity, as the unnerving experience of Pope's deaf friend Cromwell shows:

> Mr. Cromwell hearing none of the words and seeing the action to be tragical, was much astonished to find the audience laugh; and says the Prince and Princess [German-speaking Hanoverians] must doubtless be under no less amazement on the same account.[6]

Much of Gay's satirical humour, like Buckingham's, derives from the deliberate incongruity between matter and manner, between the essentially comic situation and the feigned solemnity with which it is presented.

There are, however, important differences between Buckingham and Gay, exemplified by the explicitness of Buckingham's Prologue and the irony of Gay's Preface. It is inconceivable that anyone, even someone attuned to heroic drama, should actually take the mock play in *The Rehearsal* seriously; the interwoven comments and discussions make Buckingham's intentions perfectly clear. By eschewing Buckingham's rehearsal technique in his search for subtler burlesque, Gay refuses to announce his intentions explicitly, and for the most part adopts the satirical method of uncompromising irony used by Defoe in *The Shortest Way with the Dissenters* and by Swift in *A Tale of a Tub*. Whereas Buckingham embodies his norms of Nature and Reason in Johnson and Smith, Gay's ironical approach allows him only to imply his positive aesthetic values by the indirect method of making fun of deviations from them. Gay's problem is to ensure that his mock play sufficiently clarifies the ludicrous characteristics of contemporary drama for it to be apprehended as satirical burlesque, even by an audience accustomed to pathetic tragedy.

Gay's solution of this artistic difficulty involves another significant departure from *The Rehearsal*. Both Buckingham and Gay blend the most commonplace situations of the drama they are burlesquing to form the plots of their mock plays, but Buckingham largely retains the courtly characters and milieu of heroic drama and achieves much of his satire by amplifying the language and actions of the heroic play to the point of absurdity. Gay does exaggerate certain situational features of contemporary drama, but his burlesque technique is much more consistently mock-heroic than Buckingham's. As in *The Mohocks* and *The Beggar's Opera*, Gay introduces a social world totally alien to pathetic tragedy, genteel comedy, and Italian opera. He substitutes a humble pastoral setting and a collection of low-life characters, such as servants and soldiers, for the court and city locales and the aristocratic and mythological personages of contemporary tragedy. The tender sentiments, torments of love, and spiritual anguish of high-born characters put into the mouths of peasants are ludicrously incongruous, but Gay's play is more than frivolous farce. By transferring to an earthy context the supposedly high-minded and uplifting scenes of pathos, remorse, and reconciliation found in plays tinged with sentimentalism, Gay exposes them for the tear-jerking and morally evasive incidents they often are, and reveals the overwrought language in which they are written as inflated, melodramatic rant. What Gay does, as the Preface suggests, is to create a potpourri of generic confusion – tragedy which not only makes us laugh but also has a happy ending in accordance with the conventions of comedy; farce which approaches pathos; and pastoral defying the conventions of pastoral.

In some respects, the pastoral element in *The What D'Ye Call It* resembles Gay's slightly earlier *The Shepherd's Week* (1714), a series of pastoral poems written at Pope's suggestion to ridicule the popular eclogues of Ambrose Philips. In dealing with the realities of rural existence as opposed to the life of Golden Age shepherds and shepherdesses, Philips' *Pastorals* (1709) flout the established neoclassical conventions of the genre, upheld by Pope in his *Discourse on Pastoral Poetry* (1704). Unfortunately, Philips preserved the form of the Virgilian eclogue, which was unsuitable for his intended realism. Pope and Gay recognized the incompatibility between form and content in Philips' pastorals, and in *The Shepherd's Week* Gay set out to burlesque Philips by exaggerating his defects. Gay retains such conventional pastoral forms as the debate and the lament, and uses the formal rhetoric of neoclassical pastoral as Philips had done, but by introducing the grossest aspects of English country life, thus outdoing Philips in realism, he demonstrates the incongruity between crude subject matter and extremely stylized treatment at the heart of Philips' eclogues.

In the Proeme to *The Shepherd's Week*, Gay adopts the pose of Philips and pretends to argue against the arcadian pastoralism of his contemporaries, but this is as completely ironic as the Preface to *The What D'Ye Call It*. *The Shepherd's Week* is not a purely burlesque work, but one of Gay's aims was to defend neoclassical convention against what he regarded as the literary perversions of Philips. In *The What D'Ye Call It* Gay continued his attack on what he saw as false pastoralism by treating the facts of rural life in a high style, but the satire of Philips-like pastoral is peripheral to the burlesque of drama. Nevertheless, Gay probably decided on this satirical method because in *The Shepherd's Week* he had already produced a successful burlesque by blending low life and heroic couplets. Gay's choice of couplets in *The What D'Ye Call It* to burlesque blank-verse tragedies may seem curious, but is vindicated by the mock-heroic manner in which he exploits them to deflate the emotionalism of his targets.

One feature of the ironical method of burlesque is that it tends to produce a non-burlesque as well as a burlesque level. The characters consequently exist in their own right and as antitypes. This is obvious in works as different as *The Beggar's Opera* and *Northanger Abbey*, in which Macheath, Polly Peachum, Catherine Morland, and Isabella Thorpe, for example, are both 'real' characters and burlesque equivalents of stereotypes in Italian opera and Gothic fiction respectively. In *The Shepherd's Week*, too, the shepherds and shepherdesses take on a life of their own, independent of their burlesque function. The extent to which this happens in *The What D'Ye Call It* is more limited, but the Prologue indicates that Gay himself was aware of a certain ambiguity in his play:

> This Comick Story, or this Tragick Jest,
> May make you laugh, or cry, as you like best;
> May exercise your Good, or your Ill-nature,
> Move with Distress, or tickle you with Satyr.

Allardyce Nicoll goes so far as to claim that *The What D'Ye Call It* belongs, at least in part, to the sentimental school of writing;[7] and while this view is debatable, it does recognize the presence of something more than burlesque in the play, a dimension of social criticism and genuine pathos as opposed to the false pathos of much contemporary drama.

Gay's play is neither a rehearsal piece modelled on Buckingham's work, nor an entirely self-contained mock play like Fielding's two main burlesques of Restoration and Augustan tragedy, *The Tragedy of Tragedies* and *The Covent-Garden Tragedy*. The mock play, which occupies almost the whole of *The What D'Ye Call It*, is self-contained in that it is not interrupted by interjections, questions, and discussion as is *The Rehearsal*, but it is framed by a minute comedy in which the couple playing the lovers of the inner play are themselves married. The way in which some of the actors tend to merge with the characters they are playing, so that there is a certain degree of interpenetration between frame and inner play, is quite unlike *The Rehearsal*. Gay adheres to the play-within-a-play device but reduces the outer framework to an absolute minimum so as to put all the emphasis on the inner play, which is not presented as a rehearsal by a professional company as in *The Rehearsal* but as a complete amateur production. This has been arranged as part of the Christmas celebrations of a country justice (Sir Roger) to entertain his legal friends, who provide the silent audience although they do participate in the action at one point. This again illustrates the way in which frame and inner play interpenetrate to some extent. The vegetable and weed names of the lowly actors, such as Kitty Carrot, Peter Nettle, and Jonas Dock, suggest a relationship with the 'mechanicals' in *A Midsummer Night's Dream*, who also perform a supposedly tragic drama for the entertainment of their social superiors. Sir Roger is obviously eager to impress his fellow justices with a comprehensive survey of current theatrical fashions:

> Look ye, Steward, don't tell me you can't bring them in. I will have a Ghost; nay, I will have a Competence of Ghosts. What, shall our Neighbours think we are not able to make a Ghost? A Play without a Ghost is like, is like, – i'gad it is like nothing ... And is the Play as I order'd it, both a Tragedy and a Comedy? I would have it a Pastoral too: and if you could make it a Farce, so much the better – and what if you crown'd all with a Spice of your Opera? You know my Neighbours never saw a Play before; and d'ye see, I would shew them all sorts of Play under one.

Sir Roger is well meaning, not facetious, and both the actors and the stage audience of Sir Roger and the justices take the inner play very seriously indeed, unlike the Players and the stage audience of Johnson and Smith in *The Rehearsal* who have little but contempt for Bayes' play. By using the play-within-a-play device, Gay distances the burlesque play to make his purpose clearer, and the opening scene, introducing the actors and stage audience, does contain hints that the play about to be performed is satirical, but Gay gives no unambiguous indication of his intention.[8]

The mock play itself is entirely consistent in a way that the mock plays in *The Rehearsal* and *The Critic* are not. Although Buckingham and Sheridan present their mock plays as serious examples of contemporary drama, their use of the rehearsal framework makes the composition of autonomous mock plays unnecessary; the rehearsal technique announces its burlesque intentions explicitly, and there is no point in pretending otherwise. On the other hand, Gay's choice of irony as a satirical method forces him to sustain the illusion of complete seriousness even to the point of writing a mock play that is a unified work of art. The ironic technique demands that the 'mask' should never slip, the pretence of seriousness never falter. The need to produce a mock play with a coherent action and plot leads Gay away from close parody towards general burlesque of dramatic weaknesses. Bayes' play in *The Rehearsal* is largely constructed from direct parodies and specific situational and visual burlesques loosely joined together by the commentary of the spectators. Passages of sustained parody do occur in *The What D'Ye Call It*, and their sources are identified in the anonymous *A Complete Key to the Last New Farce The What D'Ye Call It* (1715), usually attributed to Lewis Theobald and the actor Benjamin Griffin although it may have been an ironic Scriblerian venture involving Gay himself, but they are subordinated to the overall design. In the Preface to the *Complete Key*, the play is criticized for being *'a Banter on the solemn stile of Tragedy in general'* rather than *'a Satyr upon faulty Passages of our Poets'*[9] like *The Rehearsal*, but Gay's *'Banter'*, though less systematically parodic than Buckingham's *'Satyr'*, is no less directed against *'faulty Passages'*.

The mock play is woven around two main incidents, the forcible separation of two lovers, Kitty and Filbert, and the preparation for the execution of an army deserter, Peascod. Parallels to both these situations abound in tragedies of the period, and they are usually scenes of highly charged emotions aimed at arousing pity and tears. As the *Complete Key* makes clear, many of Gay's targets provided contemporary audiences with an opportunity for a 'good weep'. Filbert, falsely accused by Dorcas of making her pregnant, is ordered by the Justices to choose between marrying her and joining the army. The rivalry between Kitty and Dorcas over Filbert probably alludes to that between Octavia and Cleopatra over Antony in Dryden's *All for Love* and that between Statira and Roxana over Alexander in Lee's *The Rival Queens*. As a fallen woman, Dorcas herself bears some relation to Jane Shore in Rowe's play. Filbert grandiloquently rebuts Dorcas' charge – '"Tis false, 'tis false – I scorn thy odious Touch'(I, i) – and refuses to wed her. His manly, stoical speech, an expression of untarnished honour, mocks the exaggerated posturings of heroic protagonists by putting them in a humble context. The melodramatic contrast between the innocent Filbert and his supporters, on the one hand, and the deceitful Dorcas and the heartless Justices, on the other, burlesques those lachrymose scenes in contemporary drama intended to be full of intense pathos. By introducing such mundane realities as legal corruption and the hardships of rural life into the high-flown emotional appeals of the women pleading on Filbert's behalf, Gay converts such 'pathos' into an object of laughter, as in Kitty's appeal beginning 'Behold how low you have reduc'd a Maid' (I, i) – an allusion to Andromache's outburst to Pyrrhus, 'Behold how low you have reduced a Queen!', in *The Distrest Mother* (III, vi).

Tragic dramatists of the period often linger over spectacles of distressed virtue or penitent vice, extracting every possible nuance of emotion from the suffering of characters who are victims of circumstance or of the machinations of others. In the exchanges between Filbert and Kitty, Gay burlesques such emotional over-indulgence by transferring the typical rhetoric of high-born protagonists to the context of farmers and impressed soldiers:

> KITTY Yes, yes, my *Thomas*, we will go together;
> Beyond the Seas together will we go,
> In Camps together, as at Harvest, glow.
> This Arm shall be a Bolster for thy Head,
> I'll fetch clean Straw to make my Soldier's Bed;
> There, while thou sleep'st, my Apron o'er thee hold,
> Or with it patch thy Tent against the Cold.
> Pigs in hard Rains I've watch'd, and shall I do
> That for the Pigs, I would not bear for you?
> FILBERT Oh, *Kitty, Kitty*, canst thou quit the Rake,
> And leave these Meadows for thy Sweetheart's sake?
> Canst thou so many gallant Soldiers see,
> And Captains and Lieutenants slight for me?
> Say, canst thou hear the Guns, and never shake,
> Nor start at Oaths that make a Christian quake?
> Canst thou bear Hunger, canst thou march and toil
> A long long Way, a thousand thousand Mile?
> And when thy *Tom*'s blown up, or shot away,
> Then – canst thou starve? – they'll cheat thee of my Pay. (I, i)

Kitty's promise of selfless loyalty and Filbert's extremely emotional response, which elevates her self-sacrifice on his account almost to the state of martyrdom, superficially resemble those appeals to the emotions in pathetic tragedy intended to arouse moral admiration for virtuous actions and qualities.

The first two lines of Kitty's speech parody two lines from Andromache's mournful maternal speech with which the first act of *The Distrest Mother* closes ('Yes, my *Astyanax*; we'll go together! / Together to the Realms of Night we'll go!'), but the main source of this dialogue, the first scene between Belvidera and Jaffeir in *Venice Preserv'd*, shows even more clearly how close Gay is at times to his targets and yet how subtly he distorts them to achieve deliberate bathos. Belvidera's declaration of love verges on hysteria:

> Oh I will love thee, even in Madness love thee:
> Tho my distracted Senses should forsake me,
> I'd find some intervals, when my poor heart

>   Should swage it self and be let loose to thine.
>   Though the bare Earth be all our Resting-place,
>   It's Root's our food, some Clift our Habitation,
>   I'l make this Arm a Pillow for thy Head;
>   As thou sighing ly'st, and swell'd with sorrow,
>   Creep to thy Bosom, pour the balm of Love
>   Into thy Soul, and kiss thee to thy Rest;
>   Then praise our God, and watch thee 'till the Morning.   (I, i)

Belvidera imagines Jaffeir and herself living like Lear's 'poor, bare forked animal', but for her this is not a state of deprivation but proof that their love is victorious over everything that stands in its way. The 'bare Earth' positively glows with romantic feeling; the lovers will find themselves in nature as they have never done before. Kitty's depiction of the actualities of life in the harsh conditions of an army camp contrasts markedly with Belvidera's rapture at the prospect of life with Jaffeir in the open, without even Filbert's torn tent for protection. Kitty's remarks about shielding Filbert from the cold with her apron may also contain a burlesque reference to Lady Easy's notorious speech over her sleeping husband in the last act of Colley Cibber's *The Careless Husband* (1704) when she finds him with her maid. After Lady Easy's initial shock and anger have given way to concern for her husband because he is without his wig, she takes a steinkirk from her neck and lays it gently on his head to keep him warm.

Kitty and Filbert's struggle against authority is of no avail, and they are finally forced to part. Their separation provides Gay with a superb opportunity for burlesquing the heartbreaking farewell scenes found in pathetic tragedy, such as those of Essex and his wife in *The Unhappy Favourite*, of Oroonoko and Imoinda in *Oroonoko*, and of Hastings and Alicia in *Jane Shore*, all of which are prolonged emotional orgies. After nearly two hundred lines of preparation in the closing scene of Southerne's play, Oroonoko make moves to kill his wife and then himself in order to escape their enemies:

>   It must be –
>   But first a dying Kiss –
>   This last Embrace –
>   And now –   (v, iv)

but nearly fifty lines later they are still taking their final leave of each other:

>   OROONOKO They shannot overtake us. This last Kiss.
>   And now farewell.
>   IMOINDA   Farewel, farewel for ever.   (v, iv)

Even these are not their last words. The antiphonal chanting of

Gay's lovers, culminating in the sudden descent to Kitty's banal doggerel about letter writing, ridicules the exclamatory clichés intended to convey the spiritual agonies endured by noble heroes and heroines and to tug the heartstrings of the audience:

> KITTY O Justice most unjust!
> FILBERT　　　　　　　O Tyranny!
> KITTY How can I part?
> FILBERT　　　　　　Alas! and how can I?
> KITTY O rueful Day!
> FILBERT　　　　　　Rueful indeed, I trow.
> KITTY O Woeful Day!
> FILBERT　　　　　　A Day indeed of Woe!
> KITTY When Gentlefolks their Sweethearts leave behind,
> 　They can write Letters, and say something kind;
> 　But how shall *Filbert* unto me endite,
> 　When neither I can read, nor he can write?　　(I, ii)

Part of this exchange is adapted from Hobnelia's monologue, *Thursday*, the fourth of the eclogues in *The Shepherd's Week*. As Kitty and Filbert are hauled apart, the antiphonal rhetoric returns, this time descending into moans and groans that deride 'the frequent Exclamations and Agonies of parting Lovers', as the *Complete Key* notes.[10] Gay's satire embodies his recognition that professional dramatists like Banks and Southerne, who catered for current tastes, were often tempted to stimulate easily aroused emotions and stock responses.

The second half of the mock play introduces Dorcas' soldier brother, Timothy Peascod, who is about to be executed for desertion. A number of Gay's principal targets, including *Venice Preserv'd*, *The Unhappy Favourite*, *The Albion Queens*, and *Jane Shore*, contain scenes in which condemned prisoners prepare themselves for execution and take leave of their friends. While the firing squad prepare themselves, Peascod gives an account of his gradual immersion in evil and crime, and explains the inevitable consequences of such a life. The mock-heroic discrepancy between his extremely trivial delinquencies and his sober, remorseful language produces a superb burlesque of the maudlin and didactic speeches of penitence that are common in the dénouements of pathetic tragedies (and genteel comedies too):

> O Fellow-Soldiers, Countrymen and Friends,
> Be warn'd by me to shun untimely Ends:
> For Evil Courses am I brought to Shame,
> And from my Soul I do repent the same.
> Oft my kind *Grannam* told me – *Tim*, take warning,
> Be good – and say thy Pray'rs – and mind thy Learning.

> But I, sad Wretch, went on from Crime to Crime;
> I play'd at Nine-pins first in Sermon time:
> I rob'd the Parson's Orchard next; and then
> (For which I pray Forgiveness) stole – a Hen.
> When I was press'd, I told them the first Day
> I wanted Heart to fight, so ran away;
> For which behold I die. 'Tis a plain Case,
> 'Twas all a Judgment for my Want of Grace. (II, i)

The *Complete Key* cites Hastings' last speech from *Jane Shore* as a possible source of Gay's burlesque, but adds that 'there are many more, obvious to all Readers of Plays, and all of them may be shaded under this *Burlesque* last Speech of *Peascods*'.[11] Some of Jane Shore's own speeches in Rowe's tragedy are among those 'shaded', and two of Essex's speeches in *The Unhappy Favourite*, 'Where art thou *Essex*! where are now thy Glories!' (II, i) and 'My Father once too truly skill'd in Fate' (IV, i) are closely alluded to, but Calista's soliloquy shortly before she commits suicide in *The Fair Penitent* is a particularly histrionic example:

> Now think thou, curst *Calista*, now behold
> The Desolation, Horror, Blood, and Ruin,
> Thy Crimes, and fatal Folly spread around,
> That loudly cry for Vengeance on thy Head;
> Yet Heav'n, who knows our weak, imperfect Natures,
> How blind with Passions, and how prone to Evil,
> Makes not too strict Enquiry for Offences,
> But is aton'd by Penitence and Pray'r:
> Cheap Recompence! here 'twould not be receiv'd,
> Nothing but Blood can make the Expiation,
> And cleanse the Soul from inbred, deep Pollution. (V, i)

When one of the Countrymen urges Peascod to repent and encourages him by handing him a 'good book', he breaks down completely over the title page. The flow of tears and references to tears figure prominently in some of the plays ridiculed by Gay. Peascod's sobbing fit of contrition at the mention of the words, 'good book', is a particularly fine burlesque of the facility with which tears are produced in pathetic plays:

> Lend me thy Handkercher – *The Pilgrim's Pro–*
> (I cannot see for Tears) *Pro – Progress* – Oh!
> – *The Pilgrim's Progress – Eighth – Edi-ti-on*
> *Lon-don – Prin-ted – for – Ni-cho-las Bod-ding-ton:*
> *With new Ad-di-tions never made before.*
> – Oh! 'tis so moving, I can read no more. (II, i)

Peascod's reaction to the book may be aimed specifically at Cato's soliloquy over Plato's *Phaedo* shortly before his suicide in Addison's play, eight editions of which were published in 1713, the year of its first production. The *Complete Key* claims that Gay originally included the words, '*Bunyan*, thou reason'st well', parodying the opening of Cato's soliloquy, 'It must be so – *Plato*, thou reason'st well!' (v, i).[12]

The subsequent six scenes, all of which are concerned with the responses of various people to Peascod's imminent fate and his last-minute reprieve, burlesque the prolonged emotional crises of many contemporary tragedies. As the *Complete Key* notes, 'The Solemnity of parting with dying Friends, which has so often drawn Tears . . . is here made a Subject of Merriment'.[13] Filbert's distress when he discovers that his old friend Peascod is to die parallels the relationship between Jaffeir and Pierre as the latter awaits execution in *Venice Preserv'd*. The emotional pitch becomes even higher with the arrival of Peascod's bastard child, Joyce, with Dorcas, whose entry is reminiscent of Alicia's in *Jane Shore* when Hastings is being taken to execution. Overcome with guilt and remorse at her false incriminations of Filbert, Dorcas confesses that the Squire is actually the father of her unborn child.

The entry of Joyce allows Gay to burlesque the introduction of defenceless and innocent children at critical moments in contemporary plays, a stock-in-trade device of the dramatist intent on producing very touching scenes, as are extended reconciliations between erring parents and forgiving children. One of the most famous examples occurs in *All for Love* when Octavia, trying to win Antony back from Cleopatra by appealing to his honour, performs a *coup de grâce* on her husband by instructing her two young daughters to approach their father and 'pull him to me, / And pull him to your selves, from that bad Woman'. The result is the most sentimental and bathetic moment in the play:

> VENTIDIUS Was ever sight so moving! Emperor!
> DOLLABELLA Friend!
> OCTAVIA Husband!
> BOTH CHILDREN Father!
> ANTONY I am vanquish'd: take me,
>   Octavia; take me, Children; share me all.
>   I've been a thriftless Debtor to your Loves,
>   And run out much, in Riot, from your Stock;
>   But all shall be amended.   (111)

Similar agonies of guilt and similar raptures of parental tenderness sweep over Peascod when he discovers that his illegitimate daughter, whom he has ignored and abandoned, is approaching for his blessing:

> Oh! my Sins of Youth!
> Why on the Haycock didst thou tempt me, *Ruth*?

> O save me, Sergeant: – how shall I comply?
> I love my Daughter so – I cannot die.   (II, iv)

Joyce responds with a mixture of filial piety and self-pity in a speech that is 'levell'd at the solemn and melancholly Complaints and Reflections so usual in all Tragedies'.[14] Gay's verbal burlesque here is general rather than specific, but Peascod's lines undoubtedly owe something to Andromache's expressions of overpowering maternal love in *The Distrest Mother*. This scene between Peascod and Joyce is also a particularly good example of how Gay's characters transcend burlesque, and there are traces of the social criticism more fully embodied in *The Beggar's Opera* and *Polly*. The non-burlesque level of *The What D'Ye Call It* is very near the surface in Joyce's lines about her upbringing in which she exposes the corrupt reality frequently underlying the righteous appearance of parish charity – 'our Church-Wardens / Feast on the Silver, and give us the Farthings' (II, iv) – just as it is at the opening of the inner play with its attack on the petty officiousness and inhuman severity of country justices.

As Peascod is led to the stake, Filbert and the Countrymen praise his excellent ploughing, nostalgically recall his activities at May time, and drink to his 'safe Passage'. The contrast between the intense gravity of the occasion and the trite and wholly inappropriate utterances of the onlookers is responsible for the burlesque humour, which reaches its climax with Peascod's parody of Pierre's speech from the scaffold in *Venice Preserv'd*:

> Is't fit a Souldier, who has liv'd with Honour,
> Fought Nations Quarrels, and bin Crown'd with Conquest,
> Be expos'd a common Carcass on a Wheel?   (v)

Pierre's highly charged declamation about the indecorum of death on the wheel is amusingly replaced by Peascod's sense of shock at the prospect of being shot in the fields he has farmed:

> Say, is it fitting in this very Field,
> Where I so oft have reap'd, so oft have till'd;
> This Field, where from my Youth I've been a Carter,
> I, in this Field, should die for a Deserter?   (II, v)

Peascod finally distributes his possessions to his friends just as Mary, Queen of Scots does to her weeping servants before going to the block in *The Albion Queens* (v, i), but Peascod has only a ''Bacco-Box', a 'Neckcloth', a 'Bottle-Skrew', and his 'Breeches' to give, whereas Mary has what she calls 'Some few Trifles', a casket of gold and jewels as well as her personal jewellery. At this point a totally unexpected reversal of fortune occurs, which 'exposes the too sudden and unprepar'd *Peripetias* in most *Tragedies*'.[15] Peascod is suddenly saved by a reprieve, and the brutal Sergeant, who has callously been awaiting the execution, is himself charged with a capital offence. Having exposed the good Peascod to extreme danger so as to mock scenes of pathos, Gay suddenly rescues him in order to ridicule the melodramatic revelations used to ensure poetic justice. The more terrible the sufferings of the virtuous, the more arbitrary must be the device by which they are delivered to receive their rewards.

After Peascod's release, the dramatic emphasis returns to Filbert and Kitty, who wanders distracted in the fields not knowing that Dorcas' tardy confession has procured Filbert's acquittal and freedom. Kitty now replaces Peascod as the pathetic figure of the play. Her anguished monologue, punctuated by totally banal exclamations from the Chorus of Sighs and Groans, burlesques the nostalgic yearning of Rowe's pathetic heroines for a former happiness and innocence that have become unattainable. The disparity between the high-flown language and the undignified object, a rake, eulogised in Kitty's speech ridicules the distraught retrospection at the end of Rowe's 'she-tragedies' and simultaneously continues Gay's assault, begun in *The Shepherd's Week*, on Philips' *Pastorals*:

> Dear happy Fields, farewell; ye Flocks, and you
> Sweet Meadows, glitt'ring with the pearly Dew:
> And thou, my Rake, Companion of my Cares,
> Giv'n by my Mother in my younger Years:
> With thee the Toils of full eight Springs I've known,
> 'Tis to thy Help I owe this Hat and Gown;
> On thee I've lean'd, forgetful of my Work,
> While *Tom* gaz'd on me, propt upon his Fork:
> Farewell, farewell; for all thy Task is o'er,
> *Kitty* shall want thy Service now no more.   (II, viii)

Kitty's speeches in this scene are, in fact, derived from Sparabella's monologue, *Wednesday*, the third of the six pastorals constituting *The Shepherd's Week*.

Having lost all reason for living, Kitty asks her aunt to kill her and gives her a knife for the purpose, but at the last moment she is overcome by the indignity of such a death – ''Tis shameless sure to fall as Pigs have dy'd'. This incident alludes satirically to three of the best-known climaxes in contemporary tragedy, Jaffeir's stabbing of Pierre in *Venice Preserv'd*, and the suicide pacts between Ventidius and Antony in *All for Love* and between Oroonoko and Imoinda in *Oroonoko*. Kitty next turns to hanging, and with the help of her aunt prepares a noose, but again she experiences a sense of offended propriety that prevents her from continuing. Kitty's over-scrupulous dithering about her method of suicide burlesques those death scenes in pathetic tragedies in which the fallen but penitent heroines die with decorum and dignity amid a spate of both tears and rhetoric. Kitty faints before reaching her intended deathbed and is revived by having cold water poured over her. In a state of delirium, she then erupts into a speech that burlesques such monstrously inflated mad speeches as Alicia's in *Jane Shore* and Belvidera's in *Venice Preserv'd*:

> ALICIA A waving flood of bluish fire swells o'er me;
> And now 'tis out, and I am drowned in blood.
> Ha! what art thou! thou horrid headless trunk?
> It is my Hastings! See! he wafts me on!
> Away! I go! I fly! I follow thee.   (v, i)

> BELVIDERA Oh give me daggers, fire or water,
> How I could bleed, how burn, how drown the waves
> Huzzing and booming round my sinking head,
> Till I descended to the peaceful bottome!
> Oh there's all quiet, here all rage and fury,
> The Air's too thin, and pierces my weak brain,
> I long for thick substantial sleep: Hell, Hell,
> Burst from the Centre, rage and roar aloud,
> If thou art half so hot, so mad as I am.   (v)

> KITTY Hah! – I am turn'd a Stream – look all below;
> It flows, and flows, and will for ever flow.
> The Meads are all afloat – the Haycocks swim.
> Hah! who comes here! – my *Filbert*! drown not him.
> Bagpipes in Butter, flocks in fleecy Fountains,
> Churns, Sheep-hooks, Seas of Milk, and honey Mountains.
>   (II, viii)

Kitty's final couplet is a direct parody of Belvidera's subsequent lines:

> Murmuring streams, soft shades, and springing flowers,
> Lutes, Laurells, Sea of Milk, and ships of Amber.   (v)

In her half-demented condition, Kitty cannot decide whether the Filbert she sees is a ghost or the man she loves. This ridicules 'the frequent Tragick Surprises, where the despairing Lovers being suddenly brought together, fancy themselves Ghosts, and can scarce be sure each other are alive',[16] one of the best examples being Alphonso's (Osmyn's) meeting with Almeria, whom he believes to be dead, in Congreve's *The Mourning Bride*:

> Let me not stir, nor breath, lest I disolve
> That tender, lovely Form of painted Air
> So like *Almeria*. Ha! it sinks, it falls,
> I'll catch it 'ere it goes, and grasp her Shade.

> 'Tis Life! 'tis warm! 'tis she! 'tis she her self!
> Nor Dead, nor Shade, but breathing and alive!
> It is *Almeria*! 'tis my Wife!   (II, i)

A similar incident occurs at the end of the play when Almeria finds Alphonso alive and well, although she believes him to be dead. There is also a parallel to Belvidera's death scene, in which she is confronted by the blood-stained ghosts of Jaffeir and Pierre; Kitty's words, 'hah, dost thou bleed?' (II, ix), allude to Belvidera's 'My Husband bloody, and his friend too!' (v). In Kitty's case, however, all ends happily. She is restored to sanity when Filbert embraces her, and with this final reversal of fortune the inner mock play is concluded. A parallel resolution in the frame play then quickly brings the entire afterpiece to an end.

Gay's satirical burlesque of contemporary drama, especially heroic and pathetic tragedy, in *The What D'Ye Call It* is much more wide-ranging than in any other of his dramatic works, and with the exception of the ghost scene his subtle, ironic method is sustained throughout. At the end of the first half of the play, the ruthless Justices are interrupted by the ghosts of no less than five innocent people whose deaths they have directly or indirectly caused. The ghosts, one of which is an embryo, rise one by one to accuse and threaten the Justices, who vainly attempt to deny their responsibility while the ghosts dance around them singing a totally inane ditty, which 'may allude to those in our Modern *Opera*'s, where a parcel of unmeaning Words are introduc'd meerly to support the Air'.[17]

Most writers of tragedy in the late seventeenth century, even the more gifted ones such as Dryden, Lee and Otway, incorporate ghost scenes in their plays to supply gratuitous horror and stage spectacle for their audiences. There is no comparison between the appearance of Banquo's ghost in *Macbeth*, a manifestation of Macbeth's guilt, and the dramatically unjustified though theatrically startling jack-in-the-box antics of Pierre's and Jaffeir's ghosts at the end of *Venice Preserv'd*. Otway introduces these ghosts to heighten the terror of Belvidera's mad scene, but the result is the opposite of what is intended. Belvidera's demented declamations are dangerously close to self-parody as it is, and the presence of bleeding ghosts, appearing, disappearing, and reappearing through trap-doors, merely tips the dramatic belance towards bathos. The ghost scenes in Lee's *The Rival Queens*, the play travestied by Cibber in *The Rival Queans*, bear an even closer resemblance to Gay's burlesque ghost scene than the one in *Venice Preserv'd* because the ghosts are so minatory, and Gay could have had these specifically in mind. At one point in Lee's tragedy the ghost of King Philip walks across the stage shaking a truncheon at the conspirators, and at another the spirits of Darius and old Queen Statira threaten the sleeping Statira with daggers and sing over her. Gay's burlesque of such ghost scenes functions by exaggeration; the satirical intention is much nearer the surface here than elsewhere, although the pretence of seriousness is not abandoned.

In spite of this slight lapse, Gay maintains the precarious poise between tragedy and farce throughout his play almost without faltering. If the balance were pushed more towards farce, as happens momentarily in the visual burlesque of the ghost scene, the deliberate bathos would become cheap and the burlesque crude, as in Duffett's plays. On the other hand, if Gay had not transformed the situations of contemporary tragedy as much as he has done, *The What D'Ye Call It* would hardly be a burlesque at all. Gay's achievement is therefore very considerable, especially as he also succeeds in giving the play a dimension beyond burlesque, and it is surprising that *The What D'Ye Call It* has received so little attention compared with *The Rehearsal* and *The Tragedy of Tragedies*.

Gay's next play, *Three Hours after Marriage*, is a dramatic satire and grotesque comedy rather than a burlesque, but it does contain burlesque elements, although these are plainly of secondary importance and are easily overlooked. In writing this three-act play, first produced at Drury Lane on 16 January 1717, Gay collaborated with two fellow members of the Scriblerus Club, Pope and Arbuthnot, but both the Advertisement (in the published version) and a letter from Gay to Pope written shortly after the first production suggest that Gay contributed much more than the other two. It seems very likely that Gay was responsible for the overall dramatic conception and the narrative, and that Pope and Arbuthnot provided incidental Scriblerian satire. Nevertheless, it was probably Pope's participation that led to the very noisy reception of the play in 1717, for although it played to packed houses for seven consecutive nights (a longer run than any other play during that season) the actors had to contend with sporadic choruses of catcalls and hisses. Shortly afterwards, John Durant Breval, writing under the name of 'Joseph Gay', published a satirical account of the production in the form of a short farce, *The Confederates* (1717).

On the face of it, *Three Hours after Marriage* seems to be no more that a crude example of the kind of farcical intrigue comedy written by Thomas D'Urfey, Edward Ravenscroft, and Aphra Behn at the end of the seventeenth century and by Colley Cibber and Susannah Centlivre in the early eighteenth century. Indeed, in their edition of the play, Richard Morton and William M. Peterson argue that it resembles Shadwell's *The Virtuoso* (1676), D'Urfey's *Madam Fickle* (1676), Aphra Behn's *The Emperor of the Moon* (1687), and especially Ravenscroft's *The Anatomist* (1696).[18] The characters in *Three Hours after Marriage* include stock characters of contemporary intrigue comedy and the *commedia dell'arte*: an old, jealous, and almost impotent husband; a young, vain, and by no means virtuous wife; ingenious lovers determined to cuckold the husband; and a confidential chambermaid who arranges the wife's intrigues. The action concerns the fantastic adventures undergone by two beaux in their efforts to win Townley during the three hours after her marriage to the foolish pantaloon doctor, Fossile. There is no explicit indication of burlesque intention, no rehearsal framework, no parody, and only a few incidental fragments of verbal burlesque. The names of the two beaux, Plotwell and Underplot, are almost the only direct hints that the action of the play is a deliberately exaggerated burlesque version of the typical intrigue plot, not a very extravagant example of farcical comedy.

The absence of verbal parody and the reliance on situational and visual burlesque make it difficult to appreciate or even recognize most of the burlesque without seeing the play performed, and even then it may not be clear. The burlesque is essentially theatrical, and is to be found in the action, not the language. In this respect, as in its burlesque of comic drama, the play makes a considerable departure from *The Rehearsal*, *The What D'Ye Call It*, and indeed virtually the entire burlesque tradition. Much more in evidence than the burlesque of intrigue comedy is the superstructure of wide-ranging satire and personal invective built on the foundation of the plot. A few of the characters are modelled on well-known people of the time who were either enemies of the Scriblerus group or ridiculous figures in their eyes. Fossile himself, as the name suggests, corresponds to the palaeontologist and physician, John Woodward, who had attacked Pope and Gay for plagiarism. Sir Tremendous, who is introduced as 'the greatest Critick of our Age' (1), is a caricature of John Dennis, whom Gay had previously ridiculed in the dedication of *The Mohocks*. Fossile's niece, Phoebe Clinket, is probably a satirical portrait of the eccentric poet Lady Winchelsea, although she may also bear some resemblance to Susannah Centlivre; but as in the other cases she can be interpreted generically as well as specifically, and is representative of a certain kind of creative writer, not all of whom are women even though the obvious association is with contemporary bluestockings.

In the scenes that portray the activities of Fossile and his fellow doctors, Nautilus and Possum, and especially in the conversation between Fossile and Plotwell when the latter is disguised as a Polish doctor, the authors make typically Scriblerian attacks on pseudo-science, false learning, misdirected intellectual energy, and other departures from Reason and Good Sense – attacks that culminate in the Scriblerus Club's *Memoirs of Martinus Scriblerus*, Swift's *Gulliver's Travels*, and Pope's *The Dunciad*. Similarly, the ridicule of Sir Tremendous, who 'can instruct the Town to dislike what has pleased them, and to be pleased with what they disliked' (1), is more than personal abuse of Dennis' mannerisms. It satirizes doctrinaire and indiscriminately dismissive criticism, usually rooted in an obsession – about plagiarism in the case of Sir Tremendous.

Some of the satire is directed against the theatre and drama, and there are a few scraps of verbal burlesque in the episodes dealing with Clinket's play. Although neglected and abused as a poet and playwright, Phoebe Clinket is impervious to criticism and continues to disrupt the Fossil household with her creative work. She makes her maid carry a writing desk on her back so that when inspired she can immediately write down her effusions, something that occurs at the opening of the play. The authors here satirize Clinket by showing her in the process of poetic composition, a method used more than a century earlier by Thomas Dekker in *Satiromastix* to ridicule Ben Jonson. Apparently typical of her tragic idiom is the following couplet:

> *Swell'd with a Dropsy, sickly Nature lies,*
> *And melting in a Diabetes, dies.* (1)

The authors again use grotesque images and incongruous metaphors to ridicule the pompous rhetoric of contemporary dramatic poetry during the critical demolition of Clinket's play (*The Universal Deluge*) by Sir Tremendous, Plotwell, and the actors. Although Sir Tremendous recognizes the 'abominable' and 'most execrable' quality of Clinket's drama and finally dismembers it with the help of the actors by removing the fable, characters, and diction, his literal-minded objections miss the point so persistently that he is obviously as much a satirical butt as Clinket and her play:

> CLINKET [reads] *Enter* Deucalion *in a sort of Waterman's Habit, leading his Wife* Pyrrha *to a Boat* – Her first Distress is about her going back to fetch a Casket of Jewels. Mind, how he imitates your great Authors. The first Speech has all the Fire of *Lee*.
> *Tho' Heav'n wrings all the Sponges of the Sky,*
> *And pours down Clouds, at once each Cloud a Sea.*
> *Not the Spring-Tides –*
> SIR TREMENDOUS There were no Spring-Tides in the *Mediterranean*, and consequently *Deucalion* could not make that Simile.
> CLINKET A Man of *Deucalion*'s Quality might have travelled beyond the *Mediterranean*, and so your Objection is answered. Observe, Sir *Tremendous*, the Tenderness of *Otway*, in this Answer of *Pyrrha*.
>   *Why do the Stays*
> *Taper my Waste, but for thy circling Arms?*
> SIR TREMENDOUS Ah! *Anachronisms*! Stays are a modern

Habit, and the whole Scene is monstrous, and against the Rules of Tragedy. (1)

Clinket's lines are 'monstrous' illustrations of how the high style sinks to the ludicrous when poets strain too hard for effect, a characteristic fault of many tragic dramatists of the time. Instead of complaining about factual errors and anachronisms, Sir Tremendous should be objecting to the laughable '*Sponges of the Sky*' and the bathos of Pyrrha's reply.

After the abortive reading of Clinket's play, the elements of dramatic burlesque are associated with the adventures of Plotwell and Underplot, whose names indicate the aspects of drama under attack. The part of Plotwell, which was acted by the playwright and actor-manager of Drury Lane, Colley Cibber, may poke fun at the leading male roles in comedy for which Cibber was famous, but above all it satirically personifies the over-elaborate intrigue plots, packed with improbable actions and discoveries, that many comic dramatists of the period used at the expense of genuine wit and real comic invention. Underplot, who 'attends on *Plotwell* like his shadow' (1), performs a similar burlesque function, symbolizing those comic sub-plots that retard and interfere with the progress of the main plot rather than comment on it meaningfully. Much scholarly speculation and debate has focused on the issue of whether Plotwell was intended to be a satirical portrait of Colley Cibber and, if so, why he participated in ridiculing himself, but there is no persuasive internal evidence to support this view. Even if Plotwell is to some extent a send-up of the comic hero in contemporary plays, this does not reflect adversely on Cibber himself, even though he excelled in such parts. He may have enjoyed the opportunity to overplay his customary role.[19]

Many comedies produced between the re-opening of the theatres in 1660 and *Three Hours after Marriage* in 1717, from the most highly sophisticated to the most energetically farcical, contain intrigue plots with their attendant sub-plots. Yet, whereas the best writers of the period transform the mechanics of the intrigue plot into a symbolic representation of social intrigue and duplicity, the writers of farcical comedy manipulate their intrigue plots, often with inordinate ingenuity, for a succession of *coups de théâtre*. Gay, Pope, and Arbuthnot are not satirizing the artistically subtle use of intrigue, as in Congreve's *The Way of the World* (1700), but the cruder handling of intrigue plots by playwrights who sacrifice character for action and theatrical suprises. Even so, *The Way of the World* itself has never been an unqualified stage success, mainly because the intrigue plot is too involved to be easily grasped in performance. The difficulty that the three Scriblerian authors faced was how to exaggerate for the purpose of burlesque a form of comic drama that itself thrived on exaggeration. Farce often went to the limit of absurdity, so that the possibilites for burlesque were severely limited. To create a distinction between burlesque and burlesqued was much harder than in the case of tragedy.

The burlesque of the usual plot complications of intrigue comedy begins with some fun at the expense of dramatists who over-exploit letters as a way of oiling their comic machinery. At the end of Act I, Townley and her servant, Sarsnet, are working out a plan to prevent Fossile from seizing the many letters she expects from her numerous lovers, but in Act II Fossile, disguised as a footman at his own front door, receives and reads them. When Townley discovers Fossile's subterfuge, she immediately decides on a machination of her own designed to restore Fossile's previous image of her as an untarnished innocent. Townley sends Sarsnet to Plotwell with instructions to write her a letter purporting to come from a bitterly disappointed suitor who is vindictive enough to ruin her reputation and her marriage by forging a series of lewd love letters. The letter is, of course, intended for Fossile, who intercepts and reads it as expected. The use of letters to create comic situations is a conventional device that can be dramatically effective if handled with artistic tact, as in Wycherley's *The Country Wife* (1675). The letter incidents in *Three Hours after Marriage* burlesque by exaggeration the excessive reliance by some lesser writers of comedy on this particular convention for complicating the intrigue, creating comic misunderstandings, and making startling revelations. The authors demonstrate that when the convention is abused it results in dramatic inanity and the crudest of farce. They may also have had in mind the use of letters by contemporary tragic playwrights, the most famous example being the complications in Rowe's *The Fair Penitent* following Horatio's discovery of Calista's incriminating letter to her seducer, Lothario, who has accidentally dropped it.

The burlesque continues in Act II with the adventures of Plotwell and his 'evil Genius' Underplot while trying to approach their joint mistress, Townley. These adventures satirize, by a process of accumulation and consistent exaggeration, the duplicities, disguises, concealments, and hairbreadth escapes that characterize intrigue plots, especially scenes of attempted seduction, in contemporary comedy. For his second assault on Fossile's house, Plotwell disguises himself in clothes very similar to Fossile's own and succeeds in entering. As Plotwell leads Townley off to win his bet with Underplot that he will be the first to cuckold Fossile, the doctor suddenly returns, forcing Plotwell to adopt a role in keeping with his attire. Plotwell assumes the character of a Polish doctor and engages Fossile in mock-erudite conversation; but when Underplot, feigning illness, arrives at Fossile's house in pursuit of Townley, Plotwell seizes the opportunity to treat his greatest rival so as to 'cure him of these Frolicks'. Underplot, realizing that his rival intends to apply a red-hot poker to his temples, escapes before he can be 'cured'. The appearances and activities of Underplot, as in this scene, coalesce into a burlesque of those subordinate characters and incidents that repeatedly interrupt or divert the main narrative flow at critical moments. Later in Act II, for instance, it is Underplot's warning to Fossile that prevents another of Plotwell's attempts on Townley from succeeding. When Plotwell returns to Fossile's home concealed in a large chest, Underplot suggests to Fossile that its contents may not be as innocent as they seem, and Townley has to conceal Plotwell under her petticoat to rescue him from her jealous husband who arrives home triumphantly and unexpectedly to examine the chest.

The burlesque of intrigue comedy culminates in the museum scene, which occupies the first half of Act III. Plotwell and Underplot disguise themselves as a mummy and an alligator respectively, and are then delivered as new additions to Fossile's museum. Before leaving to visit his scientific friends, Fossile locks Townley in his museum believing that she will be completely safe from amorous attacks there. Plotwell is once more on the point of cuckolding Fossile when Underplot interrupts them, and Fossile makes yet another unexpected return, bringing Nautilus and Possum with him to examine the new 'specimens'. Only when the scientists decide to probe the 'specimens' with a sword and a rusty knife do the two unsuccessful lovers abandon their poses as museum pieces and show themselves to be alive, but by this time Townley has had sufficient time to fabricate, with the help of Clinket, an extraordinary explanation of the living 'specimens'. By claiming that the mummy and the alligator are part of a masquerade she has been rehearsing, Clinket saves Townley's reputation and preserves the hidden identities of Plotwell and Underplot.

The burlesque of intrigue dénouements at the very end of Act III also works by exaggeration. Unexpected discoveries, additional last-minute misunderstandings, coincidences, ambiguous statements, and improbable reversals of fortune occur in very rapid succession. Jack Capstone, a sailor from Deptford, arrives at Fossile's home with a baby he has been told to leave there. Townley, the mother, recognizes the child as her own bastard by one of her innumerable lovers, but succeeds for a time in concealing the fact. She even accuses Fossile of fathering the child on another woman and adopts the role of hurt wife. Despite Fossile's pleas of innocence, all the evidence, ludicrous as it is, points to his guilt. Even Fossile's friend Possum, who as a magistrate is examining the issue of the baby's parentage, is forced to conclude that Fossile is the father. But as soon as Possum has convinced himself and everyone else that doubts about Fossile's responsibility can no longer be entertained, a chance discovery shifts the entire burden of guilt onto Clinket. Fossile intercepts a letter from his niece to Plotwell which appears to be a confession of her motherhood (*'the Child which you father'd is return'd back upon my Hands'*), and Clinket's own words confirm rather than dispel this impression ('for Fertility and Readiness of Conception, I will yield to nobody'). Soon it emerges that Clinket has been speaking metaphorically, not literally, referring to what she calls 'the Offspring of my Brain', her tragedy. Finally, after another incorrect surmise, Townley is exposed as the true mother of the baby, but even this is not the last surprise for Fossile. Possum is astonished to discover that the woman Fossile has married is Susanne Townley, a notoriously licentious character whose real husband has just returned from three years military service in the East Indies. Possum orders her to return to her husband, but because he, Lieutenant Bengall, cannot possibly be the father of the child, Fossile is credited with its conception and at the end of the play is left literally holding the baby. It is very significant that what Clinket has gained from 'this Day's Adventure' is 'a Plot for a Comedy'.

In *Three Hours after Marriage* the authors do succeed in pushing the typical farcical incidents of intrigue comedy to the point at which even these become so ridiculous that they are transformed into burlesque. Nevertheless, the burlesque of intrigue plots is much less apparent than the burlesque of the tragic style in *The What D'Ye Call It*, even though the fusion of burlesque with personal and other kinds of satire makes *Three Hours after Marriage* substantially different from the earlier play. Since comedy was not nearly as susceptible to verbal burlesque as tragedy, the authors had to rely almost entirely on situational and visual burlesque, and this made it difficult for them to distinguish their own play clearly from its targets. The museum scene in particular, especially the preposterous wooing of Townley by the 'alligator' and the 'mummy' and the 'resurrection' of the 'specimens', can certainly be enjoyed as outrageous farce as well as burlesque. With its bizarre humour, abusive personal satire, and unusual burlesque method, *Three Hours after Marriage* is a most eccentric play, which stands apart from the main tradition of dramatic burlesque. Indeed, the primary preoccupation of the three authors is manifestly not burlesque, which is peripheral though not negligible. In some ways the play prefigures Fielding's dramatic satires of the 1730s, but there is nothing quite like it in previous English drama.

Between 1717 and 1727, when he wrote the first of his three ballad operas, *The Beggar's Opera*, Gay did not abandon drama, but he did not pursue the burlesque and satirical modes he had essayed in *The What D'Ye Call It* and *Three Hours after Marriage*. It goes without saying that *The Beggar's Opera*, first produced at Lincoln's Inn Fields on 29 January 1728, is more than a burlesque, but at one level it is a burlesque, and this side of the play has been neglected in favour of its more universal social and political satire as well as its paradoxically anti-romantic romance.[20] Yet the significance of the title itself cannot be appreciated except in relation to Gay's burlesque of Italian opera. To Gay's contemporaries a 'beggar's opera' was a startling anomaly, since by the time he wrote the work in 1727 'opera' usually meant Italian opera, which dealt with historical and mythological heroes and heroines in a dignified and elevated way. Gay's very title therefore implies that his 'opera' is not only different from Italian opera but also a reversal of it, and in *The Beggar's Opera* he succeeded in creating a completely new kind of English opera, ballad opera, while at the same time burlesquing the immensely fashionable Italian operas of the day.

Although Italian opera reached England less than twenty-five years before *The Beggar's Opera*, it rapidly established itself as the standard form of opera and, in doing so, supplanted the English dramatic opera of the Restoration. By the time of Handel's visit to London in 1710, a vogue for Italian opera was developing, and his decision to remain in England was a crucial factor in the growth of the cult. *Rinaldo* (1711) was the first of the numerous successes he wrote for the Opera House in London. By 1720, when Handel and his Swiss associate John Heidegger launched the Royal Academy of Music, the genre had proved so successful that the Opera House could afford to pay leading Italian singers very high fees to perform there. These Italians fascinated the public offstage as well as onstage, and the personal feud between the two leading ladies of Italian opera in London, Faustina Bordoni and Francesca Cuzzoni (following the former's arrival in 1726), received a great deal of publicity, especially as it exploded during an operatic performance in 1727 into mutual punching, scratching, and hair pulling. This incident prompted an anonymous author to write a short, satirical play about the leading figures associated with Italian opera in London, *The Contre Temps; or, Rival Queans* (1727), in which a quarrel between the Queen of Bologna (Faustina Bordoni) and the Princess of Modena (Francesca Cuzzoni) culminates in a ludicrous fight at the Temple of Discord (Royal Academy of Music) with its High Priest (Heidegger) and its Professor of Harmony (Handel) in attendance. The leading male singer at this time was the celebrated castrato Senesino, a tall man with a particularly high voice who was described by Gay in a letter to Swift dated 3 February 1723 as the unrivalled darling of the town.

Despite its great popularity, Italian opera did not pass uncriticized, and a few burlesques, such as Estcourt's *Prunella*, have already been discussed. The main reasons for the opposition to

Italian opera were articulated as early as 1711 by Addison in four *Spectator* papers (5, 13, 18, and 29). For Addison, the growing popularity of Italian opera posed a threat to English music and the English dramatic tradition, but his main objection was that it was intellectually trivial. He acknowledged the superficial attractiveness of Italian opera, its ability to charm the ear and the eye, but believed that art had an altogether more important function, one that the traditional forms of tragedy and comedy fulfilled. English neoclassical critics in the wake of Addison would probably have been much less incensed by the genre if the theatregoing public had taken it less seriously than they did and had not turned it into a snobbish cult. For audiences to prefer operas in a language they could not understand to serious plays in their own language was indicative not so much of bad taste as of a complete lack of common sense.

Gay certainly did not disapprove of Italian opera in the way that doctrinaire neoclassicists did. In 1718 he collaborated with Handel on *Acis and Galatea*, an 'English Pastoral Opera' which except for its language is a typical Italian opera. Nevertheless, Gay did express concern during the 1720s about the effect the continuing popularity of Italian opera was having on English taste, and in the Epilogue to his tragedy *The Captives* (1724) he ironically indicts contemporary audiences, especially the female members, for preferring '*the wonder*' of Italian opera to the '*meer sense*' of English plays. By 1727 Gay seems to have decided that some kind of corrective to Italian opera was necessary, and in planning *The Beggar's Opera* he set out to create a rival form, a comic and truly English kind of opera, while at the same time burlesquing the Italian kind, though in his characteristically genial way.[21] This dual purpose explains the considerable difference between *The Beggar's Opera* and previous burlesques of Italian opera. In *The Beggar's Opera* Gay eschews close parody and burlesque because this would have interfered with his intention of producing a work of art sufficiently independent of its burlesque purpose to be complete in itself. It is perfectly easy to obtain a great deal from the play without noticing its burlesque elements, whereas works such as *Prunella* and *Harlequin-Hydaspes* can only be understood in relation to the Italian operas they burlesque.

Musically *The Beggar's Opera* departs from Italian opera in two main ways. In the first place, much of Gay's work consists of spoken dialogue without any musical accompaniment; in this respect *The Beggar's Opera* resembles English dramatic opera rather than Italian opera. Secondly, the music for *The Beggar's Opera*, with the exception of the Overture, was not specially composed as in the case of Italian opera, but taken from existing musical sources. Gay himself chose the tunes, mostly well-known ones, for the sixty-nine airs in the play, drawing heavily on D'Urfey's popular collection of songs, *Wit and Mirth; or, Pills to Purge Melancholy*. Forty-one of the melodies come from broadside ballads – this explains the use of 'ballad opera' – but some of the others are by such contemporary composers as Henry Purcell and Handel. Gay's method was both simple and ingenious: he put new wine into old bottles, replacing the familiar words with his own though keeping or adapting phrases now and again. The sheer originality of what Gay did might have been too extreme for its first audiences, but *The Beggar's Opera* turned out to be one of the theatrical successes of the century, not only of the 1727–28 season, and Gay's innovation of the ballad opera immediately found many imitators. Italian opera did not suddenly lose its popularity, despite the coincidental collapse of the Royal Academy of Music in 1728, but it had to compete with a new vogue for ballad operas and ballad farces. Most of these are vastly inferior to *The Beggar's Opera*, and even Gay's later ballad operas do not compare at all favourably with his masterpiece, but there is no doubt that he had completely revitalized English opera.

Although Gay's burlesque of Italian opera is mostly indirect rather than parodic, he keeps an eye on Italian opera throughout the play, and a number of features of *The Beggar's Opera* can be explained only in terms of his burlesque purpose. Gay maintains a superficial resemblance to Italian opera by adopting some of its formal characteristics, especially its three-act structure as opposed to the five-act structure invariable in full-length tragedies and comedies. Gay also follows operatic precedent and departs from the normal practice of orthodox drama by dispensing with a prologue and an epilogue. Almost without exception, tragedies and comedies of the period were preceded by a prologue, spoken by an actor, and followed by an epilogue, spoken by an actress. Operas, on the other hand, opened with an instrumental overture, and Gay specifies that an Overture should be played for *The Beggar's Opera*. J. C. Pepusch, the musical director of Lincoln's Inn Fields, wrote an Overture in the French rather than the Italian style for the first production. Although Gay uses speech instead of operatic recitative, his placing of airs within the play resembles that of arias in an Italian opera. Gay's characters move from speech to song and back again very much as operatic characters alternate between recitative and aria. There is nothing incidental about Gay's songs, and their considerable number combined with their intrinsic dramatic significance make *The Beggar's Opera* appreciably different from plays containing incidental music. After the Overture, *The Beggar's Opera* does in fact begin with an air. Gay also follows operatic example in not limiting his songs to solos, which are almost invariable in the case of incidental songs in regular plays; there are several duets, one trio, and even occasional use of a chorus.

The main purpose of Gay's Introduction, which precedes the Overture and differs from the conventional prologue in being integral to the play, is to point to the various operatic parallels. The supposed author of the opera, the Beggar, explains to the Player that, although written to celebrate the marriage of two English ballad singers, his work is in most respects a conventional opera. As in the Preface to *The What D'Ye Call It*, Gay adopts a persona and announces his burlesque intention indirectly by speaking through his authorial 'mask', but in *The Beggar's Opera* he actually incorporates the 'mask' in the play instead of isolating him in a preface:

> I have introduc'd the Similes that are in all your celebrated *Operas*: The *Swallow*, the *Moth*, the *Bee*, the *Ship*, the *Flower*, &c. Besides; I have a Prison Scene which the Ladies always reckon charmingly pathetick. As to the Parts, I have observ'd such a nice Impartiality to our two Ladies, that it is impossible for either of them to take Offence. I hope I may be forgiven, that I have not made my Opera throughout unnatural, like those in vogue; for I have no Recitative: Excepting this, as I have consented to have neither Prologue nor Epilogue, it must be allow'd an Opera in all its forms.

Although the Beggar gives the same impression of seriousness as the 'author' of *The What D'Ye Call It*, Gay is again being ironic. When the Beggar says, 'I have not made my Opera throughout unnatural, like those in vogue', he appears to be apologising for not making his opera 'throughout unnatural', but the words convey Gay's own comment on the artificiality of Italian opera. Gay is implicitly bringing the neoclassical aesthetic yardstick of Nature to bear on Italian opera. The suggestion that 'Recitative' is particularly 'unnatural' is a common criticism of the time.

The rest of the Beggar's speech can also be interpreted ironically. He congratulates himself for using 'the Similes that are in all your celebrated *Operas*', and the ones he lists do appear in the play, but with the phrase 'in all your celebrated *Operas*' Gay implies that such similes have been reduced to the stalest of clichés. Since so-called simile arias were extremely common, what Gay is suggesting is near the mark, but in using them in *The Beggar's Opera* he is not so much burlesquing them as attempting to bring them back to life by making them express the unoperatic sentiments of unoperatic characters. The Beggar also seems pleased with his 'Prison Scene', such 'charmingly pathetick' scenes being very popular in Italian operas, especially at emotional climaxes so as to make these as moving as possible. Gay's irony here becomes clear when we discover that not just one poignant scene but about half of the play takes place in a prison, and that the prison is not one of the exotic ones of Italian opera, but London's main criminal prison at the time, Newgate, complete with all its corruptions and abuses. The irony carried in the Beggar's words about achieving 'a nice Impartiality to our two Ladies, that it is impossible for either of them to take Offence' is very topical because the allusion is to the quarrelling and intense competition between Francesca Cuzzoni and Faustina Bordoni over operatic roles. Several Italian operas have two heroines, and to avoid hurting the feelings of the prima donnas, composers and librettists tried to make the two parts as equal as possible. As the Beggar's remark suggests, *The Beggar's Opera* itself has two heroines (or anti-heroines), Polly Peachum and Lucy Lockit, who, like operatic heroines, are rivals for the hand of the hero. The rivalry between Polly and Lucy serves a double satirical purpose in alluding to that of the prima donnas in real life and to that of their stage roles.

Except for his substitution of speech for recitative, the Beggar calls his work 'an Opera in all its forms', but by using irony and by referring to ballad singers (often disreputable people), beggars, and the London parish of St Giles-in-the-Fields (the abode of thieves, highwaymen, and prostitutes), Gay makes it clear in the Introduction that the subject matter of *The Beggar's Opera* is completely different from that of Italian opera. While it is true that Gay adopts many of the 'forms' of Italian opera, what he actually presents is the unoperatic world of St Giles-in-the-Fields and London's criminal underworld. Gay turns the elevated characters and milieus of Italian opera upside down. In 1728 it would have been obvious that Gay had based one of the central characters, Peachum, on the most notorious criminal of the time, Jonathan Wild, and had drawn on the romantic glamour surrounding another famous criminal, Jack Sheppard, in conceiving his 'operatic hero' Macheath. Both Wild and Sheppard had been executed less than four years before the first production of *The Beggar's Opera*.

Far from being a typical operatic hero, such as Alessandro (Alexander the Great) in Handel's recent opera of the same name (1726), 'Captain' Macheath is the leader of a gang of highwaymen without any right to the military rank he assumes. Similarly, the two heroines are not like the high-born Rossane and Lisaura in *Alessandro*, but Polly Peachum, whose father is an organiser of crime and a receiver of stolen goods, and Lucy Lockit, whose father is the corrupt chief jailor of Newgate. The struggle between Polly and Lucy over Macheath is a low-life equivalent of that between Rossane and Lisaura over Alessandro and of very similar ones in other Italian operas. The other characters also belong to low life, most of the men being criminals and most of the women being prostitutes. *The Beggar's Opera* is obviously true to its paradoxical title in that it upsets all the usual operatic expectations. Instead of the noble characters, dignified behaviour, and refined sentiments of Italian opera, Gay provides the crimes, intrigues, and double-dealing of the underworld. Yet although Gay's characters are antitypes of operatic stereotypes at the burlesque level, they also exist in their own right as dramatic figures independent of their burlesque function. Gay's burlesque method is essentially the same as in *The What D'Ye Call It*, but his characters are now more 'real' than those of the earlier play, and he seizes the opportunity of using his mock-heroic inversions for social and political satire.

In pretending, through the mouthpiece of the Beggar, that his low-life 'opera' is conventional, Gay burlesques Italian opera, but by treating his criminal characters as though they were genuine operatic figures, he is asking whether in real life, as opposed to the factitiously heroic world of opera, there is any moral difference between criminals and their social superiors, such as courtiers, politicians, and army officers. Gay's handling of Macheath, who at times sounds and behaves like a true hero, illustrates this two-way irony very well. Macheath's first spoken words, 'Suspect my Honour, my Courage, suspect any thing but my Love' (I, xiii), are defiantly heroic, and in replying Polly reassures her criminal husband that she regards him as the equal of someone like Alexander the Great: 'I have no Reason to doubt you, for I find in the Romance you lent me, none of the great Heroes were ever false in Love'. Despite her doubts about Macheath's promises, Lucy also regards him as heroic, especially when she and Polly go to the condemned cell at Newgate to take their leave of him: 'There is nothing moves one so much as a great Man in Distress' (III, xv). Even Polly's cynical father commiserates with Macheath, when arresting him after he has been betrayed by two of his prostitute friends, by telling him that since 'the greatest Heroes have been ruin'd by Women' his case is by no means unique (II, v).

Macheath obviously regards himself as the equivalent of a military leader like Alexander the Great and actually behaves towards his gang with the generosity and fairness expected of an operatic hero. He defends his 'Honour and Truth to the Gang' and claims that 'in the Division of our Booty' he has never 'shown the least Marks of Avarice or Injustice' (II, ii); later he proves that he is no hypocrite by giving money to two members of his gang who are short of cash after failing to steal anything: 'When my Friends are in Difficulties, I am always glad that my Fortune can be serviceable to them' (III, iv). Macheath always addresses members of his gang as 'Gentlemen', whom he can trust and respect as true 'Men of Honour': 'But we, Gentlemen, have still Honour enough to break through the Corruptions of the World' (III, iv). The mock-heroic incongruity between the criminal characters and their 'operatic' behaviour and sentiments in such episodes must be interpreted as ironic burlesque. But the irony of these operatic inversions rebounds to undermine the 'honourable' conduct of those in high society, Parliament, and the professions who set themselves up and are regarded as 'gentlemen'. By the standards of opera it is absurd to call Macheath a 'Gentleman' and a 'great Man', but by the standards of the world is he any worse than many of those who pass for 'great'? Alexander the Great makes a striking operatic hero, but in reality his 'greatness' had much more to do with military conquest, colonial expansion, and political cunning than with love, charity, and wisdom. Gay's burlesque of operas like *Alessandro* is simultaneously a way of raising awkward questions about conventional values and the established order. The same scenes can be understood as operatic burlesque and as social satire; the two are inseparable. The cynicism expressed by Polly's parents about love and marriage amounts to a complete travesty of the courtly idealism surrounding love in Italian opera, but at the same time is a ruthless exposure of the unpleasant 'business' of love and marriage in contemporary high society.

Gay's use of ballad tunes is the musical equivalent of his making an operatic hero out of Macheath rather than someone like Alexander. Whether or not Gay intended to parody specific arias, he sometimes intensifies the burlesque by using the overworked similes listed in the Introduction to express attitudes towards love remote from the world of Italian opera. The '*Moth*' simile appears in Air IV in which Mrs Peachum reflects that once her daughter or any other virgin ('*a Moth*') '*plays about the Flame*' of love, she had better marry quickly before '*Her Honour's sing'd*' or she will end up as '*what I dare not name*' – a whore. Here, as in the similar Air VI, Gay revitalizes a typical operatic simile to convey the truth about the contemporary code of sexual morality. Burlesque and social comment are inextricably linked.

In other airs employing operatic similes there is less of a gulf between what they normally express in opera and what they express in *The Beggar's Opera*, but because of the incongruity between the conceited style characteristic of opera and the unoperatic singer as well as the popular tune, the burlesque effect is still recognizable. In Air XLVII Lucy's emotional torment at the thought of Polly '*sporting on Seas of Delight*' with her lover, Macheath, takes the form of an operatic cliché, the '*Ship*' simile mentioned in the Introduction, such outbursts of distress and jealousy being fairly common in Italian opera:

> I'm like a Skiff on the Ocean tost,
>   Now high, now low, with each Billow born,
> With her Rudder broke, and her Anchor lost,
>   Deserted and all forlorn.

To what extent Gay had particular operas in mind when writing his own songs is difficult to ascertain. The final scene in Act I, which brings Macheath and Polly together for the first time, includes as many as five airs, three of which are duets, and this great emphasis on song indicates a parallel to operatic scenes between devoted lovers who have to part; but whether Gay was modelling the scene on one between parting lovers in Handel's *Floridante* (1721), as Bertrand H. Bronson tentatively suggests in his brilliant essay on the play,[22] must remain speculative, even though one of Gay's duets, Air XVI, bears more than a slight resemblance to Floridante's and Elmira's declarations of undying love. According to Bronson a few other episodes in *The Beggar's Opera* may have specific operatic sources. The arrest of Macheath in a tavern (II, iv) could be based on the attempted murder of Ptolemy in a seraglio in Handel's *Giulio Cesare* (1724), and the violent row between Peachum and Lockit (II, x) possibly owes something to another scene between squabbling fathers in Handel's *Flavio* (1723), although the main source of this is the quarrel between Brutus and Cassius in Shakespeare's *Julius Caesar* (IV, iii). Although the specific correspondences to Italian opera suggested by Bronson may be no more than coincidences, *The Beggar's Opera* does contain a number of unmistakable though general situational parallels to opera, especially as the play moves towards its extraordinary dénouement in which the two characters from the Introduction, the Beggar and the Player, re-enter to transform the apparently tragic outcome into a comic one with the ease of magicians producing rabbits from an empty hat.

One of the best examples of burlesque imitation of opera before the closing stages of the play is Gay's first version of the kind of operatic prison scene that 'the Ladies always reckon charmingly pathetick', to use the Beggar's phrase. In opera this usually takes the form of a woman visiting her lover or husband who is under sentence of death. What Gay does in II, xiii – he does much the same later in III, xi – is to confront the imprisoned Macheath not with one woman but with two, Polly and Lucy, each of whom is his 'wife'. This essentially comic encounter between a philanderer and two of his conquests, one of whom, Lucy, is pregnant by him, is the antithesis of the dignified pathos and heart-rending intensity of operatic prison scenes. It also travesties the situation of a hero like Alessandro, who is faced with an almost impossible choice between Rossane and Lisaura, and who, like Macheath, but for very different reasons, does not know which way to turn.

Gay's use of two duets later in this scene makes the operatic parallel even clearer. In Air XXXVI the vocal line alternates between Polly and Lucy in the manner of operatic duets, especially those sung by rival heroines, but the dramatic context of the song, the discovery by the two girls that the rakish Macheath has been making identical declarations of love and promises of marriage to them, is totally alien to Italian opera. In the other duet, Air XXXVIII, the vocal line does not pass back and forth between Polly and Lucy but is divided so that each sings a stanza insulting the other. It is most relevant that the monosyllabic words at the end of the third line of each stanza, *'Dirt'* and *'made'*, must be sung in melismatic style, each word occupying nearly three bars of music and lasting for seventeen notes. Such coloratura singing is normal in operatic arias but uncommon in folk songs and broadside ballads, and is the only sustained example in *The Beggar's Opera*, in which Gay almost always fits one syllable to one note of music. For Gay to make the operatic parallel so explicit in this song is doubly significant since the rivalry between Polly and Lucy is not expressed with such acrimony and crudity anywhere else. The burlesque discrepancy between unoperatic content and operatic style is therefore very clear indeed, and this in turn draws attention to the discrepancy between the hostile behaviour of Francesca Cuzzoni and Faustina Bordoni towards each other in real life and the dignity of their operatic roles. Polly and Lucy hurl abuse at each other on stage; the prima donnas did not, except on the occasion in 1727 already mentioned when their personal enmity broke through their professional facades, but they certainly did offstage.

Lucy's attempt to poison Polly in III, vii-x is undoubtedly based on a situation found in several contemporary Italian operas, the scene set in a prison in which one of the main characters narrowly escapes death in the form of a cup of poison. These incidents differ somewhat from opera to opera, but in a couple of Handel's operas produced not long before *The Beggar's Opera*, the hero seems certain to die by drinking a cup of poison yet is saved as a result of a surprise intervention during which the cup is upset. In *Radamisto* (1720) the heroine Zenobia is forced by Tiridate to take the poison to Radamisto, her lover who is awaiting execution, but having done so she offers to drink it herself and is prevented only by the sudden entrance of Tiridate who knocks the bowl out of her hands. There is a similar scene in *Floridante*. In both of these operas the intended action of the heroine is one of heroic self-sacrifice and the treatment is intensely emotional. In *The Beggar's Opera*, on the other hand, Lucy's intended action is a cunning and unheroic attempt to murder her rival under the pretence of friendship and the treatment verges on the comic.

After assisting Macheath to escape from Newgate, Lucy suffers agonies of jealousy at the thought of Macheath using his freedom to become reunited with Polly, although he does not actually do this. Polly's visit to Newgate offers Lucy, who has 'the Rats-bane ready', the opportunity she needs to eliminate her rival, and she proposes that they have a drink together 'in the way of Friendship'. Despite Polly's refusal, Lucy is extremely insistent and is just handing Polly the poisoned drink when Macheath is escorted into the prison in chains by Peachum and Lockit after they have recaptured him. Polly, deeply upset at the sight of Macheath in Newgate again, drops the glass without tasting the drink, much to Lucy's relief when she realizes that her suspicions about Polly and Macheath were unfounded. This episode, the only part of the play in which Polly and Lucy appear alone together, carries a further burlesque significance in that it resembles the encounters between rival operatic heroines such as Rossane and Lisaura in *Alessandro*, in which they express their respective attitudes towards the hero.

The transition to the condemned cell in III, xiii is marked by a grotesque dance of prisoners in chains at the end of III, xii, which is a burlesque equivalent of the formal ballet dancing incorporated in many operas. Macheath's soliloquy in the condemned cell is sung, not spoken, and occupies ten consecutive airs, LVIII-LXVII. This is the only occasion in which airs follow one another without any speech intervening and in which Gay employs melodic excerpts from songs instead of the entire tune. Seven of these ten airs are unusually short, six consisting of two lines and one of only one line; two of the other three consist of four lines. The last of these ten airs, consisting of eight lines, is the only one of average length. Although the Beggar claims in the Introduction that there is 'no Recitative' in his opera, the frequently changing melodic line and the related changes of thought and feeling of Macheath's monologue do resemble operatic recitative, especially as it culminates in a full-length air just as recitative leads into an aria. In opera such emotional fluctuations as those experienced by Macheath are always rendered in recitative, arias invariably being consistent in tone. Since there is 'no Recitative' before this, the use of song for Macheath's soliloquy comes as a complete surprise and draws attention to the operatic parallel. Considered as burlesque, Macheath's 'recitative and aria' is an outrageous travesty of those sung by operatic heroes awaiting execution in prison. Whereas Floridante in Handel's opera reveals great fortitude and stoicism, even welcoming death as a deliverance, Macheath focuses his attention on women and alcohol, and drinks all the wine and brandy he can lay his hands on in a desperate attempt to keep his courage up and prepare himself for his ordeal.

The joint visit that Polly and Lucy make to Macheath in the condemned cell in III, xv in order to take their final leave of him gives rise to the only trio in *The Beggar's Opera*, Air LXVIII. Since Polly and Lucy sing several duets in the presence of Macheath earlier in the play, there are plenty of opportunities for the three of them to share an air, but Gay reserves his one trio for what might be regarded as the most 'charmingly pathetick' moment. In doing so, Gay is following the normal operatic practice of bringing the principal characters together at the climax of the work to sing an elaborate trio, quartet, or quintet, depending on their number. For a burlesque trio in the condemned cell, Gay's use of the tune of 'All you that must take a Leap', a ballad about the execution of two criminals, is highly appropriate. The desire of both girls to die with Macheath at Tyburn is a comic transformation of the determination of some operatic heroines to sacrifice themselves in order to save their lovers' lives:

> LUCY *Would I might be hang'd!*
> POLLY *And I would so too!*
> LUCY *To be hang'd with you.*
> POLLY *My Dear, with you.*

Macheath's cowardly but very human behaviour now that his supply of wine and spirits has run out is the antithesis of the unflinching heroism of characters like Floridante when facing death:

> *O Leave me to Thought! I fear! I doubt!*
> *I tremble! I droop! – See, my Courage is out.*

As soon as the air is over, the operatic burlesque is greatly enhanced by the unexpected entry of four more 'wives', each accompanied by a child, so that Macheath is surrounded by a total of ten dependents, six 'wives' and four children. What would be the 'charmingly pathetick' climax of an opera certain to moisten every female eye in the audience is turned into an extremely farcical situation, one in which Macheath ironically acquires the strength of an operatic hero and is only too willing to welcome death as a deliverance: 'What – four Wives more! – This is too much. – Here – tell the Sheriffs Officers I am ready.'

Gay's travesty of operatic conventions culminates in the startling dénouement of the last two scenes of the play, III, xvi-xvii. After Macheath is taken to execution at the end of III, xv, the dramatic action is broken off when the two characters from the Introduction, the Player and the Beggar, burst in to discuss the end of the Beggar's 'opera' and to alter it drastically. This interruption is a burlesque equivalent of the *deus ex machina*, the device common in heroic drama, tragicomedy, and opera by which poetic justice and happy endings are unexpectedly produced out of apparent disaster by a surprise discovery or sudden transformation of character. Although Italian operas often approach tragedy, they invariably end happily, and arbitrary contrivances are consequently essential to secure the required dénouements. In the closing stages of *Arsinoe*, one of the operas burlesqued by Estcourt in *Prunella*, Dorisbe's response to being rejected in love is to attempt suicide by stabbing herself, but shortly afterwards she joins in the finale as though nothing was wrong, explaining that her wound is not serious. Almost to a man, operatic villains behave abominably for two and a half acts and then at a stroke become penitent and conscience-stricken so that they can be reconciled with everyone, even their victims.

What causes the Player to intervene to save Macheath from the gallows is his shock at the impropriety of such a 'tragic' conclusion for an 'opera': 'But, honest Friend, I hope you don't intend that *Macheath* shall be really executed.' Although the Beggar had intended 'doing strict poetical Justice' with Macheath hanged and all the other characters destined for Tyburn or transportation, he relents when the Player points out that this would result in 'a downright deep Tragedy' and that such a 'Catastrophe is manifestly wrong, for an Opera must end happily':

> BEGGAR Your Objection, Sir, is very just; and is easily remov'd. For you must allow, that in this kind of Drama, 'tis no matter how absurdly things are brought about. – So – you Rabble there – run and cry a Reprieve – let the Prisoner be brought back to his Wives in Triumph.
>
> PLAYER All this we must do, to comply with the Taste of the Town.   (III, xvi)

With Macheath reprieved, *The Beggar's Opera* ends in a suitably operatic way with a celebratory song and dance. In this extraordinary episode Gay ingeniously manages to combine a number of things. He explicitly criticizes Italian opera and its fans, burlesques the almost magical reversals of fortune and character with which operas frequently end, and in doing so secures an appropriate conclusion for what is, after all, a comedy. Macheath's escape from death even carries a satirical allusion to Sir Robert Walpole, the Prime Minister, who narrowly escaped political extinction in 1727 after the death of George I by promising his successor, George II, more money for the Royal Family. What makes the burlesque more caustic than the similar burlesque of peripeteia in *The What D'Ye Call It* when Peascod is saved from execution by a last-minute reprieve is the completely gratuitous nature of Macheath's reprieve. Whereas Peascod is a maligned innocent, Macheath is an incorrigible criminal whose guilt is unquestioned. He does nothing to earn his reprieve and there is no evidence that it will transform him morally.

To concentrate on the burlesque in *The Beggar's Opera* is to ignore much in the play that accounts for its continuing to hold the stage as a dramatic masterpiece. Today, Gay's social and political satire retains much of its incisiveness despite the enormous changes in society during the last two and a half centuries; his satire was highly topical at the time but is also universal, relating to perennial features of human nature and society as well as to England in the 1720s. This is an important reason for the ease with which Brecht was able to refurbish the play exactly two hundred years later as *Die Dreigroschenoper* (*The Threepenny Opera*), in which the criminal underworld is identified with the capitalist establishment. It is obvious that audiences who know nothing about Gay's burlesque of Italian opera enjoy and appreciate the play. Nevertheless, it is only possible to comprehend the subtlety and sophistication of Gay's achievement in *The Beggar's Opera* by seeing how far he employs standard situations and features of Italian opera, transforming them for his own purposes. Gay succeeded in creating a new kind of opera, in effect a musical comedy, by inverting and making fun of the conventions of Italian opera, and his burlesque intention clearly lies behind the overall scheme of the work and behind the specific arrangement of some of its episodes. Yet important as the burlesque impulse was to the creation of the work, the burlesque element in the finished product virtually becomes the vehicle for other elements, which for most audiences and readers are the primary ones.

The colossal success of *The Beggar's Opera* in 1728 resulted in a spate of ballad operas and ballad farces during the ensuing years, but it would be wrong to think that because these are modelled on Gay's play they have any necessary connection with the burlesque tradition. Gay arrived at the new form of the ballad opera by means of his burlesque of Italian opera; but once *The Beggar's Opera* had established an alternative kind of opera, this new genre could continue without any burlesque purpose whatsoever. In fact very few ballad operas contain burlesque, in any sense of the word. Even Gay's sequel to *The Beggar's Opera*, *Polly*, can hardly be thought of as burlesque, despite the satire on over-sensitive and bad-tempered operatic singers in the Introduction when the Poet and one of the actors discuss the play about to be performed.

This Introduction, resembling that in *The Beggar's Opera*, promises a continuation of the operatic burlesque in the earlier work, but *Polly* fails to fulfil this. For one thing, the placing of the action in the West Indies, complete with noble savages, proves to be antipathetic to burlesque. The sharp contrast between the London underworld and the world of opera that is implicit throughout *The Beggar's Opera* is no longer possible with this more romantic setting, especially as Macheath is less central and much less attractive than in the earlier play. He does not even appear under his own name, but in disguise as a black-hearted as well as black-skinned negro, Morano; and his death by hanging does not produce the 'down-right deep Tragedy' it would have done in *The Beggar's Opera*. Furthermore, Gay's idealistic treatment of the Indians as exemplary characters, as opposed to the corrupt Europeans, means that the low-life and criminal characters are seen as conventional villains, not inverted heroes as Macheath's gang are in *The Beggar's Opera*. Polly is now linked with the admirable Indian prince, Cawwawkee, rather than Macheath. Gay's reversion to sentimentalism and orthodox morality militates against the development of subversive humour, either burlesque or any other kind. Like so many sequels, *Polly* seems stillborn in comparison with its predecessor.

This does not mean that burlesque is completely absent from *Polly*, but since there is no overall burlesque purpose as in *The Beggar's Opera*, any burlesque is incidental and some potentially burlesque elements do not have such significance. Gay's handling of the metaphor of Cupid's arrow in Polly's two songs in I, v (Airs VI and VII) is thoroughly conventional and without burlesque intent, although used differently, as many of the operatic similes in *The Beggar's Opera* are, it could easily be burlesque since the metaphor is so commonplace in Italian opera. The presence of burlesque in *Polly* can, however, be felt in Gay's use of music from Ariosti's *Coriolano* (1723). At the end of II, viii, Morano sings two identical pieces of recitative to music from the Italian opera, and the unexpectedness of their introduction, especially as they are the only examples of recitative in *Polly*, makes the operatic parallel very obvious. There is more extended use of Ariosti's music in II, i when Polly, disguised as a boy, wanders in Indian territory looking for Macheath until she collapses with fatigue. Before she sings Air XXIII, apostrophising sleep, to the Dead March in *Coriolano*, music from the March is interspersed with her soliloquy. Polly's agitated state resulting from her love is similar to that of numerous romantic heroines, in operas and elsewhere; but since she is in pursuit of an outlawed pirate who is manifestly unworthy of her, there is, from one point of view, a burlesque incongruity in the use of Ariosti's solemn music here. Nevertheless, the scene could just as well be presented so as to put all the emphasis on the self-sacrifice of Polly, the music therefore being a way of dignifying her by raising her virtually to the status of an operatic heroine.

The element of burlesque is much less equivocal in the treatment of Morano's struggles between love and honour – more accurately, lust and crime. Now married to Jenny Diver, one of the prostitutes who betrayed him to Peachum in *The Beggar's Opera*, Morano finds himself torn between his involvement with her and his leadership of the pirates. Vanderbluff, one of his associates, exclaims, 'what, hamper'd in the arms of a woman, when your honour and glory are all at stake!' (II, iv), and in Air XXXIII at the end of this scene Morano himself expresses his predicament:

> Tho' different passions rage by turns,
>   Within my breast fermenting;
> Now blazes love, now honour burns,
>   I'm here, I'm there consenting.

Since 'love', 'honour', and 'glory' can only be understood ironically in this context, Morano's dilemma amounts to a burlesque of that confronting hero after hero in contemporary drama and opera. The best moment of burlesque in *Polly* occurs in II, ix when Morano is literally as well as metaphorically pulled in two directions simultaneously, by Jenny representing 'love' and by Vanderbluff representing 'honour'. Warned by Vanderbluff that 'a woman will never take the last kiss' becuase 'she will always want another', Morano declares, 'I must go – But I cannot', and then expounds on his interior conflict in Air XLIII:

>   *Honour calls me from thy arms,*   [to him
>   *With glory my bosom is beating.*
>   *Victory summons to arms: then to arms*
>   *Let us haste, for we're sure of defeating.*
>   *One look more – and then –*   [to her
>   *Oh, I am lost again!*
>   *What a Power has beauty!*
>   *But honour calls, and I must away.*   [to him
>   *But love forbids, and I must obey.*   [to her
>   *You grow too bold;*   [Vanderbluff *pulling him away*
>   *Hence, loose your hold,*   [to him
>   *For love claims all my duty.*   [to her

What makes this so effective as burlesque of an obvious heroic target is the speed and suddenness of his changes of heart, especially as each position is held, however briefly, with apparently unswerving conviction.

Polly was published in 1729 after the Lord Chamberlain, obviously acting on behalf of Walpole, had banned its production, partly as a reprisal for Gay's outspoken satire of the Court, the Government, and Walpole himself in *The Beggar's Opera*, and partly because *Polly* itself contains some virulent satire in a similar vein beneath its deceptively innocuous surface. *Polly* did not reach the stage until 1777. Gay's only other ballad opera, *Achilles*, was performed posthumously at Covent Garden in February 1733, just over two months after his death. As a farcical comedy based on ancient mythology, *Achilles* is a new departure for Gay, although not the first of the few ballad operas to fall into E. M. Gagey's category of 'mythological' or 'classical' ones.[23] Even so, some of these are entirely serious, and only one ballad opera produced before *Achilles* foreshadows its method of travesty: *Penelope* (1728) by John Mottley and Thomas Cooke, a low version of Odysseus' return home to be reunited with his faithful wife Penelope at the end of the *Odyssey*. Part of the authors' purpose was to burlesque Pope's translations of Homer, which explains their use of couplets.

In the play, Penelope, usually referred to as 'Pen', runs a public house in London called the Royal Oak and is being pursued by a number of tradesmen during the absence of her husband, Ulysses (Odysseus). He is a Sergeant in the Grenadiers who comes back from the wars disguised as a beggar in order to find out whether Penelope has remained true to him. The Homeric deities are represented by Minerva, who descends in thunder and lightning in pursuit of Ulysses' son, Telemachus (known as Tele), and alcoholic refreshment:

> PENELOPE What brings your Highness here?
> MINERVA Why, what d'you think?
> To see my *Tele*, and to taste your Drink.
> Among the Gods I've often heard it spoke,
> We've no such Beer, as at the *Royal Oak*.   (III, iv)

There is nothing subtle about *Penelope*, which is coarser and more Duffett-like than *Achilles*, but some of its better moments recall *The What D'Ye Call It*, mainly because the authors seem to have learned from Gay's handling of the couplet in burlesque drama. Nevertheless, *Penelope* really belongs to the line of classical travesty descending from Scarron, and if it does burlesque contemporary drama and Italian opera, it does so almost entirely by implication.

Achilles is a comic version of the great hero's life on Scyros while disguised as a woman. It is much gentler and less crude than most classical travesties, and because it is mainly in prose the characters are considerably less tied to a burlesque function that those in most dramatic burlesques written in verse, where the relationship to the source is usually much closer. F. W. Bateson's suggestion that *Achilles* is best viewed as a 'modernization' of an ancient story comparable to Shaw's *Caesar and Cleopatra* has a lot to be said for it,[24] but this is not incompatible with seeing the play at least to some extent in the burlesque tradition. But does *Achilles* burlesque contemporary tragedy and Italian opera as well as travesty a classical story? Although critics seem to ignore this possibility, Gay's Prologue, with its reference to the rhetoric of contemporary tragedy, suggests an affirmative answer:

> *His Scene now shews the Heroes of Old* Greece*;*
> *But how? 'tis monstrous! In a Comic Piece.*
> *To Buskins, Plumes and Helmets what Pretence,*
> *If mighty Chiefs must speak but common Sense?*
> *Shall no bold Diction, no Poetic Rage,*
> *Fome at our Mouths and thunder on the Stage?*
> *No – 'tis* Achilles, *as he came from* Chiron,
> *Just taught to sing as well as wield cold Iron;*
> *And whatsoever Criticks may suppose,*
> *Our Author holds, that what He spoke was Prose.*

In parts of *Achilles*, unlike *Penelope*, it is virtually impossible to separate classical travesty from satirical burlesque; the one becomes the other.

Having disguised her son Achilles as a girl (Pyrrha) to prevent him from going to the Trojan War, the goddess Thetis leaves him at the court of Lycomedes, who is immediately attracted by Pyrrha and plans 'her' seduction. Lycomedes' jealous wife, Theaspe, decides to put Pyrrha out of her husband's reach by marrying 'her' off quickly to Periphas. Theaspe employs her daughter Deidamia to spy on Pyrrha, but Deidamia falls in love with the disguised Achilles when she finds out who Pyrrha really is, and becomes pregnant by him. When his true identity is revealed, Achilles marries Deidamia and then sets off for the Trojan War.

The action of *Achilles* clearly centres on the mistaken identity and mistaken sex of Achilles–Pyrrha, a typical device of farce. Instead of dignified conduct, solemn situations, and lofty eloquence, Gay presents stereotyped comic figures speaking humorous prose in a series of ludicrous scenes. Instead of a noble or a tragic love, there are the marital quarrels of Lycomedes and Theaspe, Lycomedes' unsuccessful attempts at adultery with Pyrrha, and Deidamia's desperate efforts to persuade the reluctant Achilles to marry her. In every way Gay thwarts conventional heroic expectations. He achieves burlesque by inverting the usual characteristics of Italian opera and contemporary tragedy, as well as of classical epic, but in the opposite way to *The Beggar's Opera*. In that work, criminals are elevated to the status of heroes, whereas in *Achilles* epic characters are deprived of their heroic attributes and rendered as vulnerable human beings. By reducing Achilles, Ajax, and the others to human proportions, Gay is of course having fun at the expense of classical sublimity, but is also suggesting that the extremely noble presentation of such characters in contemporary opera and tragedy is preposterous and unconvincing. In this respect *Achilles* is a natural successor to *The What D'Ye Call It* and *The Beggar's Opera*.

Although Gay's deliberate debasement of epic material to the level of farcical comedy does at times result in satirical burlesque, there is no parody in *Achilles* and even less verbal burlesque than in *The Beggar's Opera*. There are also fewer situational parallels to contemporary opera and tragedy than in *The Beggar's Opera*. The burlesque is therefore general rather than specific, more implicit than explicit, but on occasion it manifests itself so clearly that there is no doubt about Gay's intentions. The scene in which Lycomedes attempts to seduce Pyrrha (II, iv) is brilliant comedy, but much of the humour derives from the implied but unmistakable contrast with the serious treatment of similar situations in 'reforming' or 'exemplary' plays. Lycomedes believes that Pyrrha's determined rejections of his advances are 'those little Arts of Women' essential to a woman's pride and self-esteem and also employed to tantalize and excite men to extreme passion. Achilles is actually trying very hard to calm Lycomedes down in order to prevent the King from discovering Pyrrha's true identity. The situation itself is commonplace in plays with sentimental tendencies. It is the struggle of innocence and virtue, represented by a faithful wife or a naive virgin, against corruption and vice, embodied in a sophisticated rake. In *Achilles* the question of which is stronger is quickly settled because the 'naive virgin' is in fact an heroic warrior. As in serious treatments of the situation self-consciously aiming at moral uplift, virtue is triumphant, but the method here is brute force. When Lycomedes tries to rape Pyrrha, 'she' pushes him away violently, throws him to the ground, and pins him there while 'she' sings a moral song that is extremely ironic:

> *What Heart hath not Courage, by Force assail'd,*
>   *To brave the most desperate Fight?*
> *'Tis Justice and Virtue that hath prevail'd;*
>   *Power must yield to Right.*   (Air XXVII)

Lycomedes may believe that he has been 'got the better of' by a woman, but the audience knows exactly why justice and virtue have prevailed. In producing a splendid piece of knockabout comedy, Gay has achieved an effective burlesque of sentimental moralizing.

What makes this scene so effective is that the dialogue, particularly in the early stages, could almost be from a straight version of the incident. After the initial polite exchanges, Lycomedes makes clear to Pyrrha exactly what he is after, but his manner is stilted and formal: 'I know there are a thousand necessary Affectations of Modesty, which Women, in Decency to themselves, practise with common Lovers before Compliance. – But my Passion, *Pyrrha*, deserved some Distinction.' Achilles, keeping up his part of the innocent girl outraged by the King's suggestions, answers Lycomedes in an appropriately moral tone: 'I know my Duty, Sir; and, had it not been for that Sycophant *Diphilus*, perhaps you had known yours.' These formal exchanges culminate in a mock love duet immediately before Lycomedes' attempted rape and its vigorous repulse. The vocal line alternates between Lycomedes and Achilles in the manner of operatic love duets, but the kind of love sung about, Lycomedes' uncontrollable lust, is the antithesis of the selfless and noble love usually found in opera:

> LYCOMEDES   *Why such Affectation?*
> ACHILLES   *Why this Provocation?*
> LYCOMEDES *Must I bear Resistance still!*
> ACHILLES   *Check your Inclination.*
> LYCOMEDES *Dare you then deny me?*
> ACHILLES   *You too far may try me.*
> LYCOMEDES *Must I then against your Will!*
> ACHILLES   *Force shall never ply me.*   (Air XXVI)

It is interesting to compare this air with Air XIV in *Polly*, another 'love duet' between a would-be seducer, Ducat, and his victim, Polly, in which she resists the advances of her master and concludes with the words, '*You find that vertue's strong*' (I, xi). This air does not register as burlesque, because Gay's treatment of Polly's predicament is serious, and this outweighs any tendency towards ridicule of opera. In *Achilles*, on the other hand, the situation from which the duet emerges is farcical, and the burlesque potential is fully realized.

Gay's burlesque of opera and tragedy is most evident in his treatment of the code of honour and the concomitant conflict between love and honour. From the very opening of the play, Achilles exhibits enormous concern for his honour, regarding life without honour as considerably worse than death, and an honourable death to be the highest state man can attain. His mother's commonsensical replies to his outbursts have no effect on him, but they do expose his notion of honour as childish posturing, and consequently deflate the heroics of opera and tragedy. Throughout the first scene between Achilles and Thetis, Gay is deriding the extreme notion of honour often upheld in Italian opera and heroic tragedy. He removes it from the hothouse environment of these forms and places it in a comic context that provides a way of passing judgement on it.

Achilles' involvement with Deidamia necessarily leads to a clash between his sense of honour and his love. In the only scene in which they are alone together (II, x), Achilles berates himself for not being true to his honour by compromising himself with a woman. He envies Periphas because 'His Honour, his Fame, his Glory is not shackled by a Woman'. At the opening of the encounter, the pregnant Deidamia's interpolations form an extremely ironic commentary on Achilles' self-pitying protestations, revealing his honour to be a heartless and egotistical vanity:

> ACHILLES Was there ever a Man in so whimsical a Circumstance!
> DEIDAMIA Was there ever a Woman in so happy and so unhappy a one as mine!
> ACHILLES Why did I submit? why did I plight my Faith thus infamously to conceal my self? – What is become of my Honour?
> DEIDAMIA Ah *Pyrrha, Pyrrha*, what is become of mine!
> ACHILLES When shall I behave my self as a Man!
> DEIDAMIA Wou'd you had never behav'd yourself as one!

By incongruously putting a typical hero into the low situation of a man who has made a girl pregnant and who wants to avoid marriage, Gay has discovered an ingenious way of demolishing the usual operatic and tragic conception of honour; there is an obvious resemblance to Macheath and Lucy in *The Beggar's Opera*. In Achilles' case, honour simply becomes an excuse for refusing to face up to his responsibilities to Deidamia and her unborn child. His argument that Deidamia cannot truly love him 'if in every Circumstance of Life you have not a just Regard for my Honour' is utterly specious. In the circumstances, true honour, as opposed to the highly theatrical honour represented by Achilles, would manifest itself in a compassionate response to Deidamia's physical and emotional state.

Gay approaches the subject of honour somewhat differently in his presentation of Ajax, another man obsessed with honour. Ajax does not make his appearance until near the end of the play, but he is known to have succumbed to Pyrrha's charms and to believe himself to be Periphas' rival for 'her' hand. Although Periphas is not at all keen on the match, Ajax is convinced that Periphas has slighted his honour. The scene in which Ajax confronts Periphas (III, iii) consequently gives Gay a fine opportunity to continue his ridicule of the operatic and tragic code of honour, and he makes the most of it. Ajax is so busy uttering all the clichés about honour expected of theatrical heroes that he is quite incapable of explaining to Periphas the reason for his anger. Periphas replies to Ajax's incoherent rant with a series of courteous and perfectly reasonable remarks that are as devastating as Deidamia's ironies at the expense of Achilles' honour in II, x:

> AJAX Death, my Lord, I explain! I am not come here to be ask'd Questions. – 'Tis sufficient that I know the Affront, and that you know I will have Satisfaction. – So, now you are answer'd –
> PERIPHAS I can't say much to *my* Satisfaction, my Lord; for I can't so much as guess at your meaning.
> AJAX A Man of Honour, *Periphas*, is not to be trifled withal.
> PERIPHAS But a Man of Honour, *Ajax*, is not oblig'd in Courage to be unintelligible.
> AJAX I hate talking. – The Tongue is a Woman's Weapon. Whenever I am affronted; by the Gods, this Sword is my only Answer.
> PERIPHAS 'Tis not, *Ajax*, that I decline the Dispute, or wou'd upon any Account deny you the Pleasure of fighting; yet (if it is not too much Condescension in a Man of Honour) before I fight I wou'd willingly know the Provocation.

That Ajax can keep a straight face and continue to take himself very seriously when answered so politely and intelligently reveals him to be little more than a thick-skinned, narcissistic, and bad-tempered lout. He pays great allegiance to honour, but in his mouth the word is synonymous with puerile resentment. He is the schoolboy bully trying to get his own back because someone has obtained an advantage over him. Stepping on his honour is virtually the same as stepping on his toe, as Periphas recognizes: 'Now in my Opinion 'tis flinging away your Courage to fight without a Cause; though indeed the Men of uncommon Prowess, by their loving to make the most of every Quarrel, seem to think the contrary.' Ajax is evidently a lineal descendant of Buckingham's Drawcansir.

In the final scene, Ajax is the source of more burlesque humour, but this is fairly insignificant. The happy ending demands a reconciliation of all the conflicts in the play and Gay does not allow the burlesque element to obtrude, but the two scenes leading up to the conclusion (III, x-xi) are very different. As soon as Achilles' true identity is revealed, the struggle between his love and his honour becomes much more urgent than earlier in the play. The aim of Ulysses, Diomedes, and Agyrtes, the three Greek leaders who unmask Achilles, is to transport him to Troy as quickly as possible so that the Greek assault can be given a new ferocity and impetus: they appeal to him in terms of 'Honour', 'Victory', and 'Glory'. Deidamia, on the other hand, is equally determined that he should not go, and reminds him of his 'solemn Oaths and Promises' in begging him to think of her honour. Her pregnancy is now impossible to hide and she is greatly distressed at the thought of being abandoned by Achilles.

Achilles oscillates between these two forces like a pendulum. When Agyrtes blows a trumpet, Achilles is so enthralled at the prospect of battle and noble action that he is unaware of anything else, but after only one glance at the sad Deidamia he unhesitatingly rejects honour for love. Yet as soon as the trumpet sounds again, he forgets Deidamia's existence and is instantly transformed into a militant warrior. The speed and ease with which Achilles transfers his devotions is extremely funny, but what makes the burlesque so successful is that the 'epic hero', trapped between love and honour, has no will of his own. Achilles responds like an automaton or a Pavlovian dog to whatever stimulus is provided, and the use of exactly the same words and music at each blast of the trumpet helps to make Achilles' struggle seem completely mechanical:

> [Agyrtes *takes a Trumpet which lay amongst the Armour, and sounds*
> ULYSSES *Thy Fate, then, O Troy, is decreed.*
> DIOMEDES *How I pant!*
> ACHILLES *How I burn for the Fight.*
> DIOMEDES *Hark, Glory calls.*
> ACHILLES *Now great Hector shall bleed.*
> AGYRTES *Fame shall our Deeds requite.*
>   [As *Achilles* is going off, he turns and looks on *Deidamia.*
> ACHILLES *Beauty weeps. – Ah, why that Languish?*
>   *See she calls and bids me stay.*

How can I leave her? my Heart feels her Anguish.
Hence, Fame and Glory. Love wins the Day.
[He drops the Sword and Shield. Trumpet sounds, and he
takes 'em up again
ULYSSES *Thy Fate then, O Troy, is decreed.*
ACHILLES *How I pant! How I burn for the Fight!*
DIOMEDES *Hark, Glory calls. Now great Hector shall bleed.*
AGYRTES *Fame shall our Deeds requite.*
[As they are going; *Achilles* stops with his Eyes fix'd on
Deidamia. (III, x)

This episode looks back to Volscius' notorious internal conflict between love and honour in *The Rehearsal*, ludicrously rendered in terms of taking off and putting on his boots, but it is even more similar to the scene in *Polly* where Morano fluctuates violently between Jenny and Vanderbluff. Because the love–honour debate is couched in song in both of Gay's plays, his burlesque is aimed primarily at Italian opera, but is equally applicable to contemporary heroic tragedy. The resemblance to opera is maintained in III, xi when Achilles first sings of the pain he has to endure because of the contradictory voices speaking to him, '*Fame cries, Go;/Love says, No*' (Air XLIX), and then shares a trio with Deidamia and Ulysses that opens, '*O, what a Conflict's in my Breast!*' (Air L).

Another classical travesty in the form of a ballad opera, John Durant Breval's *The Rape of Helen*, was produced shortly after *Achilles* in 1733 and may have been influenced by it. This 'Mock-Opera', a comic version of the seduction of Helen by Paris, is also written in prose, but differs from *Achilles* in that the deities (including Juno, Minerva, Venus, and Mercury) play a crucial part, whereas only one, Thetis, appears in Gay's work, and she is a minor character. Throughout *The Rape of Helen*, the deities behave in anything but a godlike fashion and are not at all admirable. The Greeks, too, are far from noble; when Menelaus and Helen are together, they usually indulge in marital bickering and domestic squabbles. As a classical travesty, *The Rape of Helen* is lively, amusing, bawdy, and action-packed, and must have made a most entertaining stage play; but despite its label of 'Mock-Opera' it contains no explicit burlesque of Italian opera (or of contemporary drama), even in its twenty-five airs. Any mockery of opera is implicit. Compared with Gay in *Achilles*, Breval does not develop the possibilities of classical travesty for satirizing contemporary dramatic genres at all.

True mock opera, with recitatives, arias, duets, choruses, and Italianate music, is to be found in the 1730s, most notably in two short works by Henry Carey with music by John Frederick Lampe, the immensely popular *The Dragon of Wantley* (1737) and its inferior sequel *The Dragoness*, otherwise known as *Margery* (1738). After collaborating with composers, including Lampe, on English-language operas in the Italian style, such as *Amelia* (1732) and *Teraminta* (1732), Carey wrote these two burlesque operas in which a nonsensically comic text, mainly in mock-heroic couplets and sometimes with double rhymes, was set in a conventional operatic way, with music 'as grand and pompous as possible' according to Carey's Dedication to Lampe in the published version of *The Dragon of Wantley*. The action of this opera, issued as the work of Signior Carini to sustain the burlesque parallel, resembles that of many Italian operas in that the hero, Moore of Moore-Hall, has to undertake a courageous feat, the killing of a dragon, and is involved with two women, Margery and Mauxalinda, but Carey transforms all the operatic elements into farce. The Dragon, for example, not only sings, but eats buttered toast and drinks tea and ale; and the culminating encounter between Moore and the Dragon lasts only a few lines because the Dragon is slain by Moore's first kick to his bottom, dying with the words, 'Oh! oh! oh! / The Devil take your Toe' (III, i). It is uncertain whether there is any musical parody in these mock operas, but Carey may be alluding to an opera performed only months before *The Dragon of Wantley*, Handel's *Justin* (1737), which also featured dragons, although dragons and wild animals are not unusual in Italian opera. The discrepancy between words and music in Carey's two mock operas must have resulted in amusing burlesque, but being exuberantly playful rather than satirically parodic, they are as much comic or farcical operas in their own right as burlesques of Italian opera.[25]

Achilles is one of two 'irregular' plays that Gay wrote at the end of his life, the other being *The Rehearsal at Goatham*, which was not performed and remained unpublished until 1754, more than twenty years after his death. Despite its title, this one-act satire bears virtually no resemblance to Buckingham's play, being devoid of burlesque elements and containing little more than a hint of a rehearsal or an inner play, but it does have some affinity with Fielding's dramatic satires. *The Rehearsal at Goatham* is partly an allegory about the government ban in 1728 of the planned production of *Polly*, partly an anti-Walpole lampoon, and partly an attack on Colley Cibber, the Drury Lane theatre manager who was considered to have played a part in the action against Gay's second ballad opera. Cibber's appointment as Poet Laureate in 1730 made him a laughing stock in some circles, and he, like Walpole, was to become a recurrent target in Fielding's satirical plays. In *The Rehearsal at Goatham*, Sir Headstrong Bustle and Jack Oaf are caricatures of Walpole and Cibber respectively. Gay based his play on the episode of Peter and his puppet show in *Don Quixote*, a work that also provided Fielding with material for a play with the same title as Cervantes' novel and subsequently had an important influence on his fiction. The setting is the imaginary English town of Goatham, where plans to perform a puppet play upset all the local officials and dignitaries. Without any justification, these hyper-sensitive and paranoid worthies suspect that the puppet show is a veiled assault on themselves, designed to undermine their status and authority; in setting themselves up as a board of censors to vet what is a completely innocuous play, the aldermen emerge as truly ridiculous. The allegory operates in terms of the London theatre world and contemporary political life, and indeed ties the two together, as Fielding was to do with more devastating satirical effect in some of his last plays of 1736-37. As in *The Rehearsal at Goatham*, a 'puppet show' and criticism of Colley Cibber feature prominently in the first of Fielding's plays to incorporate burlesque, *The Author's Farce*.

NOTES

1. 'Gay's *Mohocks* and Milton', *Journal of English and Germanic Philology* 46 (1947) 164-7.
2. Quotations from Gay's plays are taken from John Fuller's two-volume edition of the *Dramatic Works* (Oxford, 1983). Two of the plays discussed in this chapter, *The What D'Ye Call It* and *Three Hours after Marriage*, are included in Trussler's *Burlesque Plays of the Eighteenth Century*.
3. See Fuller's 'Introduction' in his edition, I, 17-20.
4. *A General View of the Stage* (London, 1759) 165-6.
5. Letter to Caryll (3 March 1715), *The Correspondence of Alexander Pope*, ed. George Sherburn (Oxford, 1956) I, 283.
6. *Ibid.*, 282-3.
7. *Early Eighteenth Century Drama*, 197-8.
8. I am indebted to an unpublished paper by Jane Campanella, 'Gay's *The What D'Ye Call It* as an Absurdist *Rehearsal*-Type Play', for a few suggestions incorporated in this paragraph.
9. *Complete Key*, [vi].
10. *Ibid.*, 10.
11. *Ibid.*, 14.
12. *Ibid.*, 16.
13. *Ibid.*, 18.
14. *Ibid.*, 20.
15. *Ibid.*, 26.
16. *Ibid.*, 31.
17. *Ibid.*, 12-13.
18. *Three Hours after Marriage* (Painesville, Ohio, 1961) vii-ix.
19. In the Commentary to his edition of Gay's *Dramatic Works*, I, 438-43, Fuller provides an excellent résumé of the disagreement and speculation that this and similar issues in the play have provoked.
20. Much more has been written about *The Beggar's Opera* than the rest of Gay's dramatic work put together. My edition of the ballad opera (Edinburgh, 1973) contains a Bibliography listing

the most important scholarly and critical studies, such as those by Bertrand H. Bronson, Ian Donaldson, William Empson, and W. E. Schultz. See also *Twentieth Century Interpretations of The Beggar's Opera,* ed. Yvonne Noble (Englewood Cliffs, N.J., 1975); my *John Gay: The Beggar's Opera* (London, 1976); Howard Erskine-Hill, 'The Significance of Gay's Drama', *English Drama: Forms and Development,* ed. Marie Axton and Raymond Williams (Cambridge, 1977) 142-63 (this essay covers Gay's entire dramatic output); Carolyn Kephart, 'An Unnoticed Forerunner of *The Beggar's Opera', Music and Letters* 61 (1980) 266-71; Lowell Lindgren, *'Camilla* and *The Beggar's Opera', Philological Quarterly* 59 (1980) 44-61; and Robert D. Hume, ' "The World is all Alike": Satire in *The Beggar's Opera', The Rakish Stage,* 245-69.
21. The case for seeing Gay's burlesque as mild rather than hostile is strongly argued by William A. McIntosh, 'Handel, Walpole, and Gay: The Aims of *The Beggar's Opera', Eighteenth-Century Studies* 7 (1973-74) 415-33.
22. *'The Beggar's Opera', Studies in the Comic* (Berkeley, 1941) 197-231; reprinted in *Restoration Drama: Modern Essays in Criticism,* ed. John Loftis (New York, 1966) 298-327.
23. *Ballad Opera* (New York, 1937) 192-8.
24. *English Comic Drama 1700-1750* (Oxford, 1929) 98.
25. Trussler includes *Chrononhotonthologos* and *The Dragon of Wantley* in *Burlesque Plays of the Eighteenth Century.*

The Author's Farce

On 16 February 1728, just two weeks after the first production of *The Beggar's Opera*, Fielding's comedy *Love in Several Masques* was staged in London. A new playwright had arrived, and between 1728 and 1737, when he was still only thirty, Fielding probably wrote (or translated and adapted) as many as twenty-six plays and afterpieces. However, it was not until nearly two years after *Love in Several Masques* that another of his plays was performed – *The Temple Beau* on 26 January 1730. With this production, Fielding's seven-year period of intense dramatic activity can be said to have begun, and during the next few months three more of his plays were staged. *Love in Several Masques* and *The Temple Beau* are cleverly plotted and witty comedies of a thoroughly orthodox type descending from the major comic dramatists of the Restoration. Neither gives any indication of the striking originality characterizing his next play, *The Author's Farce; and The Pleasures of the Town*, first produced at the New Haymarket (Little Theatre in the Haymarket) on 30 March 1730. Among 'the pleasures of the town' Fielding set out to ridicule in this satirical play are most of the theatrical entertainments of the time, including opera, pantomime, and tragedy.

Fielding published both *The Author's Farce* and his next play, *Tom Thumb*, under the pseudonym of 'Scriblerus Secundus', and in doing so aligned himself artistically (though not necessarily politically) with the writers of the Scriblerus Club, such as Swift, Pope, and Gay. Considering the literary eminence of these figures, it may seem presumptuous of the twenty-two-year-old Fielding to have used 'Scriblerus Secundus', but it was a way of demonstrating his aims and allegiances and of showing that he was applying their aesthetic standards and critical weapons to the theatre. One of the best of the Scriblerian pieces that appeared intermittently after 1714 is *Peri Bathous: Of the Art of Sinking in Poetry* (1728), which was published under the mask of Martinus Scriblerus but which in its final version is largely the work of Pope. Fielding's dramatic works satirizing contemporary theatre might well be said to constitute 'The Art of Sinking in Drama', although Pope himself devotes part of his treatise to dramatic poetry.

It is well known that the original members of the Scriblerus Club did not exactly welcome the young Fielding as an ally, probably regarding him as a precocious upstart and a Grub Street hack. Pope in particular became rather hostile to Fielding after initially ignoring him, and the attacks on Fielding in *The Grub-Street Journal* have usually been thought to have had Pope's backing or at least to have voiced his opinion. As a strong supporter of the Hanoverian succession and in some ways a Whig rather than a Tory at heart, Fielding's political position was substantially different from Pope's, but in the cultural battle between Ancients and Moderns he sided with the great Tory satirists of the previous generation in defending traditional literary values against the rootless cult of modernity. If Fielding was strongly influenced by Pope and his fellow Scriblerians, it seems likely, as George Sherburn has argued, that when Pope was radically revising *The Dunciad* and adding the fourth Book he was in turn indebted to Fielding's dramatic burlesques and satires of the 1730s.[1] In these plays Fielding is engaged on the truly Scriblerian enterprise of exposing the contemporary debasement of standards, whether in art (especially dramatic art) or in life.

The Author's Farce contains such merciless ridicule of the contemporary theatre that it is sometimes described as Fielding's first dramatic burlesque, but genuine verbal and visual burlesque form a comparatively small part of the play – and this is true of both the original version and the considerably revised and expanded version produced at Drury Lane in January 1734 and published under Fielding's own name in 1750 with the slightly modified title, *The Author's Farce; with a Puppet Show called The Pleasures of the Town*. (The present study concentrates on the final version, but the most crucial changes and the reasons for them will be mentioned.) *The Author's Farce* is therefore quite unlike *The Rehearsal* and *The What D'Ye Call It*, although Fielding does incorporate a modification of Buckingham's rehearsal technique in the Puppet Show of the third and final act. Yet even here Fielding's methods are decidedly original and very different from those of his predecessors and of his own *Tom Thumb*, written at about the same time. *The Author's Farce* is more accurately described as a dramatic satire than a burlesque, especially as the burlesque elements are limited to the Puppet Show. In Acts I and II, Fielding only occasionally ridicules the theatrical shows in vogue; his main purpose is to indict the people most responsible for the decline in dramatic and literary standards, theatre managers and booksellers, and to portray the unfortunate predicament of writers dependent for their livelihood on these unscrupulous men.[2] With its comprehensive survey of current drama, the men who ran the theatres, booksellers and their hacks, and the domestic plight of impoverished playwrights, *The Author's Farce* is most ambitious, although Fielding's determination to be wide-ranging results in a series of virtually unconnected episodes only tenuously linked by the central character, Luckless. Yet such loose structuring is almost unavoidable in dramatic satires, as opposed to burlesques, and should be regarded as a necessary means rather than a fault or weakness.

The play opens in the manner of Fielding's earlier comedies, with Luckless, a penniless dramatist, in love with Harriot, the daughter of his landlady, Mrs Moneywood, who in turn desires him. Until halfway through Act I with the arrival of Luckless' friend Witmore, there is no indication in the 1734 version that the play is more than a comedy of intrigue; and although discussion of the theatre dominates the central part of this act, the action in the last four scenes reverts entirely to the comedy of intrigue. In the 1730 version, however, there is one incidental piece of burlesque, as Marsha Kinder notes in her discussion of Fielding's revisions.[3] At one point both Luckless and Harriot resort not only to verse but to rhyming couplets, with the result that 'their mutual declarations of love are expressed in the exaggerated language of the mock-sublime'.[4] The passage resembles similar declamations (also in couplets) by Filbert and Kitty in *The What D'Ye Call It*, and the target – lachrymose pathetic scenes between threatened lovers – is the same:

> LUCKLESS Say, then, my Harriot, would my charmer fly
> To the cold climes beneath the polar sky?
> Or, armed with love, could she endure to sweat
> Beneath the sultry, dry equator's heat?
> Thirst, hunger, labor, hardship, could she prove,
> From conversation of the world remove,
> And only know the joys of constant love?
> HARRIOT Oh, more than this, my Luckless, would I do.
> All places are a heaven, when with you.
> Let me repose but on that faithful breast.
> Give me thy love, the world may take the rest. (I, iii)[5]

Notwithstanding this burlesque episode, much of Act I is an almost farcical presentation of Luckless' financial and amatory problems, but a couple of important passages do reveal Fielding's opinion of current theatrical presentations and of the men responsible for them.

When he arrives at Mrs Moneywood's house, Witmore is amazed to find that Luckless is still trying to live by his pen, and he delivers a lengthy tirade against the present state of learning, wit, literature, and drama, proving that the world is upside down (this speech is very similar to the corresponding speech in the 1730 version):

> But now, when party and prejudice carry all before them; when learning is decried, wit not understood; when the theatres are

puppet-shows, and the comedians ballad-singers; when fools lead the town, would a man think to thrive by his wit? If you must write, write nonsense, write operas, write Hurlothrumbos, set up an oratory and preach nonsense, and you may meet with encouragement enough. Be profane, be scurrilous, be immodest; if you would receive applause, deserve to receive sentence at the Old Bailey; and if you would ride in a coach, deserve to ride in a cart.   (I, v)

Witmore finally extends his despairing view of the literary world to society at large. As in *The Dunciad*, the condition of scholarship and the theatre is symptomatic of the state of culture and civilization and indicative of a decline in moral standards. For Witmore, there has been a complete reversal of literary and dramatic values so that it does not matter whether Luckless writes sense or nonsense, except that he is more likely to be successful by imitating such absurd plays as the notorious *Hurlothrumbo; or, The Supernatural* by Samuel Johnson of Cheshire, a play referred to later in the Puppet Show. Although Johnson was believed to be insane, his play, with dialogue of almost incomprehensible bombast and with Johnson himself marching around the stage on stilts playing a violin, was an enormous success in 1729. Byrom's Epilogue to this play hints that it is a burlesque of current theatrical nonsense, but while the pretence of nonsense can be an excellent burlesque technique, as in the Puppet Show of *The Author's Farce*, nonsense itself does not constitute burlesque. Johnson gave a similar performance in his *The Blazing Comet: The Mad Lovers; or, The Beauties of the Poets* (1732), appearing as the mad Lord Wildfire rather than the mad Lord Flame of *Hurlothrumbo*.

One of the reasons for the purported decline in dramatic standards, the power of theatre managers such as Colley Cibber of Drury Lane, occupies Fielding briefly towards the end of Act I and at greater length in Act II. (In the 1730 version, the treatment of the managers is limited to Act II.) By far the most important difference between the 1730 and the 1734 versions lies in Fielding's treatment of the theatre managers. In the 1730 version, Fielding aimed his attack at Colley Cibber and Robert Wilks, two of the three Drury Lane managers at the time, who appear as Marplay and Sparkish respectively; Barton Booth, the third manager, is not represented in the play. After the moderate success of *Love in Several Masques* at Drury Lane in 1728, Fielding hoped that his next plays would also be performed there, but the Drury Lane managers rejected both *Don Quixote* and *The Temple Beau*. To some extent Fielding was obtaining his revenge by caricaturing Cibber and Wilks in *The Author's Farce*, but more importantly he was pointing out that, if the theatres were run by men concerned solely with financial success and not with maintaining dramatic standards, drama had no hope of improving. Marplay and Sparkish, as John Loftis argues, are 'at once types of the theatre manager and symbols of cultural corruption';[6] and since Cibber was associated with Walpole, there is at least a suggestion that the 'cultural corruption' was related to the Walpole Government.

Wilks died in 1732, so that when Fielding revised the play for the 1734 production he substituted Marplay Junior for Sparkish in order to ridicule the actor son of Colley Cibber, Theophilus Cibber, whom he regarded as an overbearing trouble-maker. Fielding's presentation of Marplay Junior is considerably more bitter than his treatment of Sparkish, a comparatively gentle caricature of Wilks, and one reason for the vehemence of this satirical portrait of Theophilus Cibber is connected with the theatre war of 1733–34. After the deaths of Wilks in 1732 and Booth in 1733, Colley Cibber sold his share of the Drury Lane patent to John Highmore, a man with little experience in the theatre. Theophilus Cibber, who had been deputy manager of Drury Lane under his father and had virtually run the theatre during the 1732–33 season, was infuriated at being under the control of Highmore and led a revolt of the Drury Lane actors, most of whom moved to the New Haymarket with him. When the 1733–34 season opened, Drury Lane was consequently in desperate straits. Fielding, who was now working for Drury Lane, decided to help Highmore by revising *The Author's Farce* to suit the new circumstances. Fielding probably hoped that the play would repeat some of its phenomenal success of 1730 and draw theatregoers to Drury Lane and away from the rebels, but above all he wanted to make Theophilus Cibber a laughing stock. Although the revised version was fairly successful, Fielding's intervention on Highmore's behalf had no lasting effect, and in February 1734 Highmore sold his share of the Drury Lane patent to Charles Fleetwood. Fleetwood soon made peace with Theophilus Cibber and the other rebellious actors, and the Drury Lane company was reunited in March 1734.

In his treatment of Marplay Senior and Marplay Junior, Fielding does indulge in both personal abuse and propaganda on behalf of Drury Lane, but as in the original version he is also deeply concerned with the responsibility of theatre managers for the state of contemporary drama. Colley and Theophilus Cibber were two of the most influential men in the London theatre world and were well known for their insensitive alterations of texts and for their attitude of superiority to playwrights, even though they themselves wrote plays. Condemnation of theatre managers for degrading drama was nothing new in the 1730s; Pope attacked them in *Peri Bathous*, and critics, notably Dennis, frequently voiced similar complaints.[7] Fielding's innovation was to put such criticisms into dramatic form. In doing so, he is blaming theatre managers even more than playwrights for the condition of drama.

When Marplay Junior visits Luckless in I, vi (there is no equivalent to this scene in the 1730 version), he talks very openly about the 'dramatic tailoring' performed by his father and himself to ensure that the plays they produce will suit the taste of the town and so be successful. Luckless' offer of a tragedy to Marplay Junior for his theatre prompts the latter into boastful remarks about the necessity for alterations, including a proud mention of his own modifications of Shakespeare; this refers to Theophilus Cibber's amalgamation of Parts II and III of *Henry VI*, performed in 1723. 'Let a play be never so good, without alteration it will do nothing', he explains to Witmore, the astonished representative of good sense, and he adds:

> Was you to see the plays when they are brought to us, a parcel of crude undigested stuff. We are the persons, sir, who lick them into form, that mould them into shape – The poet make the play indeed! the colourman might as well be said to make the picture, or the weaver the coat: my father and I, sir, are a couple of poetical tailors: when a play is brought us, we consider it as a tailor does his coat; we cut it, sir, we cut it; and let me tell you, we have the exact measure of the town; we know how to fit their taste. The poets, between you and me, are a pack of ignorant —

Whenever he appears, Marplay Junior, like Buckingham's Bayes, is exposed as asinine through his own words, and the scene at the playhouse in which the Marplays try to 'tailor' Luckless' play (II, i) is reminiscent of parts of both *The Rehearsal* and *Three Hours after Marriage* (that dealing with Clinket's tragedy), even though Fielding criticizes the managers rather than the dramatist. When Luckless reads a passage of sentimental rhetoric from his tragedy to them, Marplay Senior points out how the lines could be improved; but his 'amendments' succeed in reducing what is already fustian to complete nonsense (this passage is basically the same in both versions):

> LUCKLESS [*reads*] 'Then hence my sorrow, hence my every fear;
> No matter where, so we are blessed together.
> With thee, the barren rocks, where not one step
> Of human race lies printed in the snow,
> Look lovely as the smiling infant spring.'
> MARPLAY SENIOR Augh! Will you please to read that again, sir?
> LUCKLESS 'Then hence my sorrow, hence my every fear.'
> MARPLAY SENIOR 'Then hence my sorrow' – Horror is a much better word. – And then in the second line – 'No matter

where, so we are blessed together' – Undoubtedly, it should be, No matter where, so somewhere we're together. Where is the question, somewhere is the answer? – Read on, sir.
LUCKLESS 'With thee,' &c.
MARPLAY SENIOR No, no, I could alter those lines to a much better idea.
'With thee, the barren blocks, where not a bit
Of human face is painted on the bark,
Look green as Covent Garden in the spring.'
LUCKLESS Green as Covent Garden?
MARPLAY JUNIOR Yes, yes; Covent Garden market, where they sell greens.
LUCKLESS Monstrous!

'Monstrous' is the only response possible to such 'better ideas' and to the complacent manner in which the Marplays impose them on Luckless.

Fielding's final assault on the Marplays is the scene in which Marplay Senior gives his son his inheritance in the form of advice about running a theatre (II, ii – this is one of Fielding's additions to the 1734 version; the corresponding scene between Marplay and Sparkish in the 1730 version is much shorter and very different). The last thing that Marplay Senior has ever been concerned about is the cultivation of high dramatic standards, but there is also a more sinister motive behind his behaviour. He has conspired to prevent good plays from reaching the stage so that his own mediocrity as a dramatist would not be noticed: 'If thou writest thyself, and that I know thou art very qualified to do, it is thy interest to keep back all other authors of any merit, and be as forward to advance those of none.' His great envy of writers more gifted than himself has made him keep dramatic standards low so that he could be one of the leading figures in the theatre.

There is nothing good-humoured in Fielding's treatment of the two Marplays; his caricatures of Colley and Theophilus Cibber are savage. Fielding certainly had some justification for such severity, because Colley Cibber was notorious for his rude and brusque handling of budding dramatists. Pope eventually made Cibber the 'epic hero' in the final version of *The Dunciad*, but Fielding's play was not the first literary work to satirize him. In the anonymous *The Stage-Pretenders; or, The Actor Turn'd Poet* (1720), Cibber is one of several actors attacked for their attempts at playwriting and is accused of plagiarism, a charge also levelled by Fielding when he makes Marplay Senior tell his son how to achieve acclaim as a dramatist: 'The art of writing, boy, is the art of stealing old plays, by changing the name of the play, and new ones, by changing the name of the author' (II, ii). But the real *raison d'être* of the Marplay scenes is Fielding's indictment of theatre managers for their mercenary motives, their desire to satisfy the taste of the town, however crude, and their consequent refusal to take risks.

Fielding develops his attack in the scenes (II, iv-vi) that satirize the bookseller Bookweight, who closely resembles Marplay Senior in that both of them regard literature as a commercial product to be valued only in monetary terms. The writers who work for Bookweight have execrable literary standards, and at times they themselves recognize this, but considering the conditions in which they have to work they can hardly be blamed. They are merely drudges churning out saleable pamphlets on whatever happens to be topical. The real culprit is their employer, or more accurately their exploiter, who usually has the word 'price' on the tip of his tongue. In effect, Fielding is putting theatre managers like the Cibbers at the same low level as Grub Street booksellers like the famous Edmund Curll, one of Pope's victims in *The Dunciad*. Fielding does not actually identify Bookweight with Curll, but in the Puppet Show there is further criticism of booksellers, and there the bookseller is called Mr Curry.

The climax of *The Author's Farce* is the play-within-a-play section, which occupies most of Act III. (The Puppet Show is similar in both versions of the play, although in revising it Fielding dropped the less successful episodes of the 1730 version, introduced some new material, and sharpened the satire in a number of ways.) In the context of the whole play, Luckless' eccentric, human Puppet Show, which reverses the normal procedure by using live actors to imitate puppets, is his response to the rejection of his regular plays by the theatre managers: he now follows Witmore's earlier advice to 'write nonsense' by trying to be as outrageously odd and novel as possible. In presenting the predicament of a young playwright in this way, Fielding is to some extent dramatizing his own experience, because after Drury Lane turned down two of his comedies he himself wrote a decidedly odd, though far from nonsensical, play – *The Author's Farce* itself, whose very title points to its reflexive nature (a play about a playwright, one of whose dramatic works is incorporated). Nevertheless, Harry Luckless must not be identified with Henry Fielding despite certain parallels between them; Fielding is careful to distance himself from his comic hero, who is therefore not a self-portrait but a 'puppet' in Fielding's larger 'puppet show' of *The Author's Farce*.

Before Fielding, writers of dramatic burlesque had usually been content to ridicule one genre at a time; even if they satirized several dramatic forms in the same work, they invariably concentrated on one. Italian opera is not Gay's only dramatic target in *The Beggar's Opera*, but it is by far the most important. Fielding, on the other hand, was determined to deal with all the theatrical 'Pleasures of the Town' simultaneously, the result being that the Puppet Show gives the impression of being a rather chaotic farrago, as Jack-Pudding's announcement in the streets of London suggests:

> This is to give notice to all gentlemen, ladies, and others, that at the Theatre Royal in Drury Lane, this evening, will be performed the whole puppet-show called the Pleasures of the Town; in which will be shown the whole court of nonsense, with abundance of singing, dancing and several other entertainments:– Also the comical and diverting humours of Somebody and Nobody: Punch and his wife Joan, to be performed by figures; some of them six foot high. (II, vii)

In spite of the ambiguous reference to 'the whole court of nonsense', it is not surprising that Witmore, on reading the playbill, considers Luckless' Puppet Show to be a particularly extreme form of nonsense rather than an exposure of nonsense. The Theatre Manager too, who can 'make neither head nor tail on't' and has to ask Luckless 'what is the design or plot?', seems to regard the Puppet Show as completely absurd, and he is not reassured when Luckless tells him 'that a writer of puppet-shows might take as much more liberty than a writer of operas, as an opera-writer might be allowed beyond a writer of plays' (III, i). The Puppet Show does appear to be nonsensical, but it is nonsense with a satirical purpose, and the pretence of unadulterated nonsense is also an important part of Fielding's burlesque method. At the end of the Prologue to *The Author's Farce*, Fielding argues that, since theatregoers welcome gibberish under the label of tragedy or comedy, they can hardly object to an evening of deliberate nonsense:

> Beneath the tragic or the comic name,
> Farces and puppet-shows ne'er miss of fame.
> Since then, in borrowed dress, they've pleased the town,
> Condemn them not, appearing in their own.

A similar thrust against contemporary drama is made in II, vi when Luckless informs Bookweight that his Puppet Show is to be performed at Drury Lane. The bewildered Bookweight finds this completely incongruous, but Luckless asks with incisive irony, 'why what have been all the playhouses a long while but puppet-shows?', thus repeating Witmore's accusation that 'the theatres are puppet-shows'. Yet there is no hint either here or in the Prologue that the Puppet Show is actually a burlesque. Fielding makes his satirical point by simply suggesting that a piece of deliberate nonsense could not be more idiotic than the contemporary tragedies, comedies, operas, and pantomimes treated with such respect by theatre audiences. Complaints that the theatres offered little more than puppet shows were made in Augustan periodical literature, but even so Fielding's idea of calling his satirical burlesque a Puppet Show was an ingenious and original touch. The use by some eighteenth-century puppeteers of almost life-size puppets undoubtedly gave added significance to these accusations that there was little difference between the human theatre and the puppet theatre.[8] In production, Luckless' Puppet Show would have resembled a genuine puppet show as closely as possible, with appropriate styles of acting and voice production.

Although the Puppet Show is meant to be an actual performance at Drury Lane and not a rehearsal, Fielding makes an interesting adaptation of Buckingham's burlesque method. Luckless, the author of the Puppet Show, appears on stage throughout as the Master of the Show, introducing and explaining the various characters and episodes, just as the Interpreter did in real puppet shows.[9] In this role he serves as an intermediary between the audience and the inner play, and therefore draws attention to the nature of theatrical illusion, as Johnson and Smith do in a different way in *The Rehearsal*. In the 1734 version, the main action of the Puppet Show is concerned with the election of a poet laureate to the Goddess of Nonsense and takes place at her Court on the other side of the Styx. The main theme of the 1730 version, the love of Nonsense for Signior Opera, therefore becomes subordinate to this new theme of the election. The setting of the land of the dead ensures that all the competitors for the laureateship, including personifications of the various dramatic forms such as Signior Opera himself, will be seen to be lifeless, a satirical point Luckless is eager to stress. Fielding had the classical precedents of Aristophanes and Lucian for lowering his satirical targets into the underworld, but *The Dunciad*, containing a Goddess of Dulness and her laureate, was a more immediate model for Fielding than any classical work, and Dane Farnsworth Smith is right to call *The Author's Farce* 'a partial dramatization of *The Dunciad*'.[10] Dramatic presentations of hell and the land of the dead were not uncommon in pantomime at the time, and Fielding may even have been influenced by one of the forms he was out to attack. Nevertheless, Fielding's use of an underworld setting is something new in dramatic burlesque and totally different from the pantomimists' use of it for spectacular purposes. Besides *The Rehearsal* and *The Dunciad*, the other major influence on the Puppet Show is *The Beggar's Opera*. With its overture and numerous songs set to traditional tunes, including ones also used by Gay, the Puppet Show could be described as a miniature ballad opera; there is even a reference to Polly Peachum in Air xviii.

The Puppet Show opens, appropriately enough, with the figure of Punch, who apologizes for his appearance on the legitimate stage, as opposed to the puppet theatre, in a song recalling the lines from the Prologue quoted above:

> Whilst the town's brimful of farces,
> Flocking whilst we see her asses
>   Thick as grapes upon a bunch,
> Critics, whilst you smile on madness,
> And more stupid, solemn sadness;
>   Sure you will not frown on Punch.   (Air 1)

The critics should 'not frown on Punch' at Drury Lane because the live theatre has reached the point where it is not really more alive than the puppet theatre. The characters respresenting tragedy, farce, opera, and pantomime who enter shortly afterwards turn out to be no less wooden than Punch.

After a farcical episode featuring Punch and his wife, in which there are references to Orpheus in the underworld, the Puppet Show continues with Charon interviewing some new arrivals to the underworld who want to cross the Styx. Among these are a group of six, Don Tragedio, Sir Farcical Comic, Dr Orator, Signior Opera, Monsieur Pantomime, and Mrs Novel, introduced by Luckless as 'such a set of figures, as I defy all Europe, except our own playhouses, to equal'. Four of these obviously represent types of drama and this is their primary function, although Fielding intended to caricature individuals closely associated with each type of drama as well. A contemporary audience would have identified Sir Farcical Comic with Colley Cibber, and Monsieur Pantomine with John Rich, but scholars have disagreed about the models for Don Tragedio and Signior Opera. F. W. Bateson suggests James Thomson and Handel respectively,[11] but Charles B. Woods makes a good case for equating Lewis Theobald, the dramatist, Shakespearean scholar, and 'hero' of the first version of *The Dunciad*, with Don Tragedio, and Francesco Senesino, the most renowned operatic castrato at the time, with Signior Opera.[12] Woods also points out that the 'Don's Spanish title comes in part from the high-flown honor themes associated with Spain, but it is worthy of note that three new tragedies of the 1729–30 season had Spanish characters and a Spanish setting'.[13] The other two members of this group, Dr Orator and Mrs Novel, have no connection with the theatre, but in Fielding's eyes are just as guilty as the other four of purveying fashionable forms of nonsense. Dr Orator is a satirical portrait of John Henley, the Nonconformist minister who attracted large congregations by his flamboyant preaching from an ornate pulpit, described as a 'gilt Tub' in *The Dunciad* (Witmore's advice to Luckless in I, v, 'set up an oratory and preach nonsense, and you may meet with encouragement enough', refers to Henley's success). Mrs Novel is a caricature of Eliza Haywood, whose sensational prose romances were very popular. The satire on the theatrical figures begins when they explain in their characteristic ways how they died. Don Tragedio employs a couplet to describe his end:

> A tragedy occasioned me to die;
> That perishing the first day, so did I.

Sir Farcical Comic, even in talking about his death, resorts to 'stap my vitals', one of those vacuous exclamations popular with writers of comedy and farce in the eighteenth century, and a phrase made especially famous by Colley Cibber in his foppish stage roles. Signior Opera sings a little song, and Monsieur Pantomine, who is dumb, shows by mime that his neck is broken.

Before these characters reappear at the Court of Nonsense, four short episodes occur, two of which satirize the same aspect of current theatrical production. The completely gratuitous and thoroughly inane song and dance of Somebody and Nobody ridicules those interludes of assorted entertainment introduced into many productions without regard to their appropriateness. In the context of Luckless' Puppet Show, such arbitrary interpolations are made to seem ludicrous. One of the other two short episodes, the discussion between the Poet and the bookseller Curry, described by Luckless as 'the prime minister of Nonsense', establishes that the Goddess has fallen in love with Signior Opera at first sight and that their marriage is to be celebrated that night; but it also continues the satire on booksellers and allows further explicit denunciations of the contemporary theatre in the style of Witmore. Curry admits that he served the Goddess of Nonsense faithfully for thirty years, while the Poet, who has just died, informs Curry that the literary world is very much the same as when the bookseller left it:

> POET... authors starve, and booksellers grow fat. Grub Street harbours as many pirates as ever Algiers did. They have more theatres than are at Paris, and just as much wit as there is at Amsterdam; they have ransacked all Italy for singers, and all France for dancers.
> BOOKSELLER And all hell for conjurors.
> POET My lord mayor has shortened the time of Bartholomew Fair in Smithfield, and so they are resolved to keep it all the year round at the other end of the town.

The remark about the crude fairground entertainments of Smithfield being transported to London's West End theatres, with a consequent degradation of moral and aesthetic values, is an obvious echo of *The Dunciad*, which is about the cancerous encroachment of East End barbarism on West End culture and which opens:

> Books and the Man I sing, the first who brings
> The Smithfield Muses to the Ear of Kings.   (1728 version)

The other episode, involving Luckless and Punch, attacks lawyers, judges, and Members of Parliament, including Sir Robert Walpole (the 'great man'), and illustrates the political satire that Fielding introduced when revising the play because of his growing opposition to Walpole's administration (this episode replaces the nondescript game of quadrille in the 1730 version).[14]

The closest approximation to orthodox verbal burlesque in the play occurs at the opening of the long scene at the Court of Nonsense, but even here much of the satire consists of condemnation by the Master of the Show, Luckless. Nevertheless, there is ample scope for visual burlesque, as the dances already mentioned suggest, and in eighteenth-century performances there must have been a great deal of this. The ridicule of pantomime, for example, depends largely on the ability of the actor playing Monsieur Pantomime to guy the antics of Harlequin; Luckless' comment to the Goddess that Monsieur Pantomime 'is the only one of your votaries that sets people asleep without talking' merely reinforces the visual burlesque. Unlike Duffett, Fielding provides so few stage directions that it is impossible to gauge the extent of the visual burlesque, but with suitable posture, movement, and voice delivery, not to mention costume, the actors representing tragedy, farce, and opera would also have generated considerable burlesque humour. On the page, the Goddess of Nonsense's welcome to her disciples, 'Let all my votaries prepare / To celebrate this joyful day', seems to be without a trace of burlesque. Yet Luckless' subsequent remark, 'observe what a lover of recitative Nonsense is', establishes that these lines should be delivered in operatic style; depending on the skill of the actress, they could be excellent mimicry of a prima donna.

The verbal burlesque of tragedy is quite unlike that in *The Rehearsal* or *The What D'Ye Call It*. Buckingham and Gay satirically imitate particular plays or stock situations and speeches of contemporary drama, whereas Fielding provides only a stylistic burlesque. Don Tragedio's speech, although written in the ranting rhetoric of heroic tragedy, is a boastful self-introduction in which he unwittingly condemns himself and the kind of drama he stands for. His use of couplets may be thought to reflect particularly on the rhymed heroic play, but he embodies the heroic strain throughout Restoration and Augustan drama, both rhymed and unrhymed, and may be particularly representative of tragedy in the 1720s, to judge from the way in which he refers to Dryden, Lee, and Rowe:

> Yes, Tragedio is indeed my name,
> Long since recorded in the rolls of fame,
> At Lincoln's Inn, and eke at Drury Lane.
> Let everlasting thunder sound my praise,
> And forked lightning in my scutcheon blaze;

> To Shakespeare, Johnson, Dryden, Lee, or Rowe,
> I not a line, no, not a thought, do owe.
> Me, for my novelty, let all adore,
> For, as I wrote, none ever wrote before.

His series of verbal repetitions in reply to the Goddess' over-enthusiastic greeting, 'Thou art doubly welcome, welcome', provides an amusing burlesque of the more self-indulgent and mannered dramatic poetry of the time:

> That welcome, yes, that welcome is my due,
> Two tragedies I wrote, and wrote for you;
> And had not hisses, hisses me dismayed,
> By this, I'd writ two-score, two-score, by jayed!

Don Tragedio is not the only figure representing a dramatic form to damn himself through his own mouth while ostensibly describing his characteristics with pride. Sir Farcical Comic's speech to the Goddess, while not verbal burlesque, highlights a characteristic of farce, the crudely comic use of linguistic oddity and error, and also refers to Colley Cibber's notorious inability to write correct English and his unintentional use of malapropisms:

> I have made new words, and spoiled old ones too, if you talk of that; I have made foreigners break English, and Englishmen break Latin. I have as great a confusion of languages in my play as was at the building of Babel.

Later Sir Farcical Comic himself admits that his humour is based entirely on 'puns, and quibbles, and conundrums'.

The last theatrical figure to present himself to the Goddess is Signior Opera. Oddly enough, there is nothing very obviously satirical about Fielding's treatment of Signior Opera, even though he is awarded the laureateship, which suggests that Fielding regarded opera as the height of dramatic nonsense (Luckless' remark to the Theatre Manager quoted earlier also suggests this). Nevertheless, ironical humour would have been created in performance when Signior Opera burst into an English song, especially as he would have sung falsetto to imitate the castrati. Yet the song itself (Air VIII), ostensibly in celebration of wealth and worldliness, could almost be from *The Beggar's Opera*. Like one of Macheath's songs, '*The Modes of the Court so common are grown*' (Air XLIV), it is set to the tune of 'Lillibolera', and the verbal similarity to Gay's play is obvious in a line like 'When you cry he is rich, you cry a great man', which alludes to Walpole. What is uncertain is whether this is a straightforward imitation of Gay or whether Fielding intended an extremely subtle satirical touch by making Signior Opera's song resemble one of the best-known songs in a work that itself burlesques Italian opera.

Although Nonsense is overwhelmed by Signior Opera's song and says that she longs to marry him, his victory is short-lived. Mrs Novel reveals that she is his wife, and the Goddess, deeply disappointed at not being able to wed Signior Opera, rejects him. The subsequent reconciliation scene between Mrs Novel and Signior Opera burlesques the love scenes of sentimental drama and Italian opera in a way that recalls both *The What D'Ye Call It* and *The Beggar's Opera*. In the first place, Mrs Novel's promise of life-long devotion even in the face of great hardships has affinities with Kitty's corresponding speech to Filbert, but is more patently farcical:

> Were we cast on Ireland's soil,
>   There confined in bogs to dwell,
> For thee potatoes I would boil,
>   No Irish spouse should feast so well.   (Air XII)

Furthermore, this duet is modelled on and sung to the tune of 'Over the Hills and far away', which Gay uses for one of Macheath and Polly's love duets (Air XVI) in *The Beggar's Opera*. Since Fielding's duet is virtually a parody of Gay's, which itself burlesques operatic duets, it achieves a double-strength burlesque by reinforcing Gay's while at the same time generating its own.

With Signior Opera temporarily discredited, the struggle for the laureateship is renewed with Dr Orator dominating proceedings for some time, although there are brief interruptions such as Don Tragedio's eruption of hurt pride at being refused the chaplet:

> Is it for this, for this, ye gods, that I
> Have in one scene made some folks laugh, some cry?
> For this does my low blust'ring language creep?
> At once to wake you, and to make you sleep?

Except for the fact that Dr Orator resorts mainly to song to impress the Goddess, who after her infatuation with Signior Opera cannot be moved 'unless by music', the ridicule of John Henley contains only one reference to drama. Charon's announcement that 'an odd sort of a man . . . Hurloborumbo – rumbo – Hurloborumbolo' (clearly Johnson's *Hurlothrumbo*) is on his way to the Court of Nonsense spurs Dr Orator into one final fit of nonsense because he realizes that he will have no hope of winning the Goddess once Hurlothrumbo arrives. His efforts fail, and Nonsense, now declared the Goddess of Wit, relents and gives the chaplet to Signior Opera after all, even though marriage is impossible. The furious Don Tragedio threatens to kill Signior Opera, whom he calls 'that singing vermin', but the latter's banal swan-song calms Don Tragedio ('Methinks I feel my flesh congealed to bone, / And know not if I'm flesh and blood, or stone') while burlesquing the highly embellished style of operatic arias. On this occasion there is no doubt about how the song should be sung since Fielding indicates the melismata:

> More fierce than men on the high roads,
>   On the high – – – roads,
>   On the high – – – roads,
>   . . .
>   And can – – –
>   – – – – – – n,
>   He gentler prove than man?   (Air XVIII)

Before the extraordinary dénouement of the play, Fielding introduces yet another satirical sketch of a celebrated contemporary figure, 'Count' Heidegger (this episode is present only in the 1734 version). Well known for his work on behalf of Italian opera in London, Heidegger was by this time even more closely associated with another 'pleasure of the town', the masquerades at the Opera House on the evenings when Italian opera was not being performed. Fielding had previously attacked Heidegger and his very fashionable masquerades in a Swiftian poem called *The Masquerade* (1728), published under the pseudonym of 'Lemuel Gulliver, Poet Laureat to the King of Lilliput', a pseudonym resembling 'Scriblerus Secundus' in that it links Fielding with the aims of the Scriblerus Club. Heidegger was noted for his ugliness and in the Puppet Show appears as Count Ugly. He arrives at the Court of Nonsense too late to compete for the chaplet, but Nonsense rewards him for struggling on behalf of her 'noble cause' and for teaching her 'precepts' while alive by making him manager of her actors. His credentials are impeccable because on his own admission his masquerades are an unadulterated mixture of dullness and nonsense.

The dénouement of *The Author's Farce* is not unlike that of *The Beggar's Opera* in that a completely unexpected interruption leads to a surprising reversal of fortune, yet its burlesque significance has usually been ignored by scholars, notable exceptions being Valerie C. Rudolph, whose essay on the levels of illusion and reality in the play and on its 'ordered disorder' is invaluable,[15] and Susan K. Ahern, who is particularly interested in the social and moral satire released by the relationship between frame play and inner play.[16] What may look like pure farce is burlesque of sentimental dénouements such as that of Steele's *The Conscious Lovers* (1722), quite probably Fielding's specific target. When the Puppet Show is disrupted by the entry of Sir John Bindover and a Constable to arrest Luckless 'for abusing Nonsense ... when the whole town supports it' and for libelling the diversions of 'people of quality', the prospect for Luckless is even bleaker than it was at the beginning of the play. (Sir John Bindover replaces the Presbyterian parson Murdertext of the 1730 version, but otherwise the two versions are very similar). But immediately afterwards, Luckless' problems fly out of the window when Witmore, Moneywood, Harriot, and a Bantamite tutor bring him the news that he is the long-lost son of the King of Bantam, an exotic place in the East Indies fabled for its wealth. This astonishing peripeteia resembles Macheath's reprieve at the end of *The Beggar's Opera*, because both Fielding and Gay are undermining, for satirical purposes, a dramatic convention employed to ensure manifestly false yet wished-for resolutions. Sentimental comedies often end with highly improbable revelations that produce a happy ending out of apparent disaster. Close friends or relations given up for lost are serendipitously discovered in emotional 'recognition scenes', often with protestations of undying love and everlasting loyalty.

Fielding's dénouement approximates to this pattern, but the tone is comic rather than heart-rending, and the result is burlesque. When Luckless was a boy, his Bantamite tutor had taken him on a tour of the world but had lost him in London. Years later, an English merchant had arrived at the court of Bantam and presented the King with a jewel that had belonged to Luckless as a child but which he had been forced to pawn. Coincidences like this are common enough in sentimental comedy, but the hero would have either lost the jewel in sad circumstances or had it stolen from him; he would not have parted with something he probably regarded as more precious than his life in a pawnshop. It is partly by injecting such realistic touches into a conventional climax that Fielding shows how unconvincing and laughable are the contrivances intended to make audiences' tears flow at the end of sentimental plays. Another excellent instance of this satirical method occurs during the Bantamite tutor's explanation of how he set about finding Luckless once it was known that he was still alive; the Bantamite's down-to-earth practicality is deliberately at odds with the sentimental situation:

> I did intend to have advertised you in the Evening Post, with a reward; but being directed by the merchant to the pawnbroker, I was accidentally there inquiring after you when your boy brought your nab. (Oh, sad remembrance, that the son of a king should pawn a hat!)

The parenthesis here is itself a superb example of Fielding's mock sentimentality.

Fielding's other way of satirizing sentimental dénouements is by sufficiently exaggerating the stock-in-trade devices of their writers to make them appear absurd. Changes of fortune and startling revelations follow each other so rapidly that a potentially sentimental conclusion is converted into a farcical scene, although what appears to be farce is situational burlesque, as in Gay's *Three Hours after Marriage.* No sooner does Luckless learn that he is the son of the King of Bantam than a messenger arrives to announce the death of the old King; Luckless consequently possesses the throne immediately he finds he is heir to it. Mrs Moneywood quickly changes her mind about Luckless and does not object to his marrying Harriot now that her daughter will be queen. It is at this point, just before the end of the play, that Fielding introduces two hilarious recognition scenes in very quick succession. Earlier, when Luckless and his former tutor are reunited, there is an amusing burlesque of sentimental recognition scenes, but it is by the accumulation of such incidents that Fielding exposes the device to ridicule. In order to 'let all the audience know / I am no common fellow', Punch unexpectedly explains that Mrs Moneywood is really the Queen of Old Brentford (an allusion to *The Rehearsal* with its two Kings of Brentford), that Harriot is therefore Henrietta, Princess of Old Brentford, and that he himself is Mrs Moneywood's son. Even though Punch has not seen his mother or his sister since the latter was an infant, he recognizes Moneywood by her 'phiz'. The exclamations of astonishment at these revelations, and the subsequent ones when Punch's wife Joan realizes to whom she is related, provide the actors with a splendid opportunity for burlesquing the performances in sentimental plays:

> MRS MONEYWOOD Oh, my son!
> HARRIOT Oh, my brother!
> PUNCH Oh, my sister!
> MRS MONEYWOOD I am sorry in this pickle to remember who I am. But alas! too true is all you've said. Though I have been reduced to let lodgings, I was the queen of Brentford; and this, though a player, is a king's son.
> JOAN Then I am a king's daughter, for this gentleman is my husband.
> MRS MONEYWOOD My daughter!
> HARRIOT and LUCKLESS My sister!
> PUNCH My wife!

This final cry from Punch provides the *coup de grâce*; his recognition of his wife as though he has not seen her for years is particularly fatuous since they have been together in the Puppet Show. Farcical as Fielding's dénouement seems, it is not all that much an exaggeration of the recognition scene in *The Conscious Lovers* when Mr Sealand is reunited with both his daughter and his sister:

> ISABELLA If yet there wants an Explanation of your Wonder, examine well this Face, (yours, Sir, I well remember) gaze on, and read, in me, your Sister *Isabella*!
> MR SEALAND My Sister!

ISABELLA But here's a Claim more tender yet – your *Indiana*, Sir, your long lost Daughter.
MR SEALAND O my Child! my Child!
INDIANA All-Gracious Heaven! is it Possible! do I embrace my Father!
MR SEALAND And do I hold thee – These Passions are too strong for Utterance – Rise, rise, my Child, and give my Tears their Way – O my Sister! (v, iii)

What makes the burlesque dénouement of *The Author's Farce* particularly noteworthy is the way in which the distinctions sustained during the rest of the work between the comic, realistic frame play and the inner play, Luckless' Puppet Show, finally dissolve completely. The arrival of the fairy-tale Bantamite tutor establishes a new level of illusion and signals a deliberate breakdown of dramatic coherence as characters cross the established boundaries. Punch, a character in the Puppet Show, turns out to be Mrs Moneywood's son, and Mrs Moneywood herself is not what she seemed in the frame play because she is apparently the Queen of a King from another burlesque play. If the Puppet Show invades the frame play, the frame play is itself invaded by the fairy-tale world of Bantam, so that fantasy prevails at the end. In Valerie C. Rudolph's words, 'Luckless, as Master of the Puppet Show, loses control of his characters, some of whom begin to act independently', yet Fielding certainly does not, and we 'see the Master of *The Author's Farce* manipulating his characters and retaining control over them'.[17] Fielding's wildly incredible but carefully calculated contrivance clarifies what is really going on in sentimental plays beneath the pretence of verisimilitude: recognition scenes and the like involve the surreptitious invasion of fantasy into would-be realism.

Although Fielding develops his burlesque of sentimental dénouements at some length in *The Author's Farce*, the ending of his comedy, *Rape upon Rape; or, The Justice Caught in his own Trap*, also produced for the first time in 1730, is an almost perfect example of a sentimental dénouement. Throughout *Rape upon Rape*, retitled *The Coffee-House Politician* because of protests about the original title, Ramble believes that his wife, Isabella, and her fortune have been lost at sea, but both are restored to him in the final scene. Ramble also turns out to be Politic's long-lost son and Hilaret's long-lost brother, and since Hilaret's fiancé, Constant, is Ramble's companion, the play ends with practically all the good characters united in one family. Like a number of writers, Fielding was quite capable of making fun of a device yet of using the same device himself in certain contexts. This ambivalence over sentimental dénouements nevertheless supports Brian McCrea's thesis about what he calls Fielding's 'literary uncertainty' during his years as a dramatist,

Plate 1: Pallas pouring wine from her lance (frontispiece to the
play in the 1714 edition of Buckingham's *Works*).

Plate 2: Stage design for the final scene of Settle's *The Empress of Morocco* (one of the plates in the 1673 edition).

Plate 3: Satirical view of a scene from Handel's *Flavio*, with Senesino (left), Francesca Cuzzoni, and Berenstadt (Hogarth? 1723).

Plate 4a: Macheath in Newgate Prison with Lucy (left), Polly and their fathers (detail from Hogarth's 1728 depiction of III, xi) and (b) key identifying those represented in the print. Performers: 1. Macheath – Mr Walker. 2. Lockitt – Mr Hall. 3. Peachum – Mr Hippisley. 4. Lucy – Mrs Egleton. 5. Polly – Miss

Fenton, afterwards Duchess of Bolton. Audience: 6. Duke of Bolton. 7. Major Paunceford. 8. Sir Robert Fagg. 9. Mr Rich, the Manager. 10. Mr Cock, the Auctioneer. 11. Mr Gay. 12. Lady Jane Cook. 13. Anthony Henley Esq. 14. Lord Gage. 15. Sir Conyers D'Arcy. 16. Sir Thomas Robinson.

Plate 5: 'The Beggar's Opera Burlesqued', an allegorical satire incorporating John Rich's theatre at Lincoln's Inn Fields (left), a scene from Italian opera (right), and the principals of Gay's ballad opera on centre stage: Macheath (ass), Polly (pig), Lucy (cat), Peachum (dog), Mrs Peachum (owl), Lockitt (bull) (Hogarth? 1728).

Plate 6: New Haymarket Theatre (Little Theatre in the Haymarket), Fielding's own theatre in 1736-37.

Plate 7: Samuel Johnson of Cheshire as Lord Wildfire with Lady Flame in his *The Blazing Comet* (1732).

Plate 8: Hogarth's 'Masquerade Ticket', his satire on Heidegger's entertainments (1727).

Plate 9: John Rich as a dog in *Perseus and Andromeda* (detail from the frontispiece in the 1731 edition of James Miller's *Harlequin-Horace; or, The Art of Modern Poetry*).

pulled in the opposite directions of Scriblerus and Cibber, of satire and sentiment.[18]

As a fitting conclusion to *The Author's Farce*, Fielding provides a mock epilogue in which four poets attempt to write a suitable epilogue but quarrel over what should be said. Through their disagreements, Fielding makes fun of the conventional epilogue, and when the poets fail to produce anything, Luckless interrupts them with his decision to 'have the Epilogue spoken by a Cat', or at least to have a cat 'act the Epilogue in dumb-show':

> Why, pray, is that so strange in comedy?
> And have you not seen Perseus and Andromeda?
> Where you may find strange incidents intended,
> And regular intrigues begun and ended,
> Though not a word doth from an actor fall;
> As 'tis polite to speak in murmurs small,
> Sure, 'tis politer not to speak at all.

Even in the Epilogue Fielding keeps up his assault on the contemporary theatre. Theobald's popular pantomime *Perseus and Andromeda* opened less than three months before *The Author's Farce* and featured John Rich miming a dog, to which Fielding's speaking cat is a burlesque response. *The Author's Farce* is certainly one of the most unusual and original plays in the burlesque tradition, and also one of the most ambitious. In it Fielding ridicules four dramatic genres, well-known individuals closely associated with each of these, and theatre managers, not to mention booksellers, Grub Street hacks, and other people not associated with the theatre, including Walpole. Some of Fielding's subsequent dramatic burlesques and satires are more brilliantly witty and less diffuse, but none, except for *Pasquin*, has the range of *The Author's Farce*; and *Pasquin* is a very different kind of play.

Two plays having more than a little in common with *The Author's Farce* appeared in London at the same time as Fielding's play, and a third, the anonymous *Jack the Gyant-Killer*, was staged later in the year. Gabriel Odingsells' *Bays's Opera* opened at Drury Lane on the very day that *The Author's Farce* received its first peformance, and James Ralph's *The Fashionable Lady; or, Harlequin's Opera* began its run at Goodman's Fields a couple of days later on 2 April 1730. *Jack the Gyant-Killer*, an afterpiece in one act, received two performances at the New Haymarket in July 1730, once with *Rape upon Rape* as the mainpiece. As the title suggests, Odingsells' play derives to some extent from *The Rehearsal* in that it uses a full-scale rehearsal framework, unlike *The Author's Farce*. In *Bays's Opera*, Bays presents his work to two commentators, Arabella and Belinda, just as Bayes presents his heroic play to Johnson and Smith in *The Rehearsal*.

Nevertheless, *Bays's Opera* is hardly a work of orthodox dramatic burlesque, and in some ways is closer to *The Author's Farce* than to Buckingham's play. Whereas Bayes' play in *The Rehearsal* is an imitative satire of contemporary drama, the play within a play in *Bays's Opera* is not. Although it ridicules current dramatic forms, especially pantomime, Bays' play is really a complex allegory about the condition of drama. It does contain two mock-pantomimic episodes burlesquing the elaborate processions and dances of pantomime, but these form only a small part of the inner play. Three of the principal figures in the allegory are Tragedo, Cantato, and Pantomime, representing tragedy, Italian opera, and pantomime respectively. The resemblance to *The Author's Farce*, in which dramatic genres are also personified, is obvious, but plagiarism by either Fielding or Odingsells can be ruled out. The basic action of Bays' play concerns the struggle for superiority between Pantomime and Cantato, who has previously displaced Tragedo, and the final victory of Pantomime, who seizes control of the Commonwealth of Wit. In devising the inner play, Odingsells seems to have been influenced by *The Dunciad*, though not to the extent that Fielding was in the Puppet Show of *The Author's Farce*.

The weakness of Bays' play as satire is that the basic action is unnecessarily complicated by numerous sub-plots and a host of minor characters; Odingsells also overloads his allegory in an attempt to compress as much material into the work as possible. Indeed, *Bays's Opera* as a whole is not nearly as lucid as it might be, especially as Odingsells' Bays is sometimes a figure of fun, like Buckingham's Bayes, and sometimes a spokesman for the author. Nevertheless, Odingsells was deeply concerned about the state of aesthetic and moral values at the time, and in *Bays's Opera* he was making a very serious attack on debased artistic standards. He argues in his Preface:

> The only view of this Performance was to expose the Folly and Absurdities of a prevailing (and, as I thought, vitiated) Taste; which seem'd to prefer Farce and Buffoonery, as well as the unprofitable, immoral and unnatural Representations of Poetical Fiction, to the more polite and instructive Entertainments of Dramatick Poetry and Musick.

The aims of Fielding and Odingsells were very similar, but compared with *The Author's Farce*, *Bays's Opera* is deficient in vitality, humour, and satirical bite.

Ralph's *The Fashionable Lady* resembles *Bays's Opera* in that it employs a rehearsal structure, ridicules contemporary theatrical entertainments, and contains many songs, but otherwise it differs markedly from Odingsells' play. The play within a play, a ballad opera by Drama, is a comedy about Mrs Foible, the fashionable lady of the title, and her various suitors, including Harlequin. It is not an imitative satire of current drama, although like *Bays's Opera* it contains some burlesque of pantomime. The most interesting part of Ralph's play is undoubtedly the commentary by Ballad, Drama, Modely, and Meanwell surrounding the inner play. Much of this commentary is concerned with prevailing theatrical fashions and the state of drama in England, topics previously discussed by Ralph in *The Touch-Stone; or, Historical, Critical, Political, Moral, Philosophical and Theological Essays upon the Reigning Diversions of the Town* (1728), published under the bawdy pseudonym of 'A. Primcock'. (Ralph's ironic suggestion in one of these essays that the story of Tom Thumb should be turned into an opera – 'Cu---ni *in Breeches would make a delightful* Tom Thumb'[19] – may have had some effect on the genesis of Fielding's *Tom Thumb*, especially as the two men were very friendly at the time.) In the opening scene, for example, Ballad first defends ballad opera in general and *The Beggar's Opera* in particular from an attack by the fan of Italian opera, Modely, and then criticizes Italian opera in no uncertain terms: 'I sent for you to hear my Friend *Drama*'s Play; not to quarrel about squeaking, Recitative, paltry Eunuchs, and a Trill of insignificant outlandish Vowels' (I, i). Drama himself is aware that the theatre is not in a healthy state, but he nevertheless complies with the taste of the town by providing pantomimic incidents and a large number of songs in his play.

To some extent Ralph embodies in Drama, as Fielding does in Luckless, the predicament of the contemporary playwright who is virtually forced by circumstance to conform to current dramatic modishness while conscious of its limitations and absurdities. Drama is not, therefore, strictly comparable to Buckingham's Bayes. Meanwell, however, is similar to Johnson and Smith in *The Rehearsal*; he is the voice of Reason and Good Sense, and the spokesman of Ralph's own views. Because he is not impressed by theatrical novelty and gimmickry, Meanwell is highly critical of most recent dramatic developments. Like Johnson and Smith in *The Rehearsal*, he asks penetrating questions during Drama's play and is always prepared to expose what he regards as nonsense:

> MEANWELL But pray, Mr. *Drama*, what is the Reason that this Scene is nothing but Sing-Song? I think 'tis the greatest Impropriety imaginable, in a Court of Justice.
> DRAMA O, Sir! for that very Reason I contriv'd it so.
> MODELY Stupid enough o'Conscience!
> DRAMA Beside, Mr. *Meanwell*, you must consider this is only an Imitation of our modern Operas, both *Italian* and *English*; the more absurd, the more fashionable; their Authority will justify the most ridiculous things in Nature.
> MEANWELL Ay, that's true, the *Italian* justifies the most egregious Nonsense.   (III, iii)

The Fashionable Lady is a more entertaining and a better stage play than *Bays's Opera*, but is nevertheless a rather undistinguished piece of dramatic writing. Like Odingsells' play, it is interesting because it coincided with *The Author's Farce* and because it set out to do something similar in a similar way.

The description of *Jack the Gyant-Killer* on the title page as a 'Comi-Tragical Farce' suggests that this, like *Tom Thumb*, is a dramatic burlesque based on a children's story, but it resembles Fielding's play only in that it makes use of a nursery tale for satirical purposes. *Jack the Gyant-Killer* is not a burlesque of contemporary drama but a satire in dramatic form, having affinities with *The Author's Farce* in that it also derives to some extent from *The Dunciad*. The allegorical action concerns the struggle between Reason and Folly and is set in the Palace of Folly. With the aid of her giants, Princess Folly has deposed the Monarch of Reason and usurped his throne, but Reason still retains a few supporters, notably Jack, who launch a counter-attack against the new sovereign in an attempt to liberate Britain from the tyranny of Folly. At first, Jack is driven off by the giants, and his followers temporarily succumb to 'Folly and Pleasure', but Jack finally kills the giants and emerges victorious. Folly is transformed into a monster, and Reason can return to his throne. Even more interesting than the play itself is the extended Introduction in the published version, with its caustic satire of literary hacks and Grub Street writers for serving Folly rather than Reason. There is, however, little reference to the theatre in the Introduction, although near the end Plotless describes the new conception of tragic drama to Scenewell:

> Since *Folly* has ruled the Hearts of our Audiences, they are grown altogether insensible of the tender Passions; and as little Compassion is felt for the Distress of an Hero on the Stage, as for the Calamities of a poor Relation at Home. – No, no, no, nothing is now to be aim'd at in Tragedy but the Sublime.

It is this kind of tragic 'sublimity' that drew Fielding's burlesque fire in *Tom Thumb*.

NOTES
1. 'The Dunciad, Book IV', *Texas Studies in English* 24 (1944) 174-90. See also J'nan Sellery, 'Language and Moral Intelligence in the Enlightenment: Fielding's Plays and Pope's *Dunciad*', *Enlightenment Essays* 1 (1970) 17-26 (Part 1) and 108-19 (Part 2).
2. In his monumental study, *Grub Street* (London, 1972), Pat Rogers includes a short sub-section about Fielding's treatment of the phenomenon of Grub Street (327-36), nearly half of which is concerned with *The Author's Farce* and the plight of Luckless.

3. 'The Improved Author's Farce: An Analysis of the 1734 Revisions', *Costerus 6* (1972) 35-43.
4. *Ibid.*, 36.
5. This quotation is from *The Author's Farce* (1730 version), ed. Charles B. Woods (London, 1967). Except where otherwise noted, quotations from Fielding's plays, including the 1734 version of *The Author's Farce*, are taken from *The Complete Works of Henry Fielding*, ed. William Ernest Henley (London, 1903), although I have silently emended any substantive errors I have discovered.
6. *The Politics of Drama in Augustan England* (Oxford, 1963) 104. For a detailed discussion of Fielding's treatment of Colley Cibber in *The Author's Farce*, especially the 1730 version, see Charles B. Woods, 'Cibber in Fielding's *Author's Farce*: Three Notes', *Philological Quarterly 44* (1965) 145-51; also Houghton W. Taylor, 'Fielding upon Cibber', *Modern Philology 29* (1931-32) 73-90.
7. See Loftis, *The Politics of Drama in Augustan England*, 72-9.
8. See George Speaight, *The History of the English Puppet Theatre* (London, 1955) 161-3.
9. *Ibid.*, 173. In 'Fielding's Puppet Image', *Philological Quarterly 53* (1974) 71-83, Anthony J. Hassall discusses Fielding's metaphorical use of the puppet theatre in *The Author's Farce* and in his novels.
10. *Plays about the Theatre in England*, 150.
11. *English Comic Drama 1700-1750*, 124-5.
12. *The Author's Farce*, ed. Woods, 45(n) and 106-7; also 'Theobald and Fielding's Don Tragedio', *English Language Notes 2* (1964-65) 266-71.
13. *The Author's Farce*, ed. Woods, 45(n).
14. In spite of Sheridan Baker's argument, in 'Political Allusion in Fielding's *Author's Farce, Mock Doctor,* and *Tumble-Down Dick*', *Publications of the Modern Language Association of America 77* (1962) 221-6, that both versions of *The Author's Farce* contain political allusions, it is difficult to believe that Fielding intended any political satire in the original version; see *The Author's Farce*, ed. Woods, xv(n), and Bertrand A. Goldgar, *Walpole and the Wits*, 102-4.
15. 'People and Puppets: Fielding's Burlesque of the "Recognition Scene" in *The Author's Farce*', *Papers on Language and Literature 11* (1975) 31-8.
16. 'The Sense of Nonsense in Fielding's *Author's Farce*', *Theatre Survey 23* (1982) 45-54.
17. 'People and Puppets', 38.
18. *Henry Fielding and the Politics of Mid-Eighteenth-Century England*, 50-77.
19. *The Touch-Stone* (London, 1728) 26.

Tom Thumb and The Tragedy of Tragedies

Tom Thumb, ironically labelled 'A Tragedy', was staged for the first time on 24 April 1730 as a two-act afterpiece to *The Author's Farce*. It was so successful that Fielding immediately revised and expanded it, adding a Prologue, an Epilogue, and a witty Preface that cleverly guys Colley Cibber's badly written Preface to his completed version of Vanbrugh's unfinished comedy, *The Provok'd Husband* (1728); Pope had already ridiculed Cibber's Preface in *Peri Bathous*. This second version of *Tom Thumb* was issued under the authorship of Scriblerus Secundus. During the next season, *The Battle of the Poets; or, The Contention for the Laurel*, a brief satirical play probably by Thomas Cooke, was incorporated into some productions of *Tom Thumb*. This first appeared on 30 November 1730 and was published in December under the authorship of Scriblerus Tertius. *The Battle of the Poets* is essentially an attack on the new Poet Laureate, Colley Cibber (Fopling Fribble in the play), who was appointed to this position towards the end of 1730 more on political than literary grounds; but it also contains caricatures of his two main rivals for the post, Lewis Theobald (Comment Profund) and Stephen Duck (Flail), and of John Dennis (Sulky Bathos) and James Ralph (Noctifer). Cooke most probably derived the competition for 'the Laurel' in his play, with the eventual victory of the worst contender for the title, from the Puppet Show in *The Author's Farce*.

Partly because of Cooke's tampering with his play and partly because he was still not completely satisfied with the second version of *Tom Thumb*, Fielding revised it once more, making substantial alterations and additions to the text and providing a completely new framework in place of the Preface, Prologue, and Epilogue of the second edition. According to L. J. Morrissey, one of Fielding's reasons for his revisions was his desire to expand and sharpen considerably the very tentative political satire of the earlier versions,[1] but Bertrand A. Goldgar has questioned whether the play, in any of its versions, contains allusions to contemporary politics.[2] Goldgar's historical research suggests that much of the alleged political satire is a product of twentieth-century scholarship. Fielding's main purpose in reworking *Tom Thumb* as *The Tragedy of*

Tragedies, at least in the published version, was undoubtedly to widen the range of his satire in a Scriblerian manner to include contemporary scholarship and pedantry, illustrating the aberrations of the 'modern' mind. The final three-act version, *The Tragedy of Tragedies; or, The Life and Death of Tom Thumb the Great*, was first produced on 24 March 1731 together with his three-act farce, *The Letter Writers; or, A New Way to Keep a Wife at Home*. In rewriting the play, Fielding took the opportunity to remove the weakest parts of *Tom Thumb*, especially the episode involving the Physicians and dealing with the false report of the hero's death. He also removed the amusing and popular incident at the end of the play in which Lord Grizzle kills Tom Thumb's ghost, but he made amends for this surprising deletion by introducing a much more extended ghost scene. Since scholars and editors like James T. Hillhouse,[3] L. J. Morrissey,[4] and T. W. Craik[5] have examined Fielding's revisions in some detail, this study will concentrate on the final and best version of the play, *The Tragedy of Tragedies*.[6]

As this title indicates, Fielding devotes himself to ridiculing just one of his many targets in *The Author's Farce*, but 'tragedy' here means a considerable proportion of Restoration and Augustan tragedy including the rhymed heroic play. Commentators such as Hillhouse rightly argue that Fielding concentrates his burlesque on the more heroic variety of tragedy, descending from Restoration heroic drama and from Dryden's *All for Love*, rather than on pseudo-classical tragedy. But at the same time, it is often difficult to distinguish stylistically between these. Two of Fielding's targets, Edward Young's *Busiris* (1719) and *The Revenge* (1721), are clear-cut examples of the heroic type, but James Thomson's *Sophonisba* (1730), which comes in for quite a lot of mockery, contains both heroic and pseudo-classical features. Although pseudo-classical plays like Addison's *Cato* are in many ways more restrained than the flamboyant heroic kind, they are often written in an inflated and pompous style that is not all that different from heroic bombast.

In *The Tragedy of Tragedies* Fielding parodies at least forty-two plays, many of them from the late seventeenth century, which was the heyday of heroic tragedy, rather than from the eighteenth century. At first sight it may appear strange that Fielding should allude more frequently to Dryden, Otway, Lee, and Banks, than to Young, Thomson, Dennis, Rowe, and Addison, but the plays of the older dramatists still held the stage and were at least as popular as many of the more recent tragedies. Consequently *The Tragedy of Tragedies* cannot avoid going over some of the same ground as *The Rehearsal* and *The What D'Ye Call It*; and although Fielding employs neither Buckingham's rehearsal technique nor Gay's play-within-a-play device, he owes a great deal to both his predecessors. Because of Fielding's concentration on the heroic tradition, Samuel L. Macey sees the play as the direct heir to *The Rehearsal.*[7] Nevertheless, there are several ways in which Fielding makes his own very individual contribution to the tradition of dramatic burlesque. What Buckingham does is to retain the courtly world of heroic drama and satirize the genre largely by exaggeration, while Gay burlesques pathetic tragedy by transferring its typical actions and language to an agricultural milieu. Fielding's novel and imaginative method of adapting a children's story to the form of heroic tragedy is different from both of these. The setting is King Arthur's Court and the action is ostensibly heroic, but all the characters are travesties of heroic figures and the result is a zany burlesque. In the Preface to the second edition of *Tom Thumb,* Fielding ironically praises modern tragedy at the expense of ancient tragedy, arguing that, whereas the Greeks aimed at rousing pity and terror, modern dramatists alone succeed in producing 'mirth and laughter'; only in modern tragedy, indeed, are nonsense and absurdity such crucial ingredients. Having established this, Fielding, in the Prologue to the same version of the play, solemnly offers *Tom Thumb* as a tragedy that is intended to be utterly ludicrous throughout:

> *Since then, to laugh, to Tragedies you come,*
> *What Heroe is so proper as* Tom Thumb?
> Tom Thumb! *whose very Name must Mirth incite,*
> *And fill each merry* Briton *with Delight.*
> Britons, *awake! – Let* Greece *and* Rome *no more*
> *Their Heroes send to our Heroick Shore.*
> *Let home-bred Subjects grace the modern Muse,*
> *And* Grub-Street *from her Self, her Heroes chuse.*

Witty as the Preface and Prologue of the second edition are, they are not nearly as impressive as the mock-scholarly framework with which Fielding surrounds *The Tragedy of Tragedies.* Fielding now assumes the persona of a typical contemporary scholar and critic, H. Scriblerus Secundus, who presents the play as a tragic masterpiece of the Elizabethan period, possibly even by Shakespeare, and provides an extremely learned Preface and copious annotations. In this way Fielding is able to ridicule what he regarded as the pedantry of such men as the eminent classical scholar Richard Bentley and the distinguished critic John Dennis, while at the same time intensifying his burlesque by claiming that practically all Restoration and Augustan tragedies descend from *The Tragedy of Tragedies.* Fielding's pretence that the play is a very serious work may owe something to Gay's similar claim for *The What D'Ye Call It* in his Preface, but the recent appearance of *The Dunciad Variorum* (1729), with the Martinus Scriblerus Prolegomena and notes, must have given Fielding the idea of presenting his burlesque in a mock-critical edition. Another work likely to have influenced Fielding is *A Comment upon the History of Tom Thumb* (1711), probably written by William Wagstaffe, who parodies Addison's scholarly discussion of *Chevy Chase* in *The Spectator* (70 and 74) by providing a painstakingly thorough analysis of the nursery tale. There are also affinities with Swift's *The Battle of the Books* and *A Tale of a Tub*, especially as Fielding's 'Editor', with his ludicrous lack of judgement and common sense, is plainly a representative of the Moderns in the struggle between the Ancients and the Moderns that occupied Swift in these early satires. Fielding develops the role of H. Scriblerus Secundus to such an extent that only about half of the mock edition is devoted to the text of the play. As a result *The Tragedy of Tragedies* is as much a masterpiece of literary irony as of dramatic burlesque, which helps to explain why it is one of the very few dramatic burlesques still widely read. Although *The Tragedy of Tragedies* is not a rehearsal play, it does, in its printed as opposed to its stage version, bear some resemblance to the rehearsal format in that the mock play is embedded in a satirical framework intended to ridicule a representative literary figure, who is, however, a scholar and critic, not an author.

Fielding's mock preface follows the usual pattern of scholarly introductions to acknowledged classics. First of all, H. Scriblerus Secundus discusses the opinions of various authorities and arbiters of literary taste, quoting approvingly the favourable remarks supposedly made, in Latin of course, by Dr Bentley and the famous Professor Pieter Burmann of Leyden. He then turns his attention to the contrary view of John Dennis, who has had the audacity to suggest that the play is a burlesque:

> there have not been wanting some who have represented these Scenes in a ludicrous Light; and Mr. D— hath been heard to say, with some Concern, That he wondered a Tragical and Christian Nation would permit a Representation on its Theatre, so visibly designed to ridicule and extirpate every thing that is Great and Solemn among us.

He quickly repudiates such accusations by showing that Dennis based his opinion on the 1730 edition, which according to H. Scriblerus Secundus was pirated and therefore hopelessly corrupt. Even so, the Editor argues, the true tragic grandeur of *Tom Thumb* was obvious to most audiences in 1730, and he consequently attributes to malice allegations that the play was 'intended a Burlesque on the loftiest Parts of Tragedy, and designed to banish what we generally call Fine Things, from the Stage'. The Preface continues in this brilliantly ironic way with a discussion of the play's authorship and sources. Little of this has any direct relevance to the dramatic burlesque, but it does form a vital part of Fielding's attack on pedants and critics, especially Dennis, and also contains excellent gibes at the eighteenth-century reading public, the bookseller Edmund Curll, and the low standards of contemporary authors.

The preface culminates in a detailed examination of 'the Fable, the Moral, the Characters, the Sentiments, and the Diction' of the play in the manner of Dryden and subsequent critics. H. Scriblerus Secundus has no difficulty in proving that the nonsensical plot is a perfect example of neoclassical regularity and uniformity, and by reference to Aristotle that there is nothing incongruous in a tragic hero of minute proportions. He also establishes that the burlesque dénouement, a mass slaughter, carries the noble and instructive moral 'That Human Happiness is exceeding transient, and, That Death is the certain End of all Men'. The paragraphs dealing with 'the Sentiments and the Diction' are even more significant from the point of view of burlesque, because it is in these that Fielding most explicitly ridicules contemporary tragedy. The Editor explains that the best way to justify his claims for the play's greatness and influence is to quote as footnotes the many passages that Restoration and Augustan dramatists have derived, or even borrowed, from *The Tragedy of Tragedies*. Fielding thus reverses the actual literary process and presents his parodies as the sources of the 'sublime' speeches in contemporary tragedy. H. Scriblerus Secundus contends that the dramatic poetry of the play set the standard for later playwrights because it observes one simple criterion:

> That the greatest Perfection of the Language of a Tragedy is, that it is not to be understood; which granted (as I think it must be) it will necessarily follow, that the only ways to avoid this, is by being too high or too low for the Understanding, which will comprehend every thing within its Reach.

In an apparently erudite discussion of some lines form Horace, Cicero, and Ovid, the Editor tries to find classical authority for his view that 'Bombast is the proper Language for Joy, and Doggrel for Grief'; in addition, he interprets Longinus' idea of the sublime as 'a Set of big sounding Words, so contrived together, as to convey no Meaning', and sees this exemplified in *The Tragedy of Tragedies* and its 'successors'. Here, as in the subsequent remark that 'Tragedy hath of all Writings the greatest Share in the *Bathos*, which is the Profound of *Scriblerus*', Fielding is leaning heavily on Pope's *Peri Bathous*, published three years earlier. Pope, under the guise of Martinus Scriblerus, ironically converts 'bathos' into a term of praise, almost equivalent to 'sublime' or 'profound', and then commends many of his contemporaries for the high level of bathos in their work. *The Tragedy of Tragedies* is a deliberate study in literary and dramatic bathos, but for H. Scriblerus Secundus this is the measure of its achievement, the final guarantee that it conforms to the highest Restoration and Augustan conception of tragedy:

> I shall not presume to determine which of these two Stiles [bombast and doggerel] be properer for Tragedy. – It sufficeth, that our Author excelleth in both. He is very rarely within sight through the whole Play, either rising higher than the Eye of your Understanding can soar, or sinking lower than it careth to stoop.

The total inability of the Editor to distinguish between nonsensical bombast and true poetry and between burlesque and tragedy makes him a perfect example of a Swiftian Modern.

Fielding continues his satire on 'modern' scholars and critics, with Dennis again the chief victim, in H. Scriblerus Secundus' annotations to the text, although many of these merely point to the passages parodied (or, in the Editor's opinion, the passages owing their inspiration to the play). Dennis was one of the most intelligent critics in the first half of the eighteenth century, but he was notorious for an aggressive bluntness of manner that was often taken to be ill-mannered rudeness, and it is this aspect of Dennis' criticism that Fielding singles out for censure in the annotations. Fielding attributes to Dennis various remarks about the play that are either self-evidently silly or easily dismissed by H. Scriblerus Secundus as irrelevant and imperceptive. Of course, H. Scriblerus Secundus' judgement is hardly the most trustworthy, and the 'beauties' of the text that he takes great pains to point out are usually the most devastating parodies, but Fielding has to criticize Dennis, Bentley and the others through his burlesque Editor if he is to sustain his chosen method of irony.

Several authorities besides Dennis are 'quoted' in the notes. H. Scriblerus Secundus raises many difficult scholarly questions about the text and then presents the conflicting opinions of Burmann, Theobald, Salmon, and other experts about such issues as whether there were giants in the reign of King Arthur and whether there was only one Tom Thumb in history or three. One particularly amusing footnote lists the inane emendations supposedly made by three distinguished scholars to the line, 'The mighty *Thomas Thumb* victorious comes'(I, i):

> Dr. *B—y* reads the mighty Tall-mast Thumb. Mr. *D—s* the mighty Thumping Thumb. Mr. *T—d* reads Thundering. I think *Thomas* more agreeable to the great Simplicity so apparent in our Author.

Besides citing the passages in Restoration and Augustan plays 'influenced' by *The Tragedy of Tragedies* and discussing the ideas of scholars and critics, the Editor uses the notes to air his own views on the nature of tragedy and to show how the play conforms to these. Perhaps the best example is H. Scriblerus Secundus' defence of the ghost. By ingeniously misinterpreting Aristotle, he proves that 'a Ghost is the Soul of Tragedy' and implies that a tragedy without a ghost is almost a contradiction in terms.

The scholarly apparatus provided by H. Scriblerus Secundus is so extensive that *The Tragedy of Tragedies* seems to be a work intended for the library rather than the theatre, but the play in its final form was a considerable success on the stage and was revived periodically throughout the eighteenth century. Two mock-operatic versions, both called *The Opera of Operas*, appeared in 1733, one set by Arne and the other by Lampe (who later collaborated with Carey on his mock operas), but Fielding himself was not responsible for either of these adaptations. In 1780, when the play no longer held the London stage but was still being produced in the provinces, Kane O'Hara gave it a new lease of life as a burletta, *Tom Thumb*, which was as popular as the original version and continued to be performed well into the nineteenth century.

The reason for the continuing appeal of the play to every kind of audience is obvious from the opening dialogue between two courtiers:

> DOODLE Sure, such a Day as this was never seen!
>   The Sun himself, on this auspicious Day,
>   Shines, like a Beau in a new Birth-Day Suit:
>   This down the Seams embroider'd, that the Beams.
>   All Nature wears one universal Grin.
> NOODLE This Day, O Mr. *Doodle*, is a Day
>   Indeed, a Day we never saw before.
>   The mighty *Thomas Thumb* victorious comes;
>   Millions of Giants crowd his Chariot Wheels,
>   Giants! to whom the Giants in *Guild-hall*
>   Are Infant Dwarfs. They frown, and foam, and roar,
>   While *Thumb* regardless of their Noise rides on.
>   So some Cock-Sparrow in a Farmer's Yard,
>   Hops at the Head of an huge Flock of Turkeys.   (I, i)

Such banality and bathos delivered as solemn rhetoric could be taken simply as first-rate farcical nonsense and was, no doubt, enjoyed as such by less sophisticated theatregoers, but it is also nonsense with a purpose, and the burlesque purpose would have been perfectly clear to anyone familiar with contemporary tragedy. The opening of Noodle's speech is the 'source' of numerous lines in Restoration and Augustan drama according to the notes, in which four such lines are cited. Fielding's burlesque humour in this fairly typical passage is much broader and perhaps less subtle than Gay's in *The What D'Ye Call It*, but not necessarily inferior. The burlesque simile with which Noodle's speech ends is so obviously fatuous that it might appear crude, but on the other hand Fielding was forced to 'sink' even lower than the dramatists he was ridiculing if he was to achieve burlesque at all. This, as the passages from the plays quoted in the notes indicate, was not easy. Furthermore, Fielding's nursery-tale 'tragedy' is closer in conception to the dramatic extravaganza of the nineteenth century (associated in particular with James Planché) than either *The Rehearsal* or *The What D'Ye Call It*, and such verbal burlesque suits it perfectly.

The extravaganza, as defined by V. C. Clinton-Baddeley, is 'burlesque without an object, burlesque weakened into farce, a whimsical entertainment conducted in rhymed couplets or blank verse' which has 'no critical purpose' and which is 'not aimed at any dramatic absurdity of the contemporary stage'.[8] Fielding's play is obviously not an extravaganza, but its playful exuberance, while having a critical purpose and being aimed at absurdities of the contemporary stage, generates a type of verbal humour and comic action that achieves a considerable degree of independence from its targets and can be enjoyed for its own sake. Most of Fielding's characters, especially the women, have nonsense names not much more extravagant than the exotic names, such as Masinissa and Dolabella, that fill the Dramatis Personae lists in heroic plays and contemporary tragedies. King Arthur's Queen is called Dollallolla, his daughter, Huncamunca, and one of the maids of honour, Mustacha; in additon there is the Queen of the Giants, Glumdalca, the nobleman in love with Huncamunca, Lord Grizzle, and the three courtiers with even more ridiculous names, Noodle, Doodle, and Foodle. All these characters are burlesque versions of the exaltedly noble figures in heroic tragedy and behave accordingly. Arthur, for example, is partial to giantesses and afraid of his wife, who is attracted to midgets and very fond of alcohol. The tragic heroine Huncamunca is a girl with a truly enormous appetite who yearns for something more than food and is determined to commit bigamy. What Fielding does in these cases is to endow the superhuman and therefore dehumanized characters of heroic tragedy with particular weaknesses so that they become preposterous.

His presentation of Tom Thumb is somewhat different although still similar to the extravaganza. In every way except physical size, Tom Thumb is the typical hero of heroic tragedy. He is a 'man' of unimpeachable honour; he is boastful, completely self-confident, able to conquer any enemy with little effort, including an army of giants, and prepared to put an immediate end to anyone who affronts him or his friends. When he opens his mouth, he sounds like a close relative of Buckingham's Drawcansir, as in the speech he makes on his return to Arthur's Court after defeating the giants:

> I ask not Kingdoms, I can conquer those,
> I ask not Money, Money I've enough;

> For what I've done, and what I mean to do,
> For Giants slain, and Giants yet unborn,
> Which I will slay – if this be call'd a Debt,
> Take my Receipt in full – I ask but this,
> To Sun my self in *Huncamunca's* Eyes. (I, iii)

But despite Dollallolla's exclamation, 'Was ever such a Godlike Creature seen' (I, iii), Tom Thumb is, of course, a dwarf, the hero seen through the wrong end of a telescope, and humorous references to his size occur throughout the play. Noodle describes him as 'a Lump of Gristle', even though 'tis a Gristle of no mortal kind' (I, i) according to Doodle. When Huncamunca is languishing for love of Tom Thumb, Mustacha tells her:

> I am surpriz'd that your Highness can give your self a Moment's Uneasiness about that little insignificant Fellow, *Tom Thumb the Great* – One properer for a Play-thing, than a Husband. – Were he my Husband, his Horns should be as long as his Body. – If you had fallen in Love with a Grenadier, I should not have wonder'd at it – If you had fallen in Love with Something; but to fall in Love with Nothing! (II, iii)

Later, when Huncamunca and the polyandrous giantess Glumdalca are struggling over who should marry Tom Thumb, Glumdalca makes this extremely self-denying offer to the hero:

> Oh! stay, *Tom Thumb*, and you alone shall fill
> That Bed where twenty Giants us'd to lie. (II, vii)

Finally, Tom Thumb is ignominiously swallowed by a cow 'of larger than the usual Size' (III, x). The burlesque incongruity between Tom Thumb's dimensions and his actions and speeches is consequently well established in the text, but must have been even more effective and hilarious on the stage, especially as Tom Thumb was usually played by child actors, sometimes girls and sometimes as young as five, who would have spoken the heroic bombast with high-pitched voices. The relative sizes of the characters is one of the main visual jokes in a play with little obvious visual burlesque except for the ghost scenes (III, i-ii), the *'bloody Engagement between the two Armies'* in III, ix, and the pile of corpses in III, x. The physical contrast between Tom Thumb and Glumdalca, who was often played by a large man, clearly recalls Swift's satirical use of different-sized people in *Gulliver's Travels*, especially in the land of the giants, Brobdingnag, where Gulliver is the lilliputian 'hero' and his devoted nurse is called Glumdalclitch.

Although *The Tragedy of Tragedies* is to a considerable extent constructed from parodies of single lines and short passages (Clinton-Baddeley calls it 'a nest-full of souvenirs, an anthology of nonsense'),[9] Fielding has welded these together so invisibly that the resulting mock play is even more coherently organized than *The What D'Ye Call It*; as a consequence the specific parodies are transmuted into a general burlesque of contemporary tragedy. In outline, the plot, in which the all-conquering hero becomes entangled in a web of relationships and passions, is fairly typical of heroic tragedies. Tom Thumb's return to the Court after his military victory to claim his reward, the hand of Huncamunca in marriage, precipitates an imbroglio of love and jealousy culminating in civil war and the deaths of almost all the characters. Despite his reciprocated devotion to Huncamunca, Tom Thumb is pursued by both Dollallolla and Glumdalca, with whom Arthur falls desperately in love at first sight:

> I feel a sudden Pain within my Breast,
> Nor know I whether it arise from Love,
> Or only the Wind-Cholick. (I, iii)

To complicate matters still further, Tom Thumb's enemy, Grizzle, is himself in love with Huncamunca, and he resorts to rebellion as an act of revenge following her marriage to Tom Thumb. It is after putting down Grizzle's revolt that Tom Thumb meets disaster in the form of a cow. By placing his mock-heroic figures in a conventional heroic framework, Fielding presents the stock situations of heroic tragedy in a ridiculous light, and caricatures the complex love relationships, the unbearable torments of envy and jealousy, and the conflicts between love and honour that are central in many tragedies of the age. The annotations often clarify Fielding's situational and verbal burlesque, as in the case of the superb confrontation scene between Huncamunca and Glumdalca over who should marry Tom Thumb (II, vii). This, as the note suggests, is an extended parody of the meeting between Cleopatra and Octavia in Dryden's *All for Love*, but at the same time it burlesques all such highly charged encounters in contemporary tragedy. Here, as elsewhere, exuberant extravagance is the hallmark of Fielding's situational burlesque.

When Tom Thumb is describing his love for Huncamunca to his friend Noodle, he is interrupted by a bailiff and his companion who have come to take Noodle into custody for debt. As a creature of supreme honour, Tom Thumb regards this as an insult to himself and immediately acts with the utmost violence in the manner of Drawcansir:

> BAILIFF Oh, Sir! I have an Action against you.
> NOODLE At whose Suit is it?
> BAILIFF At your Taylor's, Sir.
>   Your Taylor put this Warrant in my Hands,
>   And I arrest you, Sir, at his Commands.

TOM THUMB Ha! Dogs! Arrest my Friend before my Face!
  Think you *Tom Thumb* will suffer this Disgrace!
  But let vain Cowards threaten by their Word,
  Tom Thumb shall shew his Anger by his Sword.
                               [*Kills the* Bailiff *and his* Follower
BAILIFF Oh, I am slain!
FOLLOWER I am murthered also,
  And to the Shades, the dismal Shades below,
  My Bailiff's faithful Follower I go.
NOODLE Go then to Hell, like Rascals as you are,
  And give our Service to the Bailiffs there.
TOM THUMB Thus perish all the Bailiffs in the Land,
  Till Debtors at Noon-Day shall walk the Streets,
  And no one fear a Bailiff or his Writ.   (II, ii)

As this is one of the few passages containing couplets, it is probably aimed in particular at the incredibly honourable conduct of Almanzor and his fellow supermen in Restoration heroic drama. Bailiffs and their associates have no place in heroic plays, so the mere presentation of a 'hero' communicating with such unworthy beings, let alone bothering to kill them, would have created burlesque humour for an eighteenth-century audience. The speed with which Tom Thumb acts, added to the fact that by non-heroic standards it is completely wrong of him to slay innocent men simply carrying out their legal duty, considerably intensifies the burlesque effect. What finally ensures the reduction of heroic codes of behaviour to absurdity is the farcical quality of the language, most obvious in the well-worn pun on 'Suit' and in Tom Thumb's aggressively indignant jingles.

Perhaps the highest point of Fielding's situational burlesque is the very end of the play, which H. Scriblerus Secundus describes as 'this charming and bloody Catastrophe'. When Noodle announces to the Court the news of Tom Thumb's humiliating fate, the Queen is overcome with grief and triggers off a chain of violent deaths, with a murder to almost every line:

NOODLE Her Majesty the Queen is in a Swoon.
QUEEN Not so much in a Swoon, but I have still
  Strength to reward the Messenger of ill News. [*Kills* Noodle
NOODLE Oh! I am slain.
CLEORA My Lover's kill'd, I will revenge him so.
                                              [*Kills the* Queen
HUNCAMUNCA My Mamma kill'd! vile Murtheress, beware.
                                              [*Kills* Cleora
DOODLE This for an old Grudge, to thy Heart.
                                           [*Kills* Huncamunca
MUSTACHA And this

>   I drive to thine, Oh *Doodle*! for a new one.   [*Kills* Doodle
> KING Ha! Murtheress vile, take that   [*Kills* Mustacha
>   And take thou this.   [*Kills himself, and falls*
>   So when the Child whom Nurse from Danger guards,
>   Sends *Jack* for Mustard with a Pack of Cards;
>   Kings, Queens and Knaves throw one another down,
>   'Till the whole Pack lies scatter'd and o'erthrown;
>   So all our Pack upon the Floor is cast,
>   And all I boast is – that I fall the last.   [*Dies*   (III, x)

This pantomimic game of human ninepins, which also resembles the game of Pass the Parcel except that it is a case of Pass the Dagger, was greatly appreciated to judge from the Editor's note:

> No Scene, I believe, ever received greater Honours than this. It was applauded by several *Encores*, a Word very unusual in Tragedy – And it was very difficult for the Actors to escape without a second Slaughter.

It has obvious appeal just as knockabout farce, but it also successfully burlesques the fondness of English tragic dramatists, in spite of neoclassical influence, for littering the stage with corpses at the end of a play. Although H. Scriblerus Secundus singles out Dryden's *Cleomenes* (1692), in which five main characters lie dead when the curtain falls, as the play coming closest to *The Tragedy of Tragedies* in its tragic dénouement, Fielding is not parodying any particular play but satirizing in general 'those bloody Spectacles daily exhibited in our Tragedies', as the note puts it. Fielding's attention to the telling detail that does so much to enhance his burlesque throughout the play is obvious in the solemn exclamations that accompany these almost arbitrary killings. Particularly effective are the repetition of the words 'vile Murtheress' (reversed on the second appearance) and Doodle's and Mustacha's explanations of the motives for the seemingly motiveless murders they commit – there is no clue as to what Doodle's 'old Grudge' and Mustacha's 'new one' are. And why the King should commit suicide, unless death has become contagious or the prospect of surviving alone is unbearable to him, is just as mysterious. His act does, of course, lead to the fine burlesque of dying speeches, built on a ludicrous equivalent of an epic simile, with which the play ends.

It is above all the language of the play that makes it one of the classics of dramatic burlesque and the most easily enjoyable. Fielding could have modelled his mock tragedy on the standard situations of heroic tragedy without providing, for example, all the extended burlesque similes that add so much to the final effect. The burlesque simile is certainly amongst Fielding's chief weapons in his attack on the rhetorical bombast of contemporary poetic drama.

Hillhouse notes in his edition that 'abuse of the simile is one of the most striking weaknesses of the tragic style, both heroic and classic'.[10] Indeed some of the similes and metaphors from serious plays listed in the annotations are so inappropriate or exaggerated that Fielding has only to reproduce them in the context of his play to make them laughable. One of the most famous passages in the play, Glumdalca's outburst when she finds that Tom Thumb has chosen Huncamunca as his wife instead of herself, is of this kind:

> Left, scorn'd, and loath'd for such a Chit as this;
> I feel the Storm that's rising in my Mind,
> Tempests, and Whirlwinds rise, and rowl and roar.
> I'm all within a Hurricane, as if
> The World's four Winds were pent within my Carcass.
> Confusion, Horror, Murder, Guts and Death.   (II, vii)

Fielding achieves this burlesque of the 'tempests in the soul' so frequently experienced by thwarted or overwrought heroes and heroines by judicious quotation from three separate speeches employing exactly the same simile. 'Tempests, and Whirlwinds', like 'Left, scorn'd, and loath'd', is taken directly from a speech by Cassandra in Dryden's *Cleomenes* (IV, i); 'the Storm that's rising in my Mind' is a slightly modified version of a line spoken by Aureng-Zebe in Dryden's play of the same name (1675) (IV, i); and 'as if / The World's four Winds were pent within my Carcass' is, with the exception of 'my', a part of a speech by Northumberland in Banks' *Vertue Betray'd; or, Anna Bullen* (1682) (I, i). Although the last line of Glumdalca's speech does not form part of the 'storm' simile, it is, owing to Fielding's careful placing of the unexpected and incongruous word 'Guts', a truly brilliant burlesque of the heroic oaths that Lee, in particular, was very fond of using, although Banks again provides a very close parallel in *The Unhappy Favourite*: 'Repentance, Horrors, Plagues, and deadly Poysons'(V, i).

Fielding also possessed the comic imagination necessary to produce a large number of completely fatuous similes ideal for burlesquing the rant of heroic tragedy. A couple of good examples will have been obvious in the passages already quoted, but the following lines, spoken by the Parson shortly after marrying Tom Thumb and Huncamunca, contain a *pièce de résistance* of grotesquery:

> Long may they live, and love, and propagate,
> Till the whole Land be peopled with *Tom Thumbs*.
> So when the *Cheshire* Cheese a Maggot breeds,
> Another and another still succeeds.
> By thousands, and ten thousands they increase,
> Till one continued Maggot fills the rotten Cheese.   (II, ix)

The play is full of these brilliant burlesque similes, and in his brief discussion of the play Clinton-Baddeley rightly maintains that 'Fielding's favourite joke was certainly the simile'.[11] At one point Fielding even makes an explicit attack on the 'abuse of the simile' by poetic dramatists. The Ghost's warning to the King about Grizzle's rebellion culminates in a catalogue of typical poetic similes; the long-suffering Arthur voices Fielding's own opinion:

> GHOST Thy Subjects up in Arms, by *Grizzle* led,
>   Will, ere the rosy finger'd Morn shall ope
>   The Shutters of the Sky, before the Gate
>   Of this thy Royal Palace, swarming spread:
>   So have I seen the Bees in Clusters swarm,
>   So have I seen the Stars in frosty Nights,
>   So have I seen the Sand in windy Days,
>   So have I seen the Ghosts on *Pluto's* Shore,
>   So have I seen the Flowers in Spring arise,
>   So have I seen the Leaves in *Autumn* fall,
>   So have I seen the Fruits in Summer smile,
>   So have I seen the Snow in Winter frown.
> KING D—n all thou'st seen! – Dost thou, beneath the Shape
>   Of Gaffer *Thumb*, come hither to abuse me,
>   With Similes to keep me on the Rack?   (III, ii)

And a few lines later, after the departure of the Ghost, Arthur adds:

> Curst be the Man who first a Simile made!
> Curst, ev'ry Bard who writes! – So have I seen
> Those whose Comparisons are just and true,
> And those who liken things not like at all.   (III, iii)

Just as the plot is a methodical burlesque of commonplace situations in heroic tragedy, the language of the play systematically burlesques its poetry and rhetoric. The 'abuse of the simile' is only one of several targets. In the context of Fielding's play, such typical exclamations as 'Oh! ye Gods!' and 'Be still my Soul' (I, iii) that were intended to be momentous are exposed, as they are in *The Rehearsal*, for the empty formulas they were. Fielding is particularly successful in burlesquing the passionate outbursts of defiance, determination, love, jealousy, and grief that are never far away from the lips of heroic characters. He usually does this by slightly exaggerating conventional speeches so that they become patently ridiculous, especially in the mouths of his mock-heroic figures. When Dollallolla is trying to prevent 'this hated Match' between Huncamunca and Tom Thumb, Lord Grizzle comes to her aid with protestations of such heroic bravado that the Queen has to restrain his enthusiasm. The particular source of this speech is, oddly enough, a poem, Edward Young's Pindaric ode *The Merchant, A Naval Lyrick* (1730), but the burlesque is equally applicable to

Young's tragic style and to that of many other dramatists:

> We will; not Fate it self,
> Should it conspire with *Thomas Thumb*, should cause it.
> I'll swim through Seas; I'll ride upon the Clouds;
> I'll dig the Earth; I'll blow out ev'ry Fire;
> I'll rave; I'll rant; I'll rise; I'll rush; I'll roar;
> Fierce as the Man whom smiling Dolphins bore,
> From the Prosaick to Poetick Shore.
> I'll tear the Scoundrel into twenty Pieces.   (I, v)

Near the end of the play, when Arthur hears of Tom Thumb's death, he reacts even more vehemently than heroic characters do at the news of catastrophe. Hillhouse cites the King's speech, 'Th'are gone, th'are gone, where I must n'ere aspire, / Run, sally out, and set the World on fire', from the end of Otway's *Don Carlos* (1676) (v, i) as a possible origin of Fielding's burlesque, but similar speeches are widespread in the plays of the period:

> Shut up again the Prisons, bid my Treasurer
> Not give three Farthings out – hang all the *Culprits*,
> Guilty or not – no matter – Ravish Virgins,
> Go bid the Schoolmasters whip all their Boys;
> Let Lawyers, Parsons, and Physicians loose,
> To rob, impose on, and to kill the World.   (III, x)

The speeches of chaos and confusion in contemporary tragedies are usually expressed in cosmic and metaphysical terms, with plentiful reference to Earth, Nature, Heaven, Hell, and Harmony, to make them as impressive as possible. In Arthur's speech, Fielding wittily burlesques such hollow grandiloquence by rendering exactly the same sentiment in terms of the mundane and the concrete; instead of Gods, for example, there are 'Lawyers, Parsons, and Physicians'. The result is devastating. Glumdalca's 'tempest in the soul', mentioned earlier in connection with the burlesque simile, is another fine burlesque of the emotional eruptions to be expected in heroic characters, this time of the rage and jealousy that accompany unrequited love.

Fielding's best treatment of another common feature of heroic love, the debate between love and honour, is Dollallolla's extended soliloquy when she finds that she 'can't live / Without my Virtue, or without *Tom Thumb*'. Believing that a woman without her virtue is a 'Stocking with a Hole in't', she tries to find a way out of her dilemma by balancing her love against her honour in the way usual in heroic plays. But Fielding literalizes the metaphor of the balance so that he presents a concrete picture of Tom Thumb and the Queen's virtue being physically weighed together:

> Then let me weigh them in two equal Scales,
> In this Scale put my Virtue, that, *Tom Thumb*.
> Alas! *Tom Thumb* is heavier than my Virtue.   (I, vi)

The irony of the last line reinforces the travesty. The Queen may well cry 'Alas!' when she discovers that the virtue she has been making so much fuss about is less substantial than the minute Tom Thumb. The Queen finally solves her problem in a most unheroic way by hoping to become a widow.

Fielding's linguistic mixture of farcical exuberance and mock solemnity is particularly evident in many of the King's lines, as in the regal pronouncement he makes when Dollallolla tells him she is weeping for joy at Tom Thumb's victory over the giants:

> If it be so, let all Men cry for Joy,
> 'Till my whole Court be drowned with their Tears;
> Nay, till they overflow my utmost Land,
> And leave me Nothing but the Sea to rule.   (I, ii)

Although this is excellent burlesque of the 'floods of tears' cliché, Fielding had to do little more than quote from one of many plays to produce burlesque. H. Scriblerus Secundus cites six passages, two from Lee (including the following lines from *Mithridates* (1678), three from Banks, and one from Theobald, that verbally differ very little from Arthur's speech:

> Pouring forth Tears at such a lavish Rate,
> That were the World on Fire, they might have drown'd
> The Wrath of Heav'n, and quench'd the mighty Ruin.   (I, i)

The real difference is, of course, one of context. The tragic dramatist intended his 'flood of tears' to express the anguish and suffering of his characters and to arouse pathos. But in relying on stereotyped rhetoric and overworked diction, he was appealing to stock responses, and Fielding ridicules what had become a cliché by giving it a deliberately ludicrous twist. Arthur is not expressing his grief or describing someone else's, as would be the case in contemporary tragedy; he is commanding his entire court to weep profusely, to weep an ocean in fact, not because they should be sad but because they are going to celebrate.

One of the pinnacles of verbal burlesque in the play is the King's great boast about Tom Thumb's heroic prowess when Dollallolla objects to the proposed marriage between Tom Thumb and Huncamunca:

> *Tom Thumb*! Odzooks, my wide extended Realm
> Knows not a Name so glorious as *Tom Thumb*.
> Let *Macedonia*, *Alexander* boast,
> Let *Rome* her *Caesar's* and her *Scipio's* show,

> Her Messieurs *France*, let *Holland* boast *Mynheers*,
> *Ireland* her O's, her *Mac's* let *Scotland* boast,
> Let *England* boast no other than *Tom Thumb*. (1, iii)

The casual yet outrageous linking of leaders of the ancient world with 'Messieurs' and '*Mac's*', as though these were the modern equivalents of Alexander and Caesar, is a mock-heroic touch of genius. It also makes the final line equivocal. Is Tom Thumb to be associated with the Roman '*Caesar's*' or the Irish 'O's'? Fielding's great achievement in verbal burlesque is in sustaining such amusing and satirical heroic nonsense from the beginning to the end of the play.

One further issue concerning Fielding's burlesque must be raised in the light of J. Paul Hunter's discussion of the play in *Occasional Form*; this is the issue of Shakespearean echoes in *The Tragedy of Tragedies*, echoes that H. Scriblerus Secundus fails to note even though he tentatively attributes the authorship to Shakespeare. To take one example already discussed, the corpse-filled dénouement does bring to mind the end of *Hamlet*, and there are a number of similar parallels, both situational and verbal. Is Fielding actually burlesquing Shakespeare himself? The answer, as Hunter demonstrates, must be in the negative, because what Fielding is really doing is bringing to mind Shakespeare at the same time as he is burlesquing later plays in order to draw attention to the sometimes narrow but always distinct demarcation between true tragedy and pretentious sensationalism, between great dramatic poetry and factitious bombast. The end of *Hamlet* is genuinely tragic, but handled with less control and sensitivity it would become laughably melodramatic. Fielding's point is that in trying to imitate and emulate Shakespeare without possessing his vision, subsequent dramatists crossed the line into absurdity, retaining only the bare mechanics of Shakespearean drama and losing its inner logic and purpose. Exactly the same is true of their treatment of language, especially figurative language, with Shakespearean poetry being debased to elaborate but empty, hackneyed, and even inane rhetoric. The result in Hunter's words is the transformation of the Shakespearean model into 'nothing better than a collection of improbable situations, dead metaphors artificially rejuvenated into absurdity, and a total language of sound and fury without significance'.[12] Fielding is in fact treating Shakespeare as a touchstone for Restoration and Augustan dramatists.

The Tragedy of Tragedies is one of the funniest and best burlesques in the language, but in its published version it is also a brilliant piece of mock scholarship. By means of his ingenious 'critical edition', Fielding achieves a perfect synthesis of dramatic burlesque and ridicule of pedantry. But does the play have an even wider satirical range? Is it, like *The Beggar's Opera*, also a political satire of Walpole and his Government? Nowhere does Fielding give an explicit indication that the play has any political reference, yet it is possible, as F. Homes Dudden[13] and L. J. Morrissey[14] argue, to interpret Tom Thumb as a caricature of Walpole. The ironical description of Walpole as 'the Great Man' by his opponents was so well known that the mere labelling of Tom Thumb as 'the Great' might have been sufficient to arouse expectations of political satire, and there are certain resemblances. Tom Thumb belongs very much to the court world, as did Walpole, and is close to both the King and Queen. Tom Thumb is also presented as the saviour and virtual leader of his nation, and is consequently greatly respected and even worshipped: to his admirers, Walpole also appeared as a national leader of great calibre. But Tom Thumb is, in fact, a pigmy, a travesty of a hero; for members of the Opposition, Walpole was a fraud, the reverse of a truly noble and dedicated man. Fielding's way of deflating the pomposity and pretentiousness of contemporary tragedy by mock-heroic incongruity, especially by presenting the apparently great and noble personages of the nation as figures of fun rather than of awe, would seem to produce political satire of its own accord, just as Gay's ironic inversions do in *The Beggar's Opera*. Indeed, L. J. Morrissey claims that *The Tragedy of Tragedies* is as rich in political allusion as Gay's ballad opera.[15] Nevertheless Bertrand A. Goldgar has demonstrated that there is no shred of external contemporary evidence to support this theory and that even the internal evidence is capable of contradictory political readings.[16] Commenting on Goldgar's argument, Brian McCrea suggests that while *The Tragedy of Tragedies*, like some other plays by Fielding of 1730–31, contains hits at Walpole, these are 'unsystematic', serving 'no party program, no dogma', and consequently would not have been seen 'as party or even political works'.[17] This may explain why Fielding's contemporaries, who were extremely sensitive to political innuendo in literature, did not interpret the play as an anti-Walpole satire in spite of its oblique allusions to the politician. In any case, Fielding was not aligned with the Opposition writers at this time and his attitude towards Walpole was opportunistic and uncertain rather than hostile, although in his next play he certainly did caricature him.

More than a year elapsed between the first night of *The Tragedy of Tragedies* and the production of Fielding's next dramatic burlesque, *The Covent-Garden Tragedy*, but it proved to be another very busy period for Fielding in the theatre. On 22 April 1731 his two-act ballad opera, *The Welsh Opera; or, The Grey Mare the Better Horse* was produced at the New Haymarket as an afterpiece to *The Tragedy of Tragedies*. Following its initial success, Fielding expanded it into three acts and renamed it *The Grub-Street Opera*. The revised version was scheduled for performance in June 1731, but the production was abandoned as a result of political pressure. It was published later in 1731 under the authorship of Scriblerus Secundus. Although *The Grub-Street Opera* obviously derives from *The Beggar's Opera* and imitates other contemporary ballad operas as well, it does not actually burlesque Italian opera and resembles Gay's work most strongly in its political satire. Indeed, the theatrical success of *The Welsh Opera* was largely due to Fielding's very daring and almost scurrilous caricatures of the Royal Family and the leading politicians of the nation, including Walpole. Nevertheless, Fielding does not completely overlook the current state of drama. The Introduction to the revised version, in which the author Scriblerus discusses his play with a young actor and explains its change of name, combines severe criticism of 'that learned society' of Grub Street with caustic observations on the theatre; the implication is that the contemporary theatre is merely an extension of the 'learned society'. The Introduction to *The Welsh Opera* is even more explicit in its criticism of contemporary dramatists and their methods:

> SCRIBLERUS ... the town is too well acquainted with modern authors to expect anything from a title. A tragedy often proves a comedy, a comedy a tragedy, and an opera nothing at all. I have seen a tragedy without any distress, a comedy without a jest, and opera without music.
> PLAYER I wish, sir, you had kept within the rules of probability in your plot, if I may call it so.
> SCRIBLERUS It is the business of a poet to surprise his audience, especially a writer of operas. The discovery, sir, should be as no one could understand how it could be brought about, before it is made.
> PLAYER No, and I defy them to understand yours after it is made.
> SCRIBLERUS Well, but I have a witch to solve all that. I know some authors who have made as strange discoveries without any witch at all.[18]

Although *The Grub-Street Opera* is so reminiscent of *The Beggar's Opera* that several of the airs and speeches could easily belong to Gay's play, Fielding only occasionally combines burlesque with personal satire in the way that Gay does. The main example is the love scene between Robin the butler and Sweetissa the waiting woman (I, vi), which ridicules both Walpole's affair with his mistress, Maria Skerrett, and the abuse of the simile by contemporary dramatists. In trying to express their love, both lovers, but especially Robin, utter similes that become increasingly inappropriate and that finally express the exact opposite of what they intend. At first they stick to the stalest of clichés, as in Robin's speech:

> Oh my Sweetissa, thou art straighter than the straightest tree, sweeter than the sweetest flower. Thy hand is white as milk, and as warm; thy breast is as white as snow, and as cold. Thou art, to sum thee up at once, an olio of perfections; or in other words, a garden of bliss which my soul delights to walk in. Oh, I will take such strides about thy form, such vast, such mighty strides –

The more adventurous they attempt to be with their similes, the more absurd these become:

> ROBIN Oh my Sweetissa, how impatient am I till the parson hath stitched us together; then, my dear, nothing but the scissors of the Fates should ever cut us asunder.
> SWEETISSA How charming is thy voice! sweeter than bagpipes to my ear. I could listen ever.
> ROBIN And I could view thee ever; thy face is brighter than the brightest silver. Oh could I rub my silver to be as bright as thy dear face, I were a butler indeed!

In the end Robin and Sweetissa chant in counterpoint unintentionally ironic similes about the depth of their love until, running out of similes, they stumble into inarticulacy:

> ROBIN Mine is as deep as the knowledge of physicians.
> SWEETISSA Mine as the projects of statesmen.
> ROBIN Mine as the virtue of whores.
> SWEETISSA Mine as the honesty of lawyers.
> ROBIN Mine as the piety of priests.
> SWEETISSA Mine as – I know not what.
> ROBIN Mine as – as – as – I'gad I don't know what.

By linking 'the projects of statesmen', 'the honesty of lawyers', and 'the piety of priests' with 'the virtue of whores', Fielding makes clear what value should be attached to such 'projects', 'honesty', and 'piety'. At the same time he uses the lovers' exercise in simile, which unwittingly reduces their protestations of love to mere pretence, to comment acidly on the relationship between Walpole and Maria Skerrett. Fielding transforms the burlesque simile into an instrument of personal satire.

Harold Gene Moss has drawn attention to the many references and allusions to contemporary plays in *The Grub-Street Opera*, a feature he interprets as a ploy by Fielding to pretend that the work is not primarily a political satire.[19] Although many of these parallels with other plays are not burlesque or parodic imitations, Moss, following a suggestion by Ernest Bernbaum,[20] argues that the subplot of *The Grub-Street Opera* dealing with Owen's attempted seduction of Molly does travesty George Lillo's *Silvia; or, The Country Burial* (1730) by 'reducing the elevated concerns of Lillo's opera to a wanton farce of lewd characters'.[21] Lillo's ballad opera, involving the victory of virtue over vice and the reformation of a rake, differs from the general run of such works in its seriousness and sentimentalism. It was not a success on the stage, and is an obvious target for a burlesquer, although Fielding's fun as its expense is very much secondary to his political allegory. Nevertheless, Fielding chose the same tunes as Lillo for a few of his songs, and these airs do contain parodic echoes of Lillo's lyrics.

As Jack Richard Brown has noted, *The Welsh Opera* contains another burlesque episode, which Fielding discarded when revising the play.[22] In the closing stages (II,v), Goody Scratch, a minor character who is omitted from *The Grub-Street Opera*, is exposed as a witch by the servants, but she saves her life by promising to reveal a secret that will make them all rich and happy. She declares that they 'are all people of quality and great fortunes', the men being the sons of Sir George Wealthy and the women the daughters of Lord Truelove. This is confirmed by the discovery of a birthmark in the shape of a star, 'the particular mark of Lord Truelove's children', on the right arms of the women, and of swellings behind the ears of the men, 'the witness of a happy birth'. Goody Scratch explains that all the women have fortunes of £19,355 and that all the men have annual incomes of £3,000 left to them by deceased relatives. Several marriages are instantly arranged, including a particularly bizarre one between the witch herself and the parson Puzzletext. This episode, with its completely unexpected revelations and astonishing outcome, burlesques in a suitably exaggerated way the contrived happy endings of sentimental plays, and obviously resembles the dénouement of *The Author's Farce*. In itself this burlesque scene is very effective, but it is extraneous to the main concerns of the play, and Fielding's decision to delete it when rewriting the play was dramatically sound.

The Lottery, the first of Fielding's plays for Drury Lane after becoming its resident playwright in 1731, was produced on 1 January 1732. This ballad opera exposes the corrupt practices of dealers in tickets at State Lotteries who made fortunes for themselves at the expense of the public. Although it contains less reference to the theatre than *The Grub-Street Opera*, Fielding still manages to include one touch of burlesque. Wrongly believing that the gullible country girl Chloe is extremely wealthy, the unscrupulous rogue Jack Stocks assumes the appearance of an aristocrat, Lord Lace, in an attempt to marry her for her fortune. Some of Lord Lace's speeches of courtship burlesque the stilted and verbose idiom becoming increasingly familiar with the growing popularity of sentimental drama:

I shall never forgive myself being guilty of so great an error; and unless the breath of my submission can blow up the redundancy of your good nature, till it raise the wind of compassion, I shall never be able to get into the harbour of quiet . . . Oh! ravishing! exquisite! ecstacy! joy! transport! misery! flames! ice! How shall I thank this goodness that undoes me! (I, ii)

Although Chloe is as impressed by this verbal extravagance as any sentimental heroine would be, in the context of the play's vigorous colloquial style such bombast is unmistakably ludicrous. To ensure that the burlesque intention could not possibly be missed, Fielding provides Jack Stocks' father with the following aside: 'Well said, faith – (the boy has got something by following plays, I see.)'

Fielding's next play for Drury Lane, *The Modern Husband*, opened six weeks after *The Lottery*. This was by far his most serious and morally earnest play to date, and in his Prologue he virtually renounces all his previous work as 'frolic flights of youth'. It is because *The Modern Husband* and the later *The Universal Gallant* prefigure the social-problem plays of the late nineteenth century, including his own, that Shaw, in his Preface to *Plays Unpleasant*, made his well-known claim for Fielding as a major dramatist. Although *The Modern Husband* is without any trace of burlesque, it contains a few passages concerning the theatre and current drama that complement Fielding's actual burlesques by revealing his opinion of fashionable theatregoers. Instead of setting high standards, these people exhibit a complete lack of artistic taste and discrimination. Lord Richly praises very highly a new opera entitled 'the Humours of Bedlam' because 'it has not one syllable of sense in it from the first page to the last'(II, v). Deploring the 'dull writers of the late reigns', he explains his great admiration for sheer nonsense: 'The design of a play is to make you laugh; and who can laugh at sense?' It is not surprising that he would much prefer 'a company of tumblers and ballad singers' to 'a company of players'. Gaywit agrees with Lord Richly; after claiming that the absence of any manifestation of reason virtually ensures a successful run for the new opera, he asserts that English playwrights 'have improved on the Italians' because whereas 'they wanted only sense – we have neither sense nor music'. Gaywit also believes that 'to turn the best of our tragedies and comedies into operas' would be a very worthwhile enterprise. Only Bellamant regrets the degeneration of the theatre into a place of inane entertainment.

In a further discussion of 'the Humours of Bedlam', Lord Richly says that Mrs Bellamant 'is grown a perfect deserter from the Beau Monde' because she does not share the normal reverence for the new opera. Mrs Bellamant, the only genuine representative of reason and good sense in the play, replies with her usual incisive intelligence:

> I am only for indulging reason in our entertainments, my lord. I must own, when I see a polite audience pleased at seeing Bedlam on the stage, I cannot forbear thinking them fit for no other place.   (III, vii)

In deploring the beau monde's love of fatuous novelty in the theatre, especially at the expense of aesthetic and moral standards that alone give drama substance and dignity, Mrs Bellamant implies what Fielding states in his Prologue: that drama should 'instruct and mend' as well as 'divert', and that 'low farce' is a perversion of the proper function of the stage.

Mrs Bellamant's remarks are particularly applicable to Lady Charlotte Gaywit, who typifies the most frivolous kind of regular playgoer. For Lady Charlotte, attendance at the theatre is a social necessity and little else. She seems to be totally uninterested in the plays she so frequently goes to, and finds entertainment mainly in her weekly visits to 'dear Bedlam', where she can watch the lunatics. When asked the title of the play she is about to see, she replies that she never actually knows what is being produced:

> Miss Rattle and I saw four acts the other night, and came away without knowing the name. I think, one only goes to see the company, and there will be a great deal to-night: for the Duchess of Simpleton sent to me this morning.   (III, v)

She finally departs for the theatre only when she believes that the first act is over; never in her life, she admits, has she seen the first act of a play. Perhaps even more damning are the remarks she makes when she discovers that her husband is accompanying the party to the theatre:

> I would as soon to the chapel with Lady Prue: I saw the ridiculous creature cry at a tragedy. . . . I would as soon laugh at a comedy, or fall asleep at an opera.   (III, v)

Fielding's irony here is caustic. The implication is that a sensitive and intelligent person truly responsive to drama would be moved by a good tragedy, would laugh at a good comedy, and would sleep through an opera. In general, Fielding treats Lady Charlotte with considerable indulgence, but there is no doubt that her attitude to the theatre is utterly reprehensible. By regarding the theatre primarily as a meeting place for herself and her friends, and by approving of plays only if they approximate to the 'performances' of Bedlam, Lady Charlotte is helping to undermine serious drama. In *The Author's Farce* Fielding condemns the theatre managers for pandering to the taste of the town. In *The Modern Husband* he shows the taste of the town itself. If the main aim of the theatres was to satisfy the beau monde and their associates, then Fielding's pessimism about 'the sinking honour of the stage', voiced in the Prologue to this play, was fully justified.

NOTES
1. 'Fielding's First Political Satire', *Anglia 90* (1972) 325-48.
2. *Walpole and the Wits,* 104-5.
3. *The Tragedy of Tragedies,* ed. Hillhouse (New Haven, 1918).
4. 'Fielding's First Political Satire', and *Tom Thumb and The Tragedy of Tragedies,* ed. Morrissey (Edinburgh, 1970). All quotations are taken from this edition.
5. 'Fielding's "Tom Thumb" Plays', in *Augustan Worlds,* ed. J. C. Hilson, M. M. B. Jones and J. R. Watson (Leicester, 1978) 165-74.
6. In *Burlesque Plays of the Eighteenth Century,* Trussler includes the text of *Tom Thumb* rather than the later version, but *The Tragedy of Tragedies* is included in another anthology, *Eighteenth Century Comedy,* ed. W. D. Taylor and Simon Trussler (London, 1969).
7. 'Fielding's *Tom Thumb* as the Heir to Buckingham's *Rehearsal*', *Texas Studies in Literature and Language 10* (1968-69) 405-14.
8. *The Burlesque Tradition,* 109.
9. *Ibid.,* 54.
10. *The Tragedy of Tragedies,* 179.
11. *The Burlesque Tradition,* 54.
12. *Occasional Form,* 34. Hunter also discusses the play, though more briefly, in 'Fielding and the Disappearance of Heroes', in *The English Hero, 1660-1800,* ed. Robert Folkenflik (Newark, 1982) 116-42.
13. *Henry Fielding,* I, 66-9.
14. *Tom Thumb and The Tragedy of Tragedies,* ed. Morrissey, 4-6.
15. 'Fielding's First Political Satire', 333-4, 346-7.
16. *Walpole and the Wits,* 104-5.
17. *Henry Fielding and the Politics of Mid-Eighteenth-Century England,* 220.
18. Quotations from *The Welsh Opera* and *The Grub Street Opera* are taken from *The Grub Street Opera,* ed. Edgar V. Roberts (London, 1969). There is another good modern edition, by L. J. Morrissey (Edinburgh, 1973).
19. 'Satire and Travesty in Fielding's *The Grub Street Opera*', *Theatre Survey 15* (1974) 38-50.
20. *The Drama of Sensibility* (Boston, 1915) 144-5.
21. 'Satire and Travesty in Fielding's *The Grub Street Opera*', 43.
22. 'Henry Fielding's *Grub Street Opera*', *Modern Language Quarterly 16* (1955) 32-41.

The Covent-Garden Tragedy

On 1 June 1732 Fielding's anti-Catholic comedy *The Old Debauchees* was staged at Drury Lane together with his new dramatic burlesque, *The Covent-Garden Tragedy*, as an afterpiece.[1] *The Old Debauchees* was successful, but the public response to *The Covent-Garden Tragedy* was so unfavourable on the first night that it was taken off immediately and very few revivals were ever attempted. Fielding quickly provided an alternative afterpiece by adapting Molière's *Le Médecin malgré lui* into a one-act play, *The Mock Doctor; or, The Dumb Lady Cured*. The initial reaction to *The Covent-Garden Tragedy*, so different from that to *Tom Thumb* in all its versions, might suggest that the later burlesque is considerably inferior to the earlier one, but this is not the case. The reasons for the thoroughgoing condemnation the play received were moral, not aesthetic. The audience was offended by the setting, characters, and tone of *The Covent-Garden Tragedy*, as many subsequent critics have been.[2] The action takes place in a brothel and the characters are prostitutes, drunkards, and ruffians; Covent Garden was, after all, the red-light district of London. An important influence on the play was Hogarth's *A Harlot's Progress*, a series of six prints that caused something of a sensation when they were issued for sale in April 1732.[3] After *The Tragedy of Tragedies*, *The Covent-Garden Tragedy* must have come as a shock because it lacks that light-hearted, extravaganza-like quality of the earlier mock tragedy. Yet to label the play as 'vulgar' or 'coarse', as Frederick S. Boas does,[4] is to approach it in the wrong way. The vulgarity is a deliberate part of the burlesque effect and must be accepted as such. Fielding's specific target in *The Covent-Garden Tragedy* is *The Distrest Mother* (1712), Ambrose Philips' adaptation of Racine's *Andromaque*, but as in *The Tragedy of Tragedies* his aim is to ridicule in general contemporary tragic drama, especially its language and rhetoric.

Fielding's choice of *The distrest Mother* as the model for his burlesque was a good one because Philips' play was probably the most popular eighteenth-century tragedy in the repertoire and was widely known. *The Distrest Mother* is consequently of considerable interest to the cultural historian because of what it tells us about the condition of tragedy and the expectations of contemporary audiences, but some aspects of it almost invite burlesque, and Gay had already made a number of satirical allusions to it in *The What D'Ye Call It*. *The Covent-Garden Tragedy* resembles *The What D'Ye Call It* and *The Beggar's Opera* in that the substitution of low life for high life is the basic burlesque method of all three; but in concentrating almost exclusively on prostitutes and their clients in a brothel, Fielding is much lower than even the Gay of *The Beggar's Opera*. Fielding's characters lack that element of redeeming romanticism that makes Macheath's gang and even his whores attractive. The tone is much closer to that of *The Dunciad*, and Fielding's method, like Pope's, is mock-heroic. Fielding does not attempt any sustained parody of Philips' dramatic poetry; instead he uses the characters and some features of the plot of *The Distrest Mother* as a basis on which to construct a mock tragedy about the criminal underworld. Fielding's characters speak in the same idiom as Philips', but because of the extreme incongruity between the subject of conversation and the pompous expression, Philips' verse is exposed for the pretentious rhetoric it frequently is.

The 'distrest mother' of Philips' play is Andromache, widow of Hector of Troy and prisoner of Achilles' son, Pyrrhus, the King of Epirus. The reason for her distress is that the Greeks want to kill her young son, Astyanax, in case he develops into a second Hector and avenges his father. Although betrothed to Menelaus' daughter Hermione, Pyrrhus has fallen in love with Andromache and refuses to give Astyanax to Orestes, the ambassador from the Greeks. Orestes himself is deeply in love with Hermione, who has come to Pyrrhus' court for her intended wedding. The action revolves around the tangled emotional relations of these four characters, all of whom are liable to experience sudden and violent changes of heart. In the dénouement, Hermione, insane with jealousy when she discovers that she has been rejected in favour of Andromache, persuades Orestes to murder Pyrrhus at his wedding ceremony. Once the deed is done, however, Hermione is overcome with horror and remorse, and kills herself after renouncing Orestes, who goes mad with grief and guilt.

The tone of the play is so overwrought, the motivation of the characters so inadequate, and the outpourings of maternal concern so cloyingly sentimental that it is now difficult to take the play seriously. The comparison with Racine's original is damning. Much of Philips' writing, especially his most elevated passages, today reads like self-parody. When Orestes meets Hermione at Epirus and finds that she still cares for him, he almost explodes with emotion:

Oh Joy! Oh Extasie! My Soul's intranced!

> Oh charming Princess! Oh transcendent Maid!
> My utmost Wish! – Thus, thus let me express
> My boundless Thanks! – I never was unhappy. –
> Am I *Orestes*?   (II, ii)

Out of context this could be mistaken for a burlesque of bombast, especially as Hermione makes the bathetic reply, 'You are *Orestes*'. Andromache's maternal speeches and, above all, the mad speeches of both Hermione and Orestes in Act V read even more like burlesque. Philips, like many contemporary writers of tragedy, seems unable to resist the temptation to raise the rhetorical pitch at the slightest opportunity.

Fielding substitutes two whores with burlesque names, Kissinda and Stormandra, for Andromache and Hermione respectively, and two rakes, Captain Bilkum and Lovegirlo, for Orestes and Pyrrhus, but he makes no attempt to exact correspondence to the characters in Philips' tragedy. The 'distrest mother' of *The Covent-Garden Tragedy* is not Kissinda, the Andromache figure, but Mother Punchbowl, the madam of the brothel where the action takes place. Mother Punchbowl, who is based on a well-known brothel keeper, Elizabeth Needham, is in distress because business at her establishment is going down:

> Oh! Bilkum, when I backward cast my thoughts,
> When I revolve the glorious days I've seen,
> (Days I shall see no more) – it tears my brain.   (I, iv)

These lines could easily belong to a contemporary tragedy, but here the highly charged emotional tone is ludicrous because the 'glorious days' refer to a time of extremely profitable prostitution. The play actually opens with Mother Punchbowl solemnly lamenting the present state of prostitution in words that burlesque the patriotic sentiments so frequently expressed in contemporary tragedies:

> Who'd be a bawd in this degenerate age!
> Who'd for her country unrewarded toil!
> Not so the statesman scrubs his plotful head,
> Not so the lawyer shakes his unfee'd tongue,
> Not so the doctor guides the doleful quill.   (I, i)

This speech, with its overtones of social criticism, recalls *The Beggar's Opera*, and Mother Punchbowl does in some ways resemble Mrs Trapes in Gay's ballad opera. That a bawd should complain about a 'degenerate age' is as paradoxical as that she should believe she is working for her country rather than herself, but by reversing conventional expectations Fielding ironically links the 'respectable' professions of politics, law, and medicine with prostitution, and suggests that morally there is no difference between them. Fielding implies that the statesman, lawyer, and doctor are out for themselves just as much as the whore is. There are similar ironic inversions later in the play, as when Kissinda speaks of prostitution as 'the best of trades' (II, vi) and when Mother Punchbowl herself declares, 'For even bawds, I own it with a blush, / May be dishonest in this vicious age' (II, ii). The social criticism in *The Covent-Garden Tragedy* is not developed extensively and is more implicit than explicit; but the influence of *The Beggar's Opera* is clear enough, and the way Fielding handles mock-heroic creates the impression of a thoroughly diseased society.

Fielding provides a burlesque parallel to Andromache's maternal love in the relationship between Mother Punchbowl and Bilkum. Although notorious for 'bilking' (cheating) his mistresses, Bilkum is a long-standing client of the brothel, and Mother Punchbowl sees him as her son:

> Come to my arms, thou best beloved of sons,
> Forgive the weakness of thy mother's fears:
> Oh! may I never, never see thee hanged! (I, iii)

Since Astyanax does not appear in *The Distrest Mother*, there is no exact model for the scene between Bilkum and Mother Punchbowl, but Fielding does base his burlesque of the sentimental way in which contemporary dramatists frequently treated parental devotion and filial loyalty on the almost hysterical tone Andromache adopts every time she mentions her son. The burlesque reaches its climax when the 'son' asks a favour of his 'mother':

> BILKUM And now a present evil gnaws my heart,
>   Oh! Mother, mother –
> PUNCHBOWL   Say, what would my son?
> BILKUM Get me a wench, and lend me half a crown.
> PUNCHBOWL Thou shalt have both.
> BILKUM   Oh, goodness
>   most unmatched! (I, iii)

It is difficult to imagine a greater perversion than this of the mother–son relationship in Philips' play.

This scene also contains probably the best burlesque in the play of a much overworked characteristic of Philips' dramatic poetry – the question, either ordinary or rhetorical. The number of question marks, not to mention exclamation marks, in *The Distrest Mother* at times suggests a cross-examination rather than a play. Some of Andromache's important speeches illustrate this tendency well, but the most extreme example is Hermione's soliloquy at the very beginning of Act V, 'What have I done? where am I? where is *Pyrrhus*?', which contains twenty-one questions and eleven exclamations in twenty-two and a half lines. Mother Punchbowl's speech when Bilkum arrives at the brothel, arguing with the Chairman who has brought him, brilliantly parodies this stylistic feature of *The Distrest Mother*:

> What is the reason, captain, that you make
> This noise within my house? Do you intend
> To arm reforming constables against me?
> Would it delight your eyes to see me dragged
> By base plebian hands to Westminster,
> The scoff of serjeants and attorneys' clerks,
> And then, exalted on the pillory,
> To stand the sneer of every virtuous whore?
> Oh! couldst thou bear to see the rotten egg
> Mix with my tears, and trickle down my cheeks,
> Like dew distilling from the full-blown rose.   (I, iii)

The topical allusion to the pillorying of Elizabeth Needham in 1731 that led to her death might seem distasteful, but the sustained disparity between the ignominious punishment described and the high style employed, culminating in a particularly grotesque simile, is superb burlesque.

The burlesque equivalent to the main action of *The Distrest Mother*, concerning the fluctuating and overheated passions of the four principal characters, is the intrigue involving Kissinda, Stormandra, Lovegirlo, and Bilkum, but Fielding does not attempt a point-by-point parallel. Unlike Andromache in Philips' play, the Andromache figure of *The Covent-Garden Tragedy*, Kissinda, is devoted to the Pyrrhus figure, Lovegirlo. This is probably Fielding's most significant departure from *The Distrest Mother*, but there are a number of others, including the highly appropriate happy ending. Nevertheless, Fielding rarely loses sight of Philips, and some of the key episodes of *The Distrest Mother*, such as Hermione's jealousy and revenge, are reproduced fairly accurately in burlesque form.

The burlesque love plot does not begin properly until the end of Act I, when Kissinda and Lovegirlo declare their love for each other in a way reminiscent at times of Kitty and Filbert in *The What D'Ye Call It*. This is especially true of Kissinda's first enraptured reply to Lovegirlo:

> Cease, my Lovegirlo, oh! thou has a tongue
> Might charm a bailiff to forego his hold.
> Oh! I could hear thee ever, could with joy
> Live a whole day upon a dish of tea,
> And listen to the bagpipes in thy voice.   (I, ix)

As there is no comparable scene between Pyrrhus and Andromache in *The Distrest Mother*, Fielding is not parodying Philips but burlesquing in general the love scenes of contemporary tragedy, as Gay had done. Knowing that 'a lady of the town, / If she give way to love, must be undone', Kissinda's only worry is that she will 'forget my trade and learn to dote'. She is consequently overcome with gratitude when she learns that Lovegirlo has decided to take her off the streets and set her up as his mistress:

> Then I am blest indeed – and I will be
> The kindest, gentlest, and the cheapest girl.
> A joint of meat a day is all I ask,
> And that I'll dress myself – A pot of beer,
> When thou dinest from me, shall be all my wine;
> Few clothes I'll have, and those too second-hand;
> Then when a hole within thy stocking's seen,
> (For stockings will have holes) I'll darn it for thee;
> With my own hands I'll wash thy soapened shirt
> And make the bed I have unmade with thee.   (I, ix)

In spite of the considerable difference between the social contexts of *The What D'Ye Call It* and *The Covent-Garden Tragedy*, Kissinda's promise of selfless devotion and thrift again recalls Kitty's avowals of undying love in Gay's burlesque play. Fielding certainly controls the tone of deliberate bathos as delicately as Gay; the mock portentousness of the parenthesis near the end is an excellent touch. This scene ends with Lovegirlo celebrating 'unlawful love' and comparing the advantages of a mistress to the disadvantages of a wife; his grotesquely distasteful similes make the mockery of the sanctimonious moralizing about marital fidelity in sentimental plays even more outrageous:

> Besides, whene'er my mistress plays me foul,
> I cast her, like a dirty shirt, away.
> But oh! a wife sticks like a plaster fast,
> Like a perpetual blister to the poll.   (I, ix)

When Stormandra, the burlesque Hermione, first appears at the opening of the second of the play's two acts, she and Bilkum are engaged on a quarrel of heroic proportions. The grandiloquent tone of their speeches suggests that a major catastrophe is at hand, but the subject of their argument is the payment necessary for her professional services. Bilkum, a satirical portrait of the notorious rake, Captain (later General) Edward Braddock, is determined not to pay Stormandra, while she is equally determined that he must: 'Not, though you were the best man in the land, / Should you, unpaid for, have from me a favour' (II, i). She becomes particularly incensed when he promises to bring the money after he has slept with her. That he could think her so naive as to be deceived in this way is a great insult to her professional pride:

> Trust thee! dost think I came last week to town,

> The waggon straws yet hanging to my tail?
> Trust thee! oh! when I trust thee for a groat,
> Hanover Square shall come to Drury Lane.　(II, i)

The mock-heroic echo of Birnam Wood coming to Dunsinane in *Macbeth* greatly enhances the ridicule of Philips' impassioned rhetoric. Fielding's burlesque bears little resemblance to the corresponding scene in *The Distrest Mother* where Orestes finds his former love, Hermione, at Pyrrhus' Court. It bears much more resemblance to the scene near the opening of Philips' play in which Andromache rejects Pyrrhus. Fielding reduces this momentous struggle to a row between a whore and a licentious bully.

Mother Punchbowl intervenes in an attempt to reconcile the warring couple, but is appalled at Stormandra's revelation that Bilkum is trying to cheat her. For the whores, such a possibility is almost unthinkable, and they behave as though this were the most monstrous of crimes. Fielding mocks the contrived and often spurious tragic intensity of Philips and his contemporaries, especially those moments of anguish and suffering that are meant to be deeply moving, by transforming it into farce:

> PUNCHBOWL What has he done?
> STORMANDRA　　　　　　Sure a design so base,
> 　Turk never yet conceived.
> PUNCHBOWL　　　　　Forbid it, virtue.
> STORMANDRA It wounds me to the soul – he would have bilked me.
> PUNCHBOWL Ha! in my house! oh! Bilkum, is this true?
> 　(II, ii)

In the long, self-pitying speeches that follow, Stormandra and Bilkum compete in recalling their past sacrifices for each other and in accusing each other of gross ingratitude. Although the blend of criminality and high-minded moral outrage recalls *The Beggar's Opera* ('Thy only title to the name of Captain?' might well refer to Captain Macheath), Fielding's handling of rhetoric in what is one of the finest burlesque passages in the play looks back to *The What D'Ye Call It*; the chiasmus in the last two lines of Stormandra's speech is strikingly similar to the opening of Kitty's speech, 'Yes, yes, my *Thomas*, we will go together; / Beyond the seas together will we go' (I, i), itself a parody of two of Andromache's lines:

> STORMANDRA Dost thou recount thy services, base wretch,
> 　Forgetting mine? Doest thou forget the time,
> 　When shivering on a winter's icy morn,
> 　I found thy coatless carcase at the Round-house?
> 　Did I not then forget my proper woes,
> 　Did I not send for half a pint of gin

> To warm th'ungrateful guts? Pulled I not off
> A quilted petticoat to clothe thy back?
> That unskinned back, which rods had dressed in red,
> Thy only title to the name of Captain?
> Did I not pick a pocket of a watch,
> A pocket pick for thee?
> BILKUM Dost thou mention
> So slight a favour? Have I not for thee
> Fled from the feather bed of soft repose,
> And, as the watch proclaimed the approaching day,
> Robbed the stage coach? – Again, when puddings hot,
> And Well-fleet oysters cried, the evening come,
> Have I not been a footpad for thy pride? (II, ii)

At the very end of this scene when the argument has subsided, Bilkum expresses his hope that he will, after all, obtain Stormandra on his own terms in words that allude directly to Orestes' speech of delight when he finds that Hermione still loves him:

> ORESTES Then is *Orestes* blest! My Griefs are fled!
> Fled like a Dream! – Methinks I tread in Air!
> . . .
> Surprizing Happiness! unlook'd-for Joy!
> Never let Love despair! – The Prize is mine! (II, iii)
>
> BILKUM And can I think Stormandra will be mine!
> Once more, unpaid for, mine! then I again
> Am blest, am paid for all her former scorn. (II, ii)

It is only here that Fielding follows the ostensibly corresponding scene (the meeting of Hermione and Orestes) in *The Distrest Mother*.

Although Bilkum is content, Stormandra most decidedly is not. The anguished soliloquy in which she compares Bilkum unfavourably with Lovegirlo, whom she believes to be dead, does not derive from any of Hermione's speeches, but from Andromache's frequent fits of self-indulgent nostalgia about her dead husband and ruined Troy:

> What shall I do? Shall I unpaid to bed?
> Oh! my Lovegirlo! oh! that thou wert here;
> How my heart dotes upon Lovegirlo's name.
> For no one ever paid his girls like him.
> She, with Lovegirlo who had spent the night,
> Sighs not in vain for the next day's masquerade,
> Sure of a ticket from him. (II, iv)

But Lovegirlo, unlike Hector, is not dead, and he arrives during Stormandra's soliloquy about him. For a moment both of them believe that they are seeing a ghost, and they question each other accordingly. This 'ghost' meeting of Lovegirlo and Stormandra, for which there is no obvious parallel in *The Distrest Mother* (the closest parallel is the meeting of Hermione and Orestes, but the resemblance is slight), is a piece of deliberate nonsense worthy of *The Tragedy of Tragedies*, although like the similar encounter between Kitty and Filbert near the end of *The What D'Ye Call It* it burlesques 'serious' versions of the device in contemporary tragedy.

As soon as Stormandra realizes that Lovegirlo is alive, she concludes that he has been false to her, and her recollections of her past affection for him give way to accusations that he has betrayed her love:

> I know thy falsehood, yet, perfidious fellow,
> I know thee false as water or as hell;
> Falser than any thing but thyself.   (II, v)

Such accusations in the mouth of a whore, 'ready to obey the porter's call, / At any hour, to any sort of guest', naturally rebound against herself; but even though appearances are against her, Stormandra maintains that her loyalty and devotion to Lovegirlo have been unswerving:

> STORMANDRA May I ne'er fetch
>   My watch from pawn, if I've been false to you!
> LOVEGIRLO Oh! impudence unmatched! canst thou deny
>   That thou hast had a thousand different men?
> STORMANDRA If that be falsehood, I indeed am false.
>   And never lady of the town was true;
>   But though my person be upon the town,
>   My heart has still been fixed on only you.   (II, v)

Stormandra's anger increases in intensity when her rival, Kissinda, enters in search of Lovegirlo. In the subsequent verbal duel between the two whores, Kissinda outdoes Stormandra in her protestations of love and wins Lovegirlo, but it is her final self-sacrificing promise that really moves him deeply:

> Or did he (fate forbid!)
> Want three half crowns his reckoning to pay,
> I'd pawn my under-petticoat to lend them.   (II, vi)

Fielding's burlesque parallel to *The Distrest Mother*, in which Pyrrhus rejects his betrothed, Hermione, for his new love, Andromache, is very obvious throughout this part of the play, even though there is no equivalent verbal duel between Hermione and Andromache in Philips' play.

The close parallel to *The Distrest Mother* continues with the spurned and vengeful Stormandra persuading Bilkum to kill Lovegirlo, just as Hermione urges Orestes to murder Pyrrhus when she has been discarded. Orestes is at first reluctant to carry out the assassination, believing it to be dishonourable, but he complies when Hermione promises that her love 'shall recompence the glorious Deed' (IV, iii). Similarly Bilkum questions Stormandra's purpose, and she offers him her love as a reward for the successful accomplishment of the task, but she also threatens him with legal proceedings if he does not do as she says:

> Instant obey my purpose, or by hemp,
> Rods, all the horrors Bridewell ever knew,
> I will arrest thee for the note of hand
> Which thou hast given me for twice one pound. (II, vii)

The words 'twice one pound', a 'poetic' version of the prosaic 'two pounds', is itself a nice satirical touch reflecting on the inflated, periphrastic idiom employed by poetic dramatists in pursuit of the sublime. Bilkum's blunt promise of immediate action, 'Lovegirlo is no more', followed by an extended burlesque simile of the kind found in *The Tragedy of Tragedies*, corresponds to Orestes' more exalted agreement to Hermione's urgings:

> Madam, he dyes by me! – Have you a Foe,
> And shall I let him live? – My Rival too?
> Ere yon Meridian Son declines, he dyes:
> And you shall say, that I deserve your Love. (IV, iii)

Stormandra has no intention of keeping her word to Bilkum about loving him, and as soon as he has left she prepares to commit suicide. Fielding here seems to be ridiculing the death scenes in Rowe's 'she-tragedies' more than anything in *The Distrest Mother*, although there is a parallel in Hermione's offstage suicide. Like Rowe's tragic heroines in *The Fair Penitent* and *Jane Shore*, Stormandra cannot die without making a martyr of herself, but coming from a common prostitute the self-sacrifice and didacticism are extremely funny:

> May women be by my example taught,
> Still to be good, and never to be naught;
> Never from virtue's rules to go astray,
> Nor ever to believe what man can say.
> She who believes a man, I am afraid,
> May be a woman long, but not a maid.
> If such blest harvest my example bring,
> The female world shall with my praises ring,
> And say, that when I hanged myself, I did a noble thing.
> (II, viii)

For this scene Fielding may well have been indebted to Kitty's attempted suicide and Peascod's penitent speeches in *The What*

D'Ye Call It, but the burlesque incongruity is even more extreme in *The Covent-Garden Tragedy* than in Gay's play. There is also a topical allusion to the suicide by hanging of Captain Braddock's sister Fanny in September 1731.

The final section of the mock tragedy burlesques the dénouement of *The Distrest Mother*. In true neoclassical style, the brothel porter Leathersides, who is based on a porter at The Rose Tavern in Drury Lane known as Leathercoat, reports the offstage duel between Bilkum and Lovegirlo, and claims that Bilkum has run his opponent through with his sword. This news metaphorically kills Kissinda who claims that Lovegirlo 'was three-fifths of me' (II, xi); her mathematical exactness in affairs of the heart is a mockery of what appears to be the more than one hundred per cent devotion of some sentimental heroines, including Andromache, whose love for both her son and her dead husband is obviously boundless. Disaster follows disaster as in Philips' play, and Bilkum, in despair, announces that he has seen Stormandra's body hanging from a curtain rod. The resultant sense of shock drives most of the remaining characters out of their senses. The mad speeches at this point do not correspond exactly to those of Hermione and Orestes in Act v of *The Distrest Mother*, but Orestes' inchoate and frenzied rant, which elicits Pylades' unintentionally comic remark, 'Oft have I seen him Rave: But never thus', is clearly Fielding's main target, especially in Gallono's speech:

> ORESTES I am dizzy! – Clouds! – Quite lost in utter Darkness!
> Guide me, some friendly Pilot, through the Storm.
> I shiver! – Oh, I freeze! – So: – Light returns:
> 'Tis the grey Dawn. – See, *Pylades*! Behold! –
> I am encompast with a Sea of Blood! –
> The crimson Billows! – Oh! my Brain's on Fire!
> . . .
> I blaze again! – See there! – Look where they come!
> A shoal of Furies! – How they swarm about me!
> My Terrour! – Hide me! – Oh their snaky Locks!
> Hark! How they hiss! – See! See their flaming Brands!
> Now they let drive full at me! – How they grin,
> And shake their iron Whips! – My Ears! What yelling! (v, v)

> GALLONO   Ha! distraction wild
> Begins to wanton in my unhinged brain.
> Methinks I'm mad, mad as a wild March hare;
> My muddy brain is addled like an egg;
> My teeth, like magpies, chatter in my head;
> My reeling head! which aches like any mad.   (II, xii)

'Was ever such a dismal scene of woe?', asks Leathersides, but even as he does so there is a total reversal of fortune, as at the end of *The Beggar's Opera* and *The Author's Farce*, with the arrival of Stormandra and Lovegirlo. It was only Stormandra's gown that was hanging from the curtain rod and only Lovegirlo's coat that was run through. The Hermione and the Pyrrhus of *The Covent-Garden Tragedy* are brought back to life. This final piece of burlesque nonsense, with its implication that there has been a great deal of fuss over nothing, completes Fielding's ridicule of *The Distrest Mother*, and indeed of contemporary tragedy in general, except for Lovegirlo's mock-didactic summing-up, 'From such examples as of this and that, / We all are taught to know I know not what' (II, xiii). Considering that *The Covent-Garden Tragedy* ends with the triumph of unlawful love, this is a particularly ironical parody of both Horatio's concluding lines in *The Fair Penitent*, 'By such Examples are we taught to prove, / The Sorrows that attend unlawful Love' (v, i), and Belmour's lines at the end of *Jane Shore*, 'Let those, who view this sad Example, know, / What Fate attends the broken Marriage Vow' (v, i).

The burlesque of Philips' love plot occupies most of *The Covent-Garden Tragedy*, but at the opening of the play there are a few burlesque incidents unrelated to *The Distrest Mother*. The first appearance of the 'mighty Captain Bilkum' resembles that of Tom Thumb in that both ridicule the grandiose entrances of heroes in Restoration and Augustan drama. Fielding's burlesque equivalent to the typical hero's complete lack of interest in anything mundane is Bilkum's refusal to pay the Chairman who has brought him to the brothel his full fare:

> CHAIRMAN Your honour, sir, has paid but half my fare.
> I ask but for my fare.
> BILKUM   Thy fare be damned.
> CHAIRMAN This is not acting like a gentleman.
> BILKUM Begone; or by the powers of dice, I swear,
> Were there no other chairman in the world,
> From out thy empty head I'd knock thy brains.   (I, ii)

Fielding's 'hero' is no more than a bully. The fact that he wrangles over the fare instead of ignoring the Chairman's demands altogether, as one might expect a 'hero' to do, increases rather than diminishes the mockery of heroic conduct. Bilkum's swearing 'by the powers of dice' travesties the solemn oaths of contemporary tragedy, often made in the name of deities.

Fielding also includes a burlesque of the love–honour debate in the form of a casuistical argument between Lovegirlo and Gallono about whether woman or wine is the greater good and the more civilizing influence:

LOVEGIRLO Man without woman is a single boot,
  Is half a pair of shears. Her wanton smiles
  Are sweeter than a draught of cool small beer
  To the scorched palate of a waking sot.
  Man is a puppet which a woman moves
  And dances as she will – Oh! had it not
  Been for a woman, thou hadst not been here.
GALLONO And were it not for wine – I would not be.
  Wine makes a cobbler greater than a king;
  Wine gives mankind the preference to beasts,
  Thirst teaches all the animals to drink,
  But drunkenness belongs to only man.   (I, vii)

The metaphor of the 'single boot' is probably a conscious allusion to Prince Volscius' soliloquy about love and honour in *The Rehearsal*. Bilkum, too, ponders this question deeply in an amusing monologue, but unlike the other two he is not partisan and concludes that 'he does wisest who takes most of both'(I, viii).

As might be expected from *The Tragedy of Tragedies*, the abuse of the simile by contemporary dramatists draws some of Fielding's wittiest burlesque fire. Extended burlesque similes are not as abundant in *The Covent-Garden Tragedy* as in the earlier and more fantastic play, but because Fielding reserves most of them for the emotional climaxes of his mock tragedy, they are particularly effective in deflating the magniloquence of contemporary dramatic poetry. A typically over-elaborate use of the simile occurs in *The Distrest Mother* when Pyrrhus reluctantly renounces Andromache:

  A long Farewel to *Hector*'s Widow.
  'Tis with a secret Pleasure I look back,
  And see the many Dangers I have pass'd.
  The Merchant thus, in dreadful Tempests tost,
  Thrown by the Waves on some unlook'd-for Coast;
  Oft turns, and sees, with a delighted Eye,
  'Midst Rocks and Shelves the broken Billows fly:
  And, while the outragious Winds the Deep deform,
  Smiles on the Tumult, and enjoys the Storm.   (II, v)

Although Fielding makes no attempt to parody Pyrrhus' speech, he provides several burlesque replies to this kind of writing, notably in Lovegirlo's and Bilkum's exclamations when they feel certain of the devotion of their respective mistresses. Especially good is Lovegirlo's ecstatic frenzy after Kissinda has pledged herself to him:

  Oh! I am all on fire, thou lovely wench,
  Torrents of joy my burning soul must quench.
  Reiterated joys!
  Thus burning from the fire, the washer lifts

> The red-hot iron to make smooth her shifts,
> With arm impetuous rubs her shift amain,
> And rubs, and rubs, and rubs it o'er again;
> Nor sooner does her rubbing arm withhold,
> 'Till she grows warm, and the hot iron cold.   (I, ix)

The burlesque shift from the stereotyped language of contemporary tragedy in the first three lines – lines that might have been taken directly from a serious play but for 'wench' and the resulting rhyme with 'quench' – to the low simile could hardly be more pronounced.

The Covent-Garden Tragedy resembles *The Tragedy of Tragedies* in that it is neither a rehearsal piece nor a play within a play but a self-sufficient mock tragedy. It also resembles the earlier play in that the published version contains a burlesque introduction, but unlike H. Scriblerus Secundus' Preface (and annotations) to *The Tragedy of Tragedies*, the Prolegomena to *The Covent-Garden Tragedy* are incidental to the dramatic burlesque rather than integrated with it, being a satire on *The Grub-Street Journal*. This famous weekly, founded in 1730 and committed to backing Pope in his battle with the Dunces, had begun to attack Fielding strongly in 1732 after the productions of *The Modern Husband*, *The Old Debauchees*, and especially *The Covent-Garden Tragedy*. At the opening of this play, Fielding identifies the almost illiterate brothel porter Leathersides with the writers of *The Grub-Street Journal*, which was a gross insult, especially as Leathersides was recognizably based on a well-known London pimp. Offence was duly taken, and Fielding was pilloried in two June issues of the weekly. His answer was the Prolegomena to *The Covent-Garden Tragedy* issued on 24 June 1732. These Prolegomena consist of two hostile but stupid critiques of the play, both written by Fielding under two different masks. The first is that of a dilettante critic who relies heavily on *The Grub-Street Journal* for his opinions. His artistic judgement is non-existent – he takes *The Covent-Garden Tragedy* to be an entirely serious tragedy – and Fielding's point is that anyone who follows the line advocated by the weekly is bound to be as idiotic as this gentleman critic. The second criticism takes the form of an extended review supposedly written for *The Grub-Street Journal* by one of its regular contributors, who is as unintelligent and foolish as the first commentator. He too mistakes the play for a serious tragedy, and on this basis likens it to *The Tragedy of Tragedies*. Using his own ludicrous definition of tragedy, he subjects *The Covent-Garden Tragedy* to a detailed analysis, but finds it wanting in almost every respect. He sees a resemblance between the play and *The Distrest Mother* but draws the conclusion that Fielding compares very unfavourably with Philips as a tragic dramatist. In this mock review, Fielding's ridicule of *The Grub-Street Journal* is even more relentless than his burlesque of contemporary tragedy in the play itself. He accuses *The Grub-Street Journal* of artistic insensitivity, abysmal ignorance, critical ineptitude, and intellectual poverty, but by assuming the persona of a Grub Street journalist in order to parade the reviewer's bigotry, stupidity, and false learning, Fielding makes his Swiftian attack far more searing than straightforward abuse would have done.

Although less exuberant than *The Tragedy of Tragedies* or even *The Author's Farce*, *The Covent-Garden Tragedy* does stand out as one of the few masterpieces of Augustan dramatic burlesque. Fielding's method of converting a popular tragedy into a mock tragedy about prostitutes and their clients suggests a more aggressive satirical purpose than in the relatively playful *The Tragedy of Tragedies*, and the burlesque of contemporary tragedy consequently seems more uncompromising. It is easy to understand why the original audience, who had, no doubt, enjoyed *The Tragedy of Tragedies*, found the satirical method and the topical allusions in bad taste, but nothing can disguise the sheer inventiveness and brilliance of Fielding's burlesque. His skill in controlling the deliberate bathos of burlesque hardly falters, and as in *The Tragedy of Tragedies* he subjects many features of contemporary tragedy to devastating criticism. Only in *The Rehearsal*, *The What D'Ye Call It*, and *The Tragedy of Tragedies* is such a high level of verbal burlesque so consistently sustained.

NOTES
1. This play is included in Trussler's *Burlesque Plays of the Eighteenth Century*.
2. See, for example, H. K. Banerji, *Henry Fielding: Playwright, Journalist and Master of the Art of Fiction* (Oxford, 1929) 40-1.
3. See Robert Etheridge Moore, *Hogarth's Literary Relationships* (Minneapolis, 1948) 96-100.
4. *An Introduction to Eighteenth-Century Drama 1700-1780* (Oxford, 1953) 227.

CHAPTER EIGHT

Pasquin and *Tumble-Down Dick*

After the theatrical failure of *The Covent-Garden Tragedy* in 1732, Fielding concentrated on comedy for a couple of years, adapting French plays, such as Molière's *L'Avare,* and writing his own, notably *The Universal Gallant* (1735). Then in 1735 he attempted a very different kind of full-length play, *Pasquin,* in which neither John Rich at Covent Garden nor Charles Fleetwood at Drury Lane showed much interest. Fielding's reaction was to take over the New Haymarket at the end of February 1736 and set himself up as a rival theatre manager. He had no difficulty in acquiring a company of actors, because some of the Drury Lane actors were already putting on plays at the New Haymarket about twice a week, and he simply organized these into a new troupe, which he ironically called 'The Great Mogul's Company of English Comedians'. The term 'Great Mogul' was frequently used to describe theatre managers, notably Theophilus Cibber, because of the dictatorial power they wielded. With his own company and his own theatre, Fielding was much more independent than he had ever been, and for the next fifteen months he used this freedom to indulge in widespread topical satire. At this time Fielding certainly did align himself with the political opposition to Walpole.

The first production by the new company took place on 5 March 1736 and was, of course, *Pasquin*. Fielding's theatrical gamble was immediately rewarded by the almost unparalleled success of his dramatic satire, which like *The Beggar's Opera* ran for more than sixty performances during its first season. The names 'Pasquin' and 'Marforio', which were derived from two old statues, Pasquino and Marforio, in different parts of Rome, were often adopted as pseudonyms by contemporary satirists, especially political writers. On St Mark's Day in sixteenth-century Rome, satirical writings were fixed to Pasquino and equally satirical replies were subsequently fastened to Marforio. The title *Pasquin* therefore suggests a panoramic satire of contemporary life, and Fielding is indeed mounting an attack on the political, social, moral, and cultural condition of Walpole's England. Just over a month after the opening night of *Pasquin,* John Rich followed the Roman precedent by producing at Covent Garden a dramatic reply called *Marforio*, but this afterpiece lasted for only one night and was never published. Undoubtedly provoked by *Marforio*, Fielding in turn produced a dramatic reply, *Tumble-Down Dick*, a scathing attack on English pantomime and its chief exponent, Rich himself, which was first produced as an afterpiece to *Pasquin* on 29 April 1736.

Although Fielding employs a modification of Buckingham's rehearsal technique in the Puppet Show of *The Author's Farce*, *Pasquin* is the first of his plays that can properly be called a rehearsal play, but even so his handling of the device is far from orthodox. For one thing, two plays are rehearsed rather than one, a comedy by Trapwit called *The Election* and a tragedy by Fustian called *The Life and Death of Common-Sense*. Secondly, Fielding does not use this double rehearsal primarily to burlesque contemporary drama but to satirize a wide range of targets having no connection with the theatre. As a result, neither *The Election* nor *The Life and Death of Common-Sense* is a mock play in the sense that Bayes' play in *The Rehearsal* or the inner play in *The What D'Ye Call It* is. In spite of the rehearsal framework, *Pasquin* is not so much a dramatic burlesque as what Fielding's description says it is, 'A Dramatick Satire on the Times'. His originality lies in adapting a structure originally designed for burlesque of plays and satire on playwrights for a new purpose.

The first half of *Pasquin* is devoted to a rehearsal of *The Election*. Although the opening of *Pasquin*, with complaints by the actors and ridicule of the two dramatists, closely resembles episodes in *The Rehearsal*, it is soon clear that *The Election* is for the most part a forthright exposure of the scandalous conduct of both candidates and officials at parliamentary elections. Any burlesque of comic drama is incidental to this main purpose. In *Don Quixote in England* (1734), a ballad opera reworked from a comedy originally sketched in 1728, Fielding had already touched on electoral malpractices, but in *The Election* he deals more thoroughly with the bribery and corruption widely employed during elections, alluding specifically to the recent one in 1734. His satire on abuses of the system is non-partisan, both Whigs and Tories coming in for their share of ridicule, but his anti-Government and anti-Walpole bias manifests itself in a few passages, such as Miss Stitch's dismissal of *The Daily Gazetteer*, the Government newspaper founded by Walpole and Walpole's own mouthpiece, as unworthy of notice. Fielding also uses *The Election* to criticize severely the beau monde and their modish habits, both sexual and social. Lord Place, one of the candidates for the Court (Government) Party, initiates Mrs Mayoress and Miss Mayoress into the mores of London high society by explaining that for a woman to be the mistress of a man of quality is the height of fashion and that 'Gaming, Intriguing, Voting, and running in Debt' are the only 'Trades' suitable for Society people (II, i).[1] Fielding's attack on the beau monde for its absorption in trivia, its lack of sexual morality, and its other false values, is not as exhaustive as in *The Modern Husband*, but it does form an important part of his satirical panorama in *Pasquin*.

In addition to its political and social satire, *The Election* contains a personal attack on Colley Cibber, who as Poet Laureate produced a succession of banal and inept odes for official occasions. When Lord Place is wooing the voters with promises of what he will do for them if they support him at the election, he offers the position of Poet Laureate to a man who explains that he 'can't make Verses'. This is no obstacle, however, because Lord Place assures the voter that he will 'be able to make Odes' and that he is 'qualified for the Place without being a Poet' (II, i). Fielding also pokes fun at Cibber by burlesquing a feature of his *Caesar in Egypt* (1724). In the published version of this play, each act is prefaced by a quotation from Lucan to clarify its didactic purpose. In *The Election* Fielding concludes each act with a trite couplet that is supposed to sum up Trapwit's intentions. The implication is that Cibber's moral instruction is as fatuous and trivial as Trapwit's.

Although Trapwit cannot be identified with Cibber or with any other single dramatist, he does seem to be a composite portrait of contemporary writers of comedy. Ridicule of authors occurs only spasmodically in *Pasquin*, especially when compared with *The Rehearsal*, but it does form part of Fielding's all-embracing satire and is one of the main justifications for his use of the rehearsal framework. Broadly speaking, Fielding models Trapwit on Buckingham's Bayes. Like Bayes, Trapwit is convinced of his own brilliance and originality as a playwright and is very irritated by Fustian's interruptions of the rehearsal, comparable to those of Smith and Johnson in *The Rehearsal*, in order to point out weaknesses in *The Election*. Trapwit also resembles Bayes in his loquacity; he gives himself away with almost every word he speaks. When Fustian inquires about the action and design of the play, Trapwit's puzzled reply is: 'you ask who is to be married!' Trapwit's view that the chief characteristic of comedy is the arranging of at least one marriage leads him into the spurious innovation of total mystification and surprise in a Bayes-like attempt to outdo his rival dramatists:

> And do you think I am like your shallow Writers of Comedy, who publish the Banns of Marriage between all the Couples in their Play, in the first Act? No, Sir, I defy you to guess my Couple 'till the thing is done, slap, all at once. (I, i)

Although Trapwit calls the marriage between Miss Mayoress and Colonel Promise the 'Plot' of *The Election*, he believes that plots should not open until the later part of a play, because otherwise they will be forgotten by both audiences and writers before the play is much more than halfway through. Consequently there is barely a hint of Trapwit's 'Plot' until the very end of his play when the lovers appear together for the first time, gazing at each other in silence from opposite sides of the stage. Trapwit is particularly proud of this scene, believing it to be 'the best Scene of Silence that ever was pen'd by Man' (III, i). Not surprisingly, Fustian is bewildered by Trapwit's dénouement, especially when Miss Mayoress talks about her 'ill Usage' of Colonel Promise, something that has not previously been mentioned or shown. 'What ill Usage, Mr. *Trapwit*?', asks Fustian, 'When, Sir? Where, Sir?', only to receive Trapwit's inane and Bayes-like response: 'Why, behind the Scenes, Sir. What, would you have every Thing brought upon the Stage?'

The dénouement of *The Election* is in fact one of the very few genuinely burlesque episodes in the play. The *coup de théâtre* when the love of Miss Mayoress and Colonel Promise is unexpectedly revealed makes fun of the startling last-minute discoveries used by dramatists to produce excitement and happy endings, but in addition the stilted speeches of the couple burlesque the formalized rant of lovers in sentimental comedy:

> MISS MAYORESS I have struggled with my self to put you to so many Trials of your Constancy; nay, perhaps have indulged my self a little too far in the innocent Liberties of abusing you, tormenting you, coqueting, lying, and jilting; which, as you are so good to forgive, I do faithfully promise to make you all the amends in my Power, by making you a good Wife. . . .
> COLONEL PROMISE And can you be so generous, so great, so good? Oh! load not thus my Heart with Obligations, lest it sink beneath its Burden: Oh! could I live a hundred thousand Years, I never could repay the Bounty of that last Speech; Oh! my Paradise! (III, i)

Another *coup de théâtre* follows. The couple leave the stage but return in less than a minute as man and wife. For Trapwit, marriage is 'the usual Reconciler at the End of a Comedy', and the wedding immediately results in the incredible reconciliation of the rival political factions. Because he 'would not have concluded without every Person on the Stage for the World', Trapwit imposes a sentimental resolution on his play in a completely arbitrary way without any regard for dramatic logic and plausibility. This is further proof of his stupidity, but it also ridicules the dénouements of sentimental comedies in which harmony and happiness are frequently achieved against the odds as a result of an unexpected revelation or a sudden twist of fortune.

The other important burlesque episode is the fight between the supporters of the Court and the Country parties, although in this case the political satire is just as significant as the dramatic burlesque. Trapwit includes this scene, in which the two mobs chant their slogans and *'cudgel one another off the Stage'*, in an attempt to liven up his comedy, which 'has gone on in great Tranquillity' until this point and now requires something 'of a more turbulent Nature' (II, i). Fielding is plainly burlesquing the more or less gratuitous insertion of scenes of violent action or great activity into plays solely in order to provide them with the illusion of vitality.

Between the rehearsals of Trapwit's comedy and Fustian's tragedy, Fielding satirizes two minor features of contemporary plays, epilogues and dedications. Epilogues, which at this time often contained an element of bawdy and seldom bore any relationship to the plays they were appended to, were normally spoken by actresses, but Trapwit has been unable to persuade any actress to speak his Epilogue. Originally 'there were not double Entendres enough in it', but having subsequently 'cram'd it as full as possible' in order to make it more palatable, he finds that he has overdone it and that now 'it has too many in it' (III, i). Dedications were frequently addressed to aristocrats and almost invariably included a glowing description of the dedicatee's character. After condemning dedications for being no more than 'nauseous fulsome Compliments', Fustian claims that he has written one without any trace of flattery, something he apparently detests. Yet it turns out to be even more sycophantic than usual, the Lord he addresses being said to possess 'more Wit, Sense, Learning, Honour and Humanity, than all Mankind put together' and a mind which 'is a Store-house, where every Virtue and every Perfection are lodged' (III, i). Fustian's argument that it would have been 'down-right rude' to address a Lord in what he calls a more 'concise' manner merely reinforces the impression that he has now replaced Trapwit as the Bayes-figure in *Pasquin*, even though he played the role of critic during the rehearsal of *The Election*.

The rehearsal of *The Life and Death of Common-Sense* occupies the last two acts of *Pasquin*. Fustian's tragedy was to have been rehearsed before Trapwit's comedy but had to be postponed because the actor who plays the first ghost was unwell. Fustian prefers to sit through *The Election*, even though he regards it as 'damned, incoherent, senseless Stuff', than to proceed with the rehearsal of his own play without the actor who, he claims, 'was born a Ghost: He was made for the Part, and the Part writ for him' (I, i). He heartily agrees with Trapwit's opinion that 'a Ghost is the Soul of Tragedy', a view also expressed by H. Scriblerus Secundus in his annotations to *The Tragedy of Tragedies*. Trapwit himself makes his escape from the theatre before the rehearsal of Fustian's play, but Sneerwell, who arrives towards the end of *The Election*, is present to act as a commentator on the tragedy. There are fewer interruptions during Fustian's play than during Trapwit's, but most of them serve to establish that Fustian is as much of a fool as Trapwit even though he believes himself to be a very skilful dramatist. His explanations of some of the inconsistencies in his play, such as why Common-Sense is asleep when she should be leading her army into battle, are as ludicrously inadequate as Trapwit's replies to Fustian's criticisms of *The Election*. Sneerwell is puzzled when he discovers that the tragedy has only three acts, not the obligatory five, but Fustian explains that he 'spun it out as long as I could keep Common-Sense alive; ay, or even her Ghost'. Like Bayes in *The Rehearsal*, Fustian is convinced that as a practising dramatist he knows much more about 'the practical Rules of Writing' than any mere critic such as Sneerwell, but his 'Rules' are the equal of Bayes' in crazy idiosyncrasy:

> ... the first and greatest of which is Protraction, or the Art of Spinning, without which the matter of a Play would lose the chief Property of all other Matter, namely, Extension; and no play, sir, could possibly last longer than half an Hour. I perceive, Mr. *Sneerwell*, you are one of those who would have no Character brought on, but what is necessary to the Business of the Play. – Nor I neither – But the Business of the Play, as I take it, is to Divert, and therefore every Character that Diverts, is necessary to the Business of the Play. (IV, i)

Although mainly in blank verse and at times very funny, *The Life and Death of Common-Sense* is no more a satirical burlesque of tragedy than *The Election* is of comedy. Like both *Jack the Gyant-Killer* and the Puppet Show in *The Author's Farce*, Fustian's tragedy is a partial dramatization of *The Dunciad*. The characters, such as Queen Common-Sense, Queen Ignorance, Physic, Law, and Firebrand (a priest), are allegorical, and the action concerns the overthrow of Common-Sense by Ignorance with the help of the others. Firebrand, Law, and Physic once accepted the sovereignty of Queen Common-Sense, but they have become so ambitious that they can no longer tolerate the restraints she imposes. Common-Sense sums up the main theme of the play in these lines:

> Religion, Law and Physick, were design'd
> By Heaven the greatest Blessings on Mankind;
> But Priests, and Lawyers, and Physicians made
> These general Goods to each a private Trade;
> With each they rob, with each they fill their Purses,
> And turn our Benefits into our Curses. (IV, i)

Although Common-Sense is deserted by her former allies and finally murdered by Firebrand, Ignorance's victory turns out to be a hollow triumph when the ghost of Common-Sense appears at the end of the play to the accompaniment of 'the Ghost of a tune' and drives off all her enemies. Sneerwell is relieved that Common-Sense gets 'the better at last', but Fustian replies cynically that his tragedy 'is almost the only Play where she has got the better lately' (v, i).

The contemporary theatre is only one of a number of Fielding's targets in *The Life and Death of Common-Sense*, but it is an important one. He establishes that Ignorance rather than Common-Sense is the patron of the most fashionable dramatic entertainments of the time. When Ignorance invades the kingdom of her rival, she comes 'With a vast Power from Italy and France / Of Singers, Fidlers, Tumblers, and Rope-dancers' (iv, i). Before the rehearsal actually begins, a similar point is made by one of the dancers who threatens to leave the company and 'go to France' if she is not treated properly, 'for now we have got all their Dancers away, perhaps they may be glad of some of ours' (III, i). In the early eighteenth century, especially during the twenty years before *Pasquin*, French and Italian actors performed various kinds of light entertainment quite frequently in London, including harlequinades, tumbling, acrobatics, and rope dancing, and usually attracted good audiences in spite of adverse criticism by nationalistic and neoclassical critics.[2] The dancer also contends that without the contribution made by dancers to an evening at the theatre, in the form of entr'actes and afterpieces, even Shakespeare would play 'to empty Benches'. At first, however, Ignorance mistakenly believes that the theatres are in the hands of Common-Sense, and when she and her retinue enter Covent Garden she fears that they have come too close to a stronghold of their enemy. But her fears are immediately allayed when Harlequin, a satirical portrait of John Rich, who imitated a dog in Theobald's popular pantomime *Perseus and Andromeda* (1730), welcomes her with open arms on behalf of the two licensed London theatres, Drury Lane and Rich's own Covent Garden, a new theatre which had opened as recently as 1732. Harlequin brings with him 'their choicest Treasure' (Fielding had previously made fun of Rich's 'dog' in his 'cat' epilogue to *The Author's Farce*):

> Two Dogs that walk on their hind Legs only, and personate human Creatures so well, they might be mistaken for them.
> A human Creature that personates a Dog so well, that he might almost be taken for one.
> Two Human Cats.
> A most curious Set of Puppies.
> A Pair of Pidgeons.
> A Set of Rope-Dancers and Tumblers from *Sadler's-Wells*. (v, i)

Ignorance is highly delighted to find that the theatres are now in league with her allies at Sadler's Wells, where acrobatic performances were given during the spring and summer at a tavern theatre notorious for its roughness and vulgarity. As a reward, she provides Harlequin with a new play lacking 'either Head or Tail', which he gladly accepts for immediate performance.

Common-Sense herself condemns the theatres in her conversation with the Poet shortly before she is killed. The Poet, downcast because his dramatic work has been damned, joins Common-Sense because she too has been rejected, but is not a true adherent of her values. In his plays he has always tried to give the impression of being dedicated to her principles, not out of conviction but in order to achieve success. In exposing the absurdity of this assumption, Common-Sense insists on the nonsensical nature of much current drama:

> Fool, thou wert damn'd because thou didst pretend
> Thy self my Friend; for hadst thou boldly dar'd,
> Like *Hurlothrumbo*, to deny me quite;
> Or like an Opera or Pantomime,
> Profest the cause of Ignorance in publick,
> Thou migh'st have met with thy desir'd Success;
> But Men can't bear even a Pretence to Me.   (v, i)

Common-Sense's dying speech about the total reversal of values that has taken place, so that the Poet can dedicate his play 'to Ignorance, and call her Common-Sense', ends with an amusing burlesque of the unfinished speeches of dying characters in some tragedies:

> *Statesmen* – but Oh! cold Death will let me say
> No more – and you must guess *et cetera*.   (v, i)

There is very little imitative burlesque in *The Life and Death of Common-Sense*, although there are a number of good rehearsal jokes arising from various mishaps. The thunder and lightning effects at the opening of the play, for example, follow Firebrand's exclamation about celestial omens, itself a burlesque of a tragic cliché, instead of preceding it. When Common-Sense is supposed to enter with her army, she is accompanied by only one drummer because the Prompter has been unable to recruit any other bit players for this scene. Perhaps the best rehearsal joke occurs when the scene in which Common-Sense is murdered is accidentally omitted, so that her Ghost appears before she has been killed. Fustian has to remove the flour from the actress' face for the omitted scene to be rehearsed. Such incidents are amusing in themselves and are a natural extension of the rehearsal play deriving from Buckingham, but they do not amount to burlesque. The only two genuinely burlesque episodes ridicule ghost scenes and battle scenes, which Fielding had previously treated in *The Tragedy of Tragedies*.

The first ghost to appear to the sleeping Common-Sense in the ghost episode is that of Tragedy, but the cock crows before he has

Fielding's Burlesque Drama

time to deliver his warning to the Queen and he has to make a hasty departure. Sneerwell is puzzled about the dramatic logic of such a gratuitous entrance and exit, but assumes that Fustian has included the ghost as 'a Character necessary to Divert'. When the Ghost of Comedy rises immediately afterwards, Sneerwell is even more perplexed. He exposes the absurdity of this by pointing out that the cock has already crowed, but Fustian blandly replies with a kind of irrefutable illogic that 'the second Ghost need not be supposed to have heard it'. The ghost scene reaches a suitably ridiculous climax when a third ghost rises to inform the Ghost of Comedy that the cock has crowed. In his long speech to the sleeping Queen, the Ghost of Comedy, who like Tragedy has been murdered by the enemies of Common-Sense, laments the collapse throughout society of the values upheld by Common-Sense and refers specifically to the state of the theatre:

> Play-houses cannot flourish, while they dare
> To Nonsense give an Entertainment's Name.
> *Shakespear* and *Johnson*, *Dryden*, *Lee*, and *Row*,
> Thou wilt not bear to yield to *Sadler's-Wells*. (IV, i)

Whereas the ghost scene is both a situational and visual burlesque of ghost scenes in contemporary tragedy, the battle scene is primarily a visual burlesque. At the beginning of the final act of his play, Fustian promises a piece of theatre that has not and never will be equalled: 'It is, Sir, so cram'd with Drums and Trumpets, Thunder and Lightning, Battles and Ghosts, that I believe the Audience will want no Entertainment after it; it is as full of Shew as *Merlin*'s Cave itself, and for Wit – no Rope-Dancing or Tumbling can come near it' (V, i); Merlin's Cave was a well-known curiosity in the Royal Gardens at Richmond, and was reproduced on stage in two different plays performed shortly before *Pasquin*.[3] In measuring the quality of his tragic dénouement by the standards of pantomime and acrobatics, Fustian proves beyond all doubt his stupidity, especially as his main reason for including the battle is to compete with 'all the Raree-fine Shows' so much loved by audiences. He does, however, raise expectations of violent action and thrilling spectacle, yet when the battle scene is rehearsed it turns out to be a fiasco. Even Fustian admits that he 'never saw a worse Battle in all my Life upon any Stage'. After some modifications, the battle is tried again but the result is no better, and this time Fustian complains that the soldiers 'are afraid to fight even in jest'. It is only at the third attempt that Fustian is satisfied with the performance of his battle scene, but Sneerwell remains unimpressed and makes the usual neoclassical objection to such scenes: 'I own my Imagination can better conceive the Idea of a Battle from a skilful Relation of it, than from such a Representation; for my Mind is not able to enlarge the Stage into a vast Plain, nor multiply half a Score into several Thousands.' The stage directions give no clue as to exactly how this ridiculous battle should be played, but Fielding clearly gives the producer an open invitation to burlesque the presentation of battle scenes on the contemporary stage.

Few aspects of the theatre escape Fielding's ridicule in *Pasquin*, but he seldom resorts to burlesque recreation of dramatic weaknesses and excesses as in *The Tragedy of Tragedies* and *The Covent-Garden Tragedy*. In *Pasquin*, as in *The Dunciad*, the condition of the theatre is just one of many symptoms of an underlying malaise in English life. Playwrights, politicians, courtiers, journalists, lawyers, doctors, clergymen, the beau monde, and even the Royal Society receive their share of Fielding's criticism. In no other play, not even *The Author's Farce*, does Fielding cast his net so widely and haul in so many victims. Even so, it is noteworthy that in the Epilogue, which departs considerably from the usual kind of mildly salacious epilogue ridiculed in the play itself, the Ghost of Common-Sense concentrates her attack on the theatre, including the popular entertainments imported from the Continent. The Epilogue is avowedly patriotic in tone, with its praise of Locke, Newton, Boyle, Shakespeare, and Jonson, and in its demand for '*Sense*' in the theatre it echoes Buckingham's Epilogue in *The Rehearsal*:

> Banish all Childish Entertainments hence;
> Let all that boast your Favour have pretence,
> If not to sparkling Wit, at least to Sense.

Although capable of standing by itself, *Tumble-Down Dick* is essentially an extension of *Pasquin* rather than a completely independent play and in this respect is most unusual for an afterpiece, probably even unique except for Fielding's later *Eurydice Hiss'd*. At the beginning of *Tumble-Down Dick*, the rehearsal of *The Life and Death of Common-Sense* has just ended and the rehearsal of Machine's pantomimic 'entertainment' is about to begin. Machine now takes over the role of Bayes from Fustian, who joins Sneerwell as a critical commentator on the rehearsal. The pattern of *Pasquin* is therefore continued in *Tumble-Down Dick*, but there are important differences too. The comedy and tragedy rehearsed in *Pasquin* are not primarily burlesques of contemporary drama, whereas the afterpiece rehearsed in *Tumble-Down Dick* is a straightforward satirical burlesque of English pantomime containing comparatively little social and political criticism. Futhermore, Trapwit and Fustian are not satirical portraits of particular individuals but of Augustan dramatists in general, whereas Machine corresponds to John Rich.

The immediate stimulus for the writing of *Tumble-Down Dick* was *Marforio*, possibly combined with Rich's rejection of *Pasquin* for

Covent Garden, but Fielding did not set out to ridicule Rich and his pantomimes simply out of pique. He had, after all, attacked them six years earlier in *The Author's Farce* as integral parts of the Court of Nonsense. In addition to the scene where Harlequin presents his theatrical 'Treasure' to Ignorance, *Pasquin* itself contains another passage critical of Rich and his afterpieces. When asked by Sneerwell how pantomimes came to be known as 'Entertainments', Fustian replies:

> Faith, Sir, out of their peculiar Modesty; intimating that after the Audience have been tired with the dull Works of *Shakespear, Johnson, Vanbrugh,* and others, they are to be entertain'd with one of these *Pantomimes*, of which the Master of the *Play-House*, two or three Painters, and half a Score Dancing-Masters are the Compilers: What these Entertainments are, I need not inform you who have seen 'em; but I have often wond'red how it was possible for any Creature of human Understanding, after having been diverted for three Hours with the Productions of a great Genius, to sit for three more, and see a Set of People running about the Stage after one another, without speaking one Syllable, and playing several Juggling Tricks, which are done at *Fawks*'s after a much better manner; and for this, Sir, the Town does not only pay additional Prices, but loses several fine Parts of their best Authors, which are cut out to make room for the said Farces. ['*Fawks*'s' refers to the James Street Tennis Court Theatre where the well-known Fawks family gave performances involving tricks of various kinds, juggling, puppetry, and clockwork devices; the family also provided this form of entertainment at fairs.]   (v, i)

At the opening of *Tumble-Down Dick*, Machine himself echoes Fustian's final point when he insists that two acts be removed from *Othello* if it is to be performed with his pantomime; otherwise, he claims, 'the audience will be palled before the entertainment begins'. Despite Fustian's indignant outburst about Shakespeare being mutilated for the sake of 'trumpery', the Prompter agrees to Machine's request because 'this gentleman brings more money to the house than all the poets put together'. This remark is not far from the truth about John Rich during his heyday.

Although English pantomime was almost synonymous with John Rich for the forty years before his death in 1761, the founder of the genre was John Weaver, a dancing master who did much to encourage dancing and mime in the theatre during the first twenty years of the eighteenth century. It was Weaver who made pantomime theatrically respectable by producing at Drury Lane in 1717 a dance play called *The Loves of Mars and Venus* and a true English pantomime called *The Shipwreck; or, Perseus and Andromeda*. But Rich, who was the first English actor to perfect the technique of mime, quickly made the form his own and was unrivalled for his pantomimic productions. Following in Weaver's footsteps, what Rich did was to synthesize various elements already existing in the theatre, such as opera, ballet, acrobatics, spectacle, and farce, into a new dramatic form. He drew heavily on the Italian *commedia dell'arte* and, using the stage name of Lun (the real name of a noted French mime), always took the central role of Harlequin himself. Nevertheless, the harlequinade in English pantomime differed from the improvised comedy of the *commedia dell'arte* in that the action was presented entirely in dumb show; the actors in Italian harlequinades used mime extensively but also sang and spoke.[4] Italian actors had performed in England during the reign of Elizabeth I, and Harlequins had appeared in a few seventeenth-century English masques and plays, especially after 1660, but it was not until the turn of the century that Harlequin really invaded England. During the early years of the eighteenth century, the antics of Harlequin became a regular feature at fairs and amusement booths in London, and dances and brief entertainments featuring him and other *commedia dell'arte* characters were sometimes presented as an added attraction to the main play by the two London theatres.[5]

The basic situation and action of the harlequinade is admirably described by one of Rich's contemporaries, Thomas Wilkes:

> Harlequin is generally supposed to be some being under the power of enchantment, in love with, and beloved by, Colombine; but crossed in all his designs by Pantaloon her father, his man Pierrot, and the Squire who courts her. Harlequin's only wit consists in his activity, displayed in escaping from them either by assuming another form, turning a bed-chamber into a garden, a tavern into a church, or hunting his pursuers with spirits. After a number of pursuits, crossings, turnings, and transformations, some god or superior being interposes in favour of the enchanter Harlequin, makes him friends with his pursuers, and gives him Colombine for a wife.[6]

The chase was therefore as important an element in pantomime as in farce, but it was made much more elaborate by the extensive use of ingenious stage machinery. The adventures of Harlequin formed an important part of Rich's pantomimes, but he normally interwove this comic *commedia dell'arte* element with a serious semi-operatic presentation of a mythological story, often taken from Ovid's *Metamorphoses*. In *Tumble-Down Dick* Machine answers some criticisms from Fustian and Sneerwell by asserting that 'the scene lies in Ovid's Metamorphoses' as though that justified anything and everything. Fielding himself gives a clear but very hostile account of the basic structure of English pantomime in *Tom Jones* (Book v,

Chapter 1), where he distinguishes between the two parts, comic and serious, but prefers the words 'duller' and 'dullest'.

Music and dancing were vital ingredients of Rich's pantomimes, but even more important was spectacle. The classical myth was staged with a visual opulence reminiscent of Stuart court masques, while the Harlequin story was enlivened by the appearance of devils, monsters, and other supernatural beings, and by highly sensational transformations produced by Harlequin's magic wand. (In the *commedia dell'arte* Harlequin always carried a short wooden 'bat', but Rich was probably the first Harlequin to treat this as a conjuror's wand.) As Wilkes suggests, these 'magical' transformations were particularly spectacular, trees being converted into houses, temples into cottages, and people into wheelbarrows at a wave of the wand. In *Tumble-Down Dick* the Genius of Gin appears to Harlequin and delivers a doggerel speech that lists some of Rich's 'machine' tricks:

> Take, Harlequin, this magic wand,
> All things shall yield to thy command:
> Whether you would appear incog.,
> In shape of monkey, cat or dog;
> Or else to show your wit, transform
> Your mistress to a butter-churn;
> Or else, what no magician can,
> Into a wheelbarrow turn a man.

As 'machine' plays depending on dazzling stage effects, pantomimes were obviously designed for the eye. Fustian rightly points out to Machine that 'tragedies do not depend so much upon the carpenter as you do'.

Like Italian opera, pantomime was very popular with the theatre-going public, but again like Italian opera and for very similar reasons it was frequently attacked by intellectuals. Even though pantomime was a peculiarly English amalgam, it did derive to a considerable extent from the Italian harlequinade and was therefore open to criticism on nationalistic grounds; and as the apotheosis of eighteenth-century theatricality, lacking any real intellectual or moral content, it was even more exposed to neoclassical criticism. Thomas Wilkes, who held that pantomimes were 'fit only for weak minds, which cannot bear the impressions of reflection',[7] complained that they were so full of 'the ridiculous and absurd' that 'their exhibition serves only to efface the impression, however useful or instructive, that may have been made upon the mind by an elegant Comedy or a fine Tragedy'.[8] Because pantomimes were performed as afterpieces, they did not actually displace tragedy and comedy from the stage, but by tending to dominate the evening's offerings they did have a debilitating effect on regular drama. Emmett L. Avery argues that after 1720 'what might be considered the normal relation of play and entertainment became reversed: the pantomime began to have extended runs, evening after evening, with the play often changed nightly'.[9] The theatres could attract good audiences without the inducement of an entertainment only at the beginning of the season after the summer holiday or when they presented a new play. Many theatregoers obviously went more for the pantomime than for the main play and were seeking nothing more than undemanding entertainment and thrilling spectacle.

By far the most famous criticism of pantomime is in Book III of *The Dunciad*, but other poems, notably James Miller's *Harlequin-Horace* (1731), and plays, including *The Author's Farce*, *Bays's Opera*, and *The Fashionable Lady*, incorporate satire of the genre. Different from all of these in that it is a single-minded burlesque of pantomime is the anonymous *The British Stage; or, The Exploits of Harlequin* (1724), the work that comes closest to *Tumble-Down Dick* in its aims and methods; Fielding may well have read it.[10] This play, which with its stage directions for audience reaction was presumably aimed at the intelligent reading public and not intended for the stage, was a satirical response to two very popular pantomimes based on the Faust legend that were staged at the end of 1723. The dancing master John Thurmond produced his *Harlequin Doctor Faustus; with The Masque of the Deities* at Drury Lane in November 1723. This was so successful that Rich followed suit at Lincoln's Inn Fields in December with *The Necromancer; or, Harlequin Doctor Faustus*, which was even more successful, remaining in the repertoire for the next fifty years.[11]

Thurmond's entertainment is a veritable anthology of stage tricks, such as Mephistophiles' entry on the back of a flying dragon which is spitting fire, and Faustus' numerous conjurings (making a table run around) and transformations (a statue on a pedestal into a woman, and the pedestal into a chariot drawn by dogs). The pantomime reaches its spectacular climax with the burning of a barn, after which Faustus is torn into pieces by devils as he descends into hell through flames. The mythological section comes at the very end as a coda. Rich's pantomime opens seriously enough with Faustus' inner struggle as in Marlowe's tragedy, but magic takes over as soon as he acquires his wand. In one scene a table prepared for a feast materializes from a wall, and when Faustus finds his servant about to drink some of the wine, he makes the bottle fly out of the servant's hand and the poured wine vanish in a flash of fire. The high point of the production was the windmill scene, where Faustus is chased up and down the mill by the miller, who has found the Doctor flirting with his wife. The scene reaches its climax when the miller is caught on one of the sails and carried round and round while Faustus runs off with his wife. Faustus returns in an extraordinary disguise rather like a giant and performs a dance, but even though the miller and his assistant cut off his arms and head he goes on dancing. When they cut open his belly, an unharmed Faustus jumps out and chases them away. After a long mythological sequence featuring Hero, Leander, and Charon, a huge dragon devours Faustus to the exultant rejoicing of a chorus of devils.

The author of *The British Stage* clearly regarded the popular success of these two pantomimes as proof that the theatre was in a very sorry state. In his ironic Preface he expresses amazement that a windmill and a dragon should not only appear on the London stage but be received more enthusiastically than any orthodox play. The opening section of *The British Stage*, which leads into a satirical burlesque of the two Faust pantomimes, actually features a Dragon and a Windmill talking about their theatrical success to an Ass, who represents London 'grown old in Stupidity, and abandon'd to all Wit', and an Owl, who symbolizes the British theatre. Much of the author's attack on the debased taste of the town is embodied in the Ass, whose approval seems to increase in direct proportion to the degree of absurdity of the mock pantomime he witnesses; but this is reinforced by stage directions showing the audience to be captivated by the entertainment. With the arrival of Harlequin, who signs a contract with the Devil and receives a magic wand in return, the parallel to Thurmond's and Rich's pantomimes becomes clear. What follows is largely a selective imitation of these two works presented with burlesque exaggeration in a framework of ironic condemnation. Harlequin's transformation of the Ass into 'a modish Citizen, with Horns exalted on your Forehead', for example, is a satirical reference to the magical horning of two countrymen in Thurmond's pantomime. The episode in which Harlequin cuts off one of his legs and puts it on again also refers to Thurmond's pantomime; here a usurer cuts off Faustus' right leg as payment for the money owed to him, but Mephistophiles arrives at once with a large selection of self-propelled legs for Faustus to choose a replacement. The burlesque reaches its climax with the entry of the Dragon spitting fire, as in Thurmond's pantomime, an episode that the Ass regards as 'Wit in Perfection'. The Dragon's 'wonderful Tricks' include walking on two legs, kissing Harlequin, shouldering a musket, dancing a jig, and singing 'like an Eunuch'. A crude version of Faustus' emergence from what appears to be his own stomach in Rich's pantomime follows when the Dragon *'opens his Tail, and evacuates a Dancing-master'*. Ridicule of Rich's work is, however, most explicit in the character of the Windmill, who is expected to sing at one point but being hoarse dances instead. Even by the standards of pantomime a dancing Windmill is somewhat absurd, but the implication is that it is hardly more absurd than the usual characteristics of pantomime.

Like *The British Stage*, the other specific burlesque of pantomime before *Tumble-Down Dick*, *The English Stage Italianiz'd* (1727), was intended for the reader, not the stage, and was never produced. Although this satirical travesty was published as the work of Thomas D'Urfey, it is almost certainly not by him since he died in 1723, but its unmitigated vulgarity looks back to the cruder side of the Restoration theatre and to D'Urfey's contributions to it. The Introduction to *The English Stage Italianiz'd* is a witty and ironic as well as xenophobic diatribe against the Italian invasion of the English stage in the eighteenth century, but there is no sign of either wit or irony in the scenario for the burlesque mime play. This is a very coarse version of the story of Dido and Aeneas, incorporating all the regular characters of pantomime; Harlequin, for example, appears as Dido's head butler and is in love with the Queen, while Colombine is a coquettish nymphomaniac. The action resembles that of a farcical intrigue comedy with amorous pursuits galore, involving love potions and procuring. At one point Harlequin leads Aeneas to Colombine's apartment where

> they strive which shall most express their Love in dumb Shew: *Æneas* kisses her Hand, *Harlequin* kisses her Foot, *Æneas* her Face, *Harlequin* her A-se. After many Struggles, *Æneas* takes the Chamber-Pot and drinks it all off. (II, xii)

When Aeneas and Colombine flee together from Dido, there is a typical pantomimic chase before Dido finally goes mad. Because she believes that her Maids of Honour are a flock of sheep, they bleat to her, and when she is brought 'a Mess of Caudle' by Pantaloon, 'she throws it in his Face and scalds him' (v, v). Harlequin hangs himself, but the Doctor

> blows Wind up his Fundament, and restores him to life; *Harlequin* not having stal'd for some time, the first Thing he does is to make Water, which he does with a Vengeance, lugging out his Wherewithal, and pissing out *Scaramouch's* Eyes, who tumbles against one and t'other, and affords great Diversion.
> (v, xi)

As these quotations illustrate, there is hardly a trace of genuine burlesque invention and humour in the entire mock pantomime, which depends for its satiric effect on the replacement of conventional pantomimic situations by silliness and gross indecency. Compared with *Tumble-Down Dick*, or even *The British Stage*, *The English Stage Italianiz'd* is puerile in conception, but its extreme abusiveness is a measure of its author's almost violent hostility to pantomime on patriotic and aesthetic grounds.

Tumble-Down Dick; or, Phaeton in the Suds is the most comprehensive and by far the best satire of pantomime in dramatic form. Fielding based his burlesque on a popular pantomime by William Pritchard called *The Fall of Phaeton: with Harlequin a Captive*, first produced in February 1736 at Drury Lane and not at Rich's Covent Garden.[12] Nevertheless, Rich seems to have been involved to some extent in this production and is the target of Fielding's superb mock dedication, addressed to him under his stage name of Lun and signed 'Pasquin'. After referring to his own ridicule of dedications in *Pasquin*, Fielding proceeds to adulate Rich but in such a way that the intention is unmistakable:

> It is to you, sir, we owe (if not the invention) at least the bringing into a fashion, that sort of writing which you have pleased to distinguish by the name of Entertainment. Your success herein (whether owing to your heels or your head I will not determine) sufficiently entitles you to all respect from the inferior dabblers in things of this nature ... for I fancy you have too strong a head ever to meddle with Common-sense, especially since you have found the way so well to succeed without her, and you are too great and good a Manager, to keep a needless supernumerary in your house.

The main title itself alludes to Rich. 'Tumble-Down' refers to the element of tumbling in his performances as Harlequin; and 'Dick', being the familiar form of 'Richard', is an oblique way of referring to both 'Rich' and 'Pritchard'. The more obvious but slightly longer and less alliterative 'Tumble-Down Richard' would have been a rather cumbersome title.

The alternative title of Fielding's play – 'in the suds' carries the meanings 'sulking' and 'perplexed' as well as alluding to the lathery shaving scene in a barber's shop during the first mock harlequinade – obviously parodies that of Pritchard's pantomime, and the extended description on the title page continues the parody. *Tumble-Down Dick* is not a dance play, but 'A Dramatic Entertainment of Walking in Serious and Foolish Characters Interlarded with Burlesque, Grotesque, Comic Interludes called Harlequin a Pick-Pocket ...Being ('tis hoped) the last Entertainment that will ever be Exhibited on any Stage'. By attributing *Tumble-Down Dick* to three foreigners, Fielding attacks the encroachment of Continental influence on the English stage and at the same time parodies the title page of *The Fall of Phaeton*, which credits Pritchard for the invention of the pantomime, Arne for the music, and Hayman for the sets. *Tumble-Down Dick* is said to have been devised by 'the ingenious Monsieur Sans Esprit', with music by 'the harmonious Signior Warblerini', and scenery by 'the prodigious Mynheer Van Bottom-Flat'.

For the most part, Fielding's mock pantomime follows the conventional form of pantomimes, including *The Fall of Phaeton*, and features the same characters as Pritchard's work. But the 'serious' is a travesty of the Phaeton story, not a solemn retelling of it as in *The Fall of Phaeton*, and the 'comic' presents Harlequin as a rogue and a thief, not as the victim of other people's machinations as he usually is in pantomime. *Tumble-Down Dick* has some affinity, therefore, with earlier classical travesties, such as Mottley and Cooke's *Penelope* and Gay's *Achilles*, although it differs from these in being a rehearsal play. Like Bayes in *The Rehearsal*, Machine presents his ludicrous pantomime to two commentators, Fustian and Sneerwell, as a very serious piece of theatre and makes considerable claims for it:

> . . . in tragedies and comedies, and such sort of things, the audiences will make great allowances; but they expect more from an entertainment; here, if the least thing be out of order, they never pass it by.

For Fustian, Machine's entertainment is 'an insipid dessert' after the 'luscious meal' of his own tragedy, while for Sneerwell it is something ridiculous to be laughed at, but Machine believes that 'things of this nature are above criticism'. When Fustian understandably mistakes the 'serious' for the 'comic', Machine patiently explains that 'the serious in an entertainment answers to the sublime in writing'; and when Fustian inquires whether there is any classical precedent for the introduction of the goddess Aurora's washerwoman, Machine smugly replies that 'if she's not in the ancients, I have improved upon the ancients'. Even though he objects to being questioned about his classical sources, Machine does claim classical authority for the harlequinade: 'You know sir, or may know, that Aristotle, in his book concerning entertainments, has laid it down as a principal rule, that Harlequin is always to escape.' Machine's presumption, ignorance, and stupidity establish him as one of the best Bayes-figures since Buckingham's original.

In *The Fall of Phaeton*, Phaeton, the son of Phoebus (the Sun God) and Clymene (a sea nymph), is upset when Epaphus (the son of Jupiter and Io) casts doubt on his paternity. Clymene's reaction to the rumour that she is promiscuous is to advise Phaeton to visit Phoebus and to *'beg some indubitable Mark, that should for ever convince the World of the Virtue of his Mother, and the Divinity of his Father'*, as Pritchard's brief Argument puts it. To convince Phaeton that he is indeed his father, Phoebus promises him anything he asks for, but immediately regrets his generosity when Phaeton announces that he wants to drive the chariot of the Sun through the sky for one day. Against his better judgement, Phoebus grants this request in order to honour his pledge. As Phoebus foresaw, Phaeton is unable to control the horses, who fall out of their usual course and nearly produce a conflagration of the world. At the request of Neptune and

Terra, Jupiter intervenes and destroys Phaeton for his presumption. Pritchard's pantomime ends with Neptune and Jupiter prevailing upon the distressed Phoebus to reassume his task. The text of *The Fall of Phaeton* indicates that two comic interludes constituting *Harlequin a Captive* were incorporated in the production, one after Phaeton's visit to Phoebus and the other after Phaeton's death, but there is no description of these harlequinades.

In his mock pantomime Fielding provides contemporary low-life parallels to these mythological events and characters, following *The Fall of Phaeton* very closely. An earthy tone and urban setting replace Pritchard's refined pastoral world. At one point Fielding even introduces a song in praise of gin and a dance by 'the rakes and whores' of King's Coffee-House, a particularly notorious haunt of prostitutes and their clients in Covent Garden. Clymene is an immoral oyster-wench married to a cobbler, Old Phaeton, a character mentioned by 'neither Ovid nor Mr. Pritchard', as Fustian observes. Phoebus is the chief of the watch. Instead of driving the chariot of the Sun, he carries a lantern, and he is not to be found in a temple but in the Roundhouse, the lock-up used as a headquarters by the watch. Fielding's presentation of Phoebus as a watchman makes him a particularly ridiculous figure because the watch were traditional figures of fun (as in Gay's *The Mohocks*) who were not noted for their courage, honesty, or competence. They were often accused of running away from trouble and of spending more time drinking in alehouses than on patrol. When they arrive to arrest Harlequin in the first comic interlude in *Tumble-Down Dick*, they are *'walking in their sleep'*. Machine's argument that a watchman's lantern is as appropriate a representation of Phoebus' chariot 'as ever you saw any thing on any stage' is consequently imbecilic. The other deities are just as un-godlike as Phoebus. Neptune appears as a Thames waterman; Terra enters dancing the White Joke with a dancing master; and Jupiter is armed with a pair of bellows to 'blow out the candle of the Sun'. In *The Fall of Phaeton*, Aurora, the Dawn Goddess, appears 'Sweet, blushing from her Lover's Bed' to usher in the sunrise:

> Now Nature all around she chears,
> For all around is Pleasure spread.

What Machine calls the 'second serious, or sublime' section of his pantomime opens with Aurora berating her maid for taking so long to wash and iron her shifts:

> Make haste, you drone, for if I longer stay,
> The Sun will rise before the break of day;
> Nor can I go till my clean linen's done:
> How will a dirty morning look in June?

Plate 10: Glumdalca and Huncamunca competing for the hand of Tom Thumb (Hogarth's frontispiece in the 1731 edition of *The Tragedy of Tragedies*).

Plate 11: First of six prints constituting Hogarth's 'Harlot's Progress' (1732).

Plate 12: 'Author's Benefit Ticket' for *Pasquin*, with Firebrand stabbing Queen Common-Sense, Queen Ignorance bestowing her favour on Italian opera (Farinelli) and pantomime (Harlequin Rich), and the Theatrical Barometer showing Folly to be very much in the ascendant (Hogarth? 1736).

Plate 13: 'The Judgment of the Queen o' Common Sense Address'd to Henry Fielding' (kneeling), an allegorical print endorsing his satire in *Pasquin* and featuring characters from it (1736).

Plate 14: 'Rich's Glory, or His Triumphant Entry into Covent Garden', a satire featuring Rich as Harlequin and marking the opening of his new theatre in Covent Garden (Hogarth? 1732).

Plate 15: 'Punch Kicking Apollo', a satire featuring Harlequin and allegorically attacking pantomimic entertainments for displacing poetry from the stage (1729?).

Plate 16: 'A Just View of the British Stage, or Three Heads Are Better than None', Hogarth's satire on the condition of the theatre, alluding to John Rich's Faustus pantomime and attacking the three Drury Lane managers, Colley Cibber, Barton Booth and Robert Wilks, for debasing the stage by competing with Rich's entertainments (1724).

Plate 17: 'The Stage Mutiny', John Laguerre's satire about the theatre war featuring Theophilus Cibber in his costume as Pistol (1733).

Plate 18: Satirical portrait of Farinelli (1737).

Plate 19: Last of eight prints constituting 'R-b-n's Progress in Eight Scenes', one of a number of satirical responses to the failure of the Excise Bill, featuring Walpole in an elevated though very precarious position and his effigy being hanged (1733).

Plate 20: 'The Festival of the Golden Rump', a satire featuring George II as a satyr on the altar, Queen Caroline as a priestess, and Walpole as chief magician (1737).

Plate 21: Queen Fadladinida and the King of the Antipodeans in *Chrononhotonthologos* (detail from the frontispiece to the 1734 edition).

At the opening of the mock pantomime, Phaeton is downcast because the parish boys, who are equivalent to the nymphs and swains in Pritchard's pantomime, have accused Clymene of being a whore and have said that his father is not Phoebus but 'a serjeant of the Foot-guards'. Phaeton goes to the Roundhouse to obtain from his father 'some indubitable mark, that should convince the world that his mother was a virtuous woman, and whore to Phoebus'. Phoebus agrees to let Phaeton carry his lantern for a day, but according to Fielding's Argument Phaeton falls asleep on duty, as the watch were often accused of doing, and 'was tumbled out of the wheelbarrow', a burlesque equivalent of Phoebus' chariot. When Phaeton falls, his lantern *'hangs hovering in the air'* and menaces the world with its heat until Jupiter arrives with his bellows. The 'serious' ends with a dismal Phoebus setting off again with his lantern, and a concupiscent Jupiter looking forward to a sexual escapade proposed by his pimp, Neptune.

As in *The Fall of Phaeton* two Harlequin episodes are incorporated in *Tumble-Down Dick*. The first occurs in the same place as in Pritchard's pantomime (after Phaeton's visit to Phoebus), but there is a significant change in the position of the second. In *The Fall of Phaeton* the second comic interlude is inserted after Phaeton's fall and before the final scene in the Palace of the Sun, which ends triumphantly with a Grand Dance of the deities. In *Tumble-Down Dick* the second Harlequin episode follows the burlesque equivalent of Pritchard's final scene instead of preceding it. Whereas Pritchard adheres to conventional pantomimic form by bringing *The Fall of Phaeton* to an end with a supposedly awesome scene among the gods, Fielding distorts that form by concluding his mock pantomime with a burlesque harlequinade.

Fielding's burlesque of pantomime differs from his burlesque of tragedy in *The Tragedy of Tragedies* and *The Covent-Garden Tragedy* in that it relies on a very close (at times, line-by-line) parody of one particular work. *The Covent-Garden Tragedy* does, of course, derive from one tragedy, but it follows *The Distrest Mother* in a much less precise way than *Tumble-Down Dick* does *The Fall of Phaeton*. Pritchard's pantomime opens in a *'Magnificent Garden'* with Phaeton, who is *'leaning against a Tree, in a pensive Posture'*, being questioned by his mother about the reason for his unhappiness:

> Why seems my *Phaeton* with Care opprest?
> What Grief, or Pain, sits heavy on thy Breast?

Fielding's mock pantomime opens in a *'Cobbler's Stall'* with Phaeton, who is *'leaning against the scene'*, being rebuked by his mother in what Machine absurdly claims to be 'the true altercative, or scolding style of the ancients':

> CLYMENE You lazy, lousy rascal, is't well done,
>   That you, the heir-apparent of the Sun,
>   Stand with your arms before you like a lout,
>   When your great father has two hours set out,
>   And bears his lanthorn all the world about?
> YOUNG PHAETON Oh mother, mother, think you it sounds well,
>   That the Sun's son in cobbler's stall should dwell?
>   Think you it does not on my soul encroach,
>   To walk on foot while father keeps a coach?

Pritchard's Clymene expresses her maternal concern in an elevated idiom. Fielding also employs rhyming couplets, but his energetic, colloquial style is a travesty of Pritchard's pompous rhetoric. Because it strains too hard to be worthy of its subject, the exclamatory idiom of *The Fall of Phaeton* thoroughly deserves Fielding's criticism, but it is certainly no worse and possibly somewhat better than that of other pantomimes incorporating dialogue.

The scene in which Phaeton visits his father shows how closely Fielding follows Pritchard on occasion, even retaining entire lines. In *The Fall of Phaeton*, Phoebus is seated *'on his Throne, in the Palace of the* Sun, *attended by the* Hours *and* Seasons':

> PHAETON What do I see! what Beams of Heav'nly Light
>   Pour on my Eyes, too strong for Mortal Sight.
> PHOEBUS O! tell me, *Phaeton*,
>   Tell, what strange Cause cou'd hither bring my Son?
> PHAETON Father! (if I may call thee by that Name)
>   I come to clear my own, and Mother's Fame:
>   But, Oh my Sire!

In *Tumble-Down Dick* Phoebus is seated '*in a great chair in the Round-house, attended by* Watchmen':

> YOUNG PHAETON What do I see? What beams of candle-light
>   Break from that lanthorn and put out my sight?
> PHOEBUS O little Phaey! pr'ythee tell me why
>   Thou tak'st this evening's walk into the sky?
> YOUNG PHAETON Father, if I may call thee by that name,
>   I come to clear my own and mother's fame:
>   To prove myself thy bastard, her thy miss.

Verbally, the two passages are similar, even identical at times, but in tone they are completely different. By substituting 'candle' for 'Heav'nly' and the ludicrous 'Phaey' for '*Phaeton*', and by making Young Phaeton state in the last line the purpose of his mission in a blunt way that would have shattered the decorous veneer of *The Fall of Phaeton*, Fielding transforms Pritchard's ponderous handling of this scene into farcical burlesque.

In *The Rehearsal* Buckingham parodies a speech in Dryden's *The Conquest of Granada* by substituting pigs for turtle doves, and Fielding's burlesque of Pritchard's emotionalism works in the same way in his close parody of Clymene's maternal lament for the dead Phaeton. Pritchard's Clymene is totally disconsolate, and in a song she compares herself to a nightingale who discovers that her young have been killed:

> *Then to some Grove retires, alone,*
> *Filling with plaintive Strains the Skies,*
> *There warbles out her tuneful Moan,*
> *'Till o'er th'unfinish'd Note she dies.*

What troubles Fielding's Clymene is that she has reached her menopause and will not be able 'to get another son'; she too sings, comparing herself not to a romantic bird but to an owl who finds 'Her young owls dead as mice':

> Then to some hollow tree she flies,
> To hollow, hoot, and howl,
> Till every boy that passes, cries,
> The devil's in the owl!

On other occasions Fielding achieves an equally amusing result by compressing a long-winded speech from *The Fall of Phaeton* into a pithy, parodic equivalent. In Pritchard's pantomime Phaeton's request to take Phoebus' place for a day is particularly orotund; he is full of self-importance and treats his proposed journey as momentous:

> Then let me, since that Vow must ne'er be vain,
> Drive thy fierce Steeds along th'Ætherial Plain;
> And guide thy fiery Chariot for a Day,
> While radiant Beams around my Temples play;
> Then wond'ring Mortals shall with Envy know,
> 'Tis *Phaeton* that lights the World below.

In *Tumble-Down Dick* this speech is reduced to a burlesque couplet, providing an extreme contrast to Pritchard's high-flown rhetoric. Young Phaeton makes his request in a completely casual way as though he were asking for nothing at all:

> Then let me, since that vow must ne'er be broke,
> Carry, one day, that lanthorn for a joke.

In the second 'serious' of *Tumble-Down Dick* Fielding sometimes abandons couplets for prose, as in the episode in which three Countrymen discuss the peculiar movement and excessive heat of the sun. Their uncouth colloquial dialogue is the opposite of the stilted utterances of the Priests who play the equivalent role in *The*

Fall of Phaeton. Fielding transforms the Second Priest's very literary cry of anguish, 'Alas! what sudden Change we've undergone! / Varying our Colour with th'approaching Sun', into the decidedly more urgent words of the Second Countryman, 'It's woundy hot, the skin is almost burnt off my face; I warrant I'm as black as a blackmoor'. The First Priest's declaration that the imminent destruction of the Earth is an act of divine retribution, 'Forgive, O *Phoebus*! for thy Beams are hurl'd / With Vengeance, to destroy an impious World!', becomes, in Fielding's handling, the expression of the Third Countryman's guilty conscience because of his recently committed adultery: 'Oh, neighbours! the world is at an end: call up the parson of the parish: I am but just got up from my neighbour's wife, and have not had time to say my prayers since.'

An even more extreme travesty is the final dialogue between the gods, equivalent to the concluding scene in *The Fall of Phaeton*. When Machine introduces this episode, he proudly claims that after 'a scene in heroics between a cobbler and his wife; now you shall have a scene in mere prose between several gods'. Puzzled by this reversal of expectation, Fustian suggests that it would have been more natural to have things the other way round, but Machine silences any opposition with his usual unanswerable illogic:

> You think it would have been more natural; so do I, and for that very reason have avoided it; for the chief beauty of an entertainment, sir, is to be unnatural.

After the death of Phaeton in Pritchard's pantomime, Jupiter, accompanied by Neptune, appeals to Phoebus to 'restore the Day' by driving his chariot through the sky:

> Take, take your Steeds, dispel the Gloom of Night,
> And chear again all Nature with your Light.

Fielding's Jupiter phrases his request very differently:

> Harkye, you Phoebus, will you take up your lanthorn and set out, sir, or no? For by Styx! I'll put somebody else in your place, if you do not; I will not have the world left in darkness, because you are out of humour.

Pritchard's Phoebus, who is very distressed at the loss of his son, at first refuses but agrees when the all-powerful Jupiter threatens him with the same fate as Phaeton unless he complies. Fielding's Phoebus also obeys Jupiter reluctantly, but as he sets out he is contemplating a sexual adventure rather than indulging in paternal grief: 'Well, if I must, I must; and since you have destroyed my son, I must find out some handsome wench and get another.'

What makes this particular scene so telling is that the deities actually discuss the presentation of pantomimes in the London theatres, including Rich's performances as Harlequin. When urging Phoebus to return to his appointed task as Sun God, Jupiter warns him that he is not indispensable:

> JUPITER I shall dispute with you here no longer; so either take up your lanthorn, and mind your business, or I'll dispose of it to somebody else. I would not have you think I want suns, for there were two very fine ones that shone together at Drury Lane play-house; I myself saw 'em, for I was in the same entertainment.
> PHOEBUS I saw 'em too, but they were more like moons than suns; and as like any thing else as either. You had better send for the sun from Covent Garden house, there's a sun that hatches an egg there, and produces a Harlequin.

Although this almost surreal suggestion of a hatching Harlequin may seem far-fetched, it refers to one of Rich's most famous pieces of pantomimic acting, the emergence of Harlequin from a shell like a chick in Theobald's *Harlequin a Sorcerer* (1729). Fielding's attack on Rich is particularly insulting because Jupiter reveals that the Harlequin-egg 'was laid by an ass'. Even Jupiter, who admits that he conferred Harlequin's magic powers on him, is worried about Harlequin's abuse of those powers and his total indifference to criticism:

> He has turned all nature topsy turvy, and not content with that, in one of his entertainments he was bringing all the devils in hell up to heaven by a machine, but I happened to perceive him, and stopt him by the way. . . . he has been damned a thousand times over; but he values it not a rush; the devils themselves are afraid of him; he makes them sing and dance whenever he pleases.

The entire stage presentation of *Tumble-Down Dick*, especially the mock harlequinades, was a visual burlesque of pantomimic spectacle, but even in the 'serious' Fielding singles out particular features for ridicule. Dances were an important ingredient of pantomime and in many cases were introduced gratuitously. In *The Fall of Phaeton*, the Hours and Seasons attending on Phoebus in his palace break into a dance without any reason whatever shortly after the arrival of Phaeton. Indeed, the dance actually interrupts the conversation between Phoebus and Phaeton just as it turns to the crucial issue of their relationship. In the equivalent scene in *Tumble-Down Dick*, there is an equally arbitrary burlesque dance of the Watchmen, which according to Phoebus shows that the gods 'lead as merry lives as folks below'. Phaeton, whose main concern is to establish that Phoebus is his father, rightly points out, as Pritchard's Phaeton does not, that the dance is hardly an answer to his problem and solves nothing. When asked by Fustian what dramatic purpose the dance serves, Machine can offer only the feeblest of explanations, but he does so with supreme confidence in his own artistic judgement:

> Why, sir? why, as all dances are introduced, for the sake of the dance. Besides, sir, would it not look very unnatural in Phoebus to give his son no entertainment after so long an absence?

As far as Machine is concerned, any excuse is good enough for a dance. He tells Neptune and Terra to 'dance a minuet by way of thanksgiving' when Jupiter puts out the candle representing the Sun, but his most absurd dance is that of Terra and the dancing master. Even though the heat of the Sun is threatening her kingdom with imminent destruction, Terra is so devoted to dancing that she refuses to stop:

> Though all the earth was one continual smoke,
> 'Twould not prevent my dancing the White Joke.

Fielding's burlesque of spectacular scenes is as closely linked with his satirical treatment of Machine as is his ridicule of dances. In the dawn section of the second 'serious', the stars are represented by *'two or three girls carrying farthing candles'*, and Machine explains that with the rising of the Sun 'the candles will go out', signifying the disappearance of the stars from sight. Fustian expresses amazement, even horror, at this ludicrous piece of 'spectacle', but Machine leaps to his own defence, arguing that he should be permitted as much artistic licence as any other pantomimist:

> Why will you not allow me the same latitude that is allowed to all other composers of entertainments? Does not a dragon descend from hell in Doctor Faustus? And people go up to hell in Pluto and Proserpine? Does not a squib represent a thunderbolt in the rape of Proserpine? And what are all the suns, sir, that have ever shone upon the stage, but candles? And if they represent the Sun, I think they may very well represent the stars.

Machine's 'defence' succeeds in damning not only himself but all other pantomimists as well. Shortly afterwards, Fielding burlesques the excessive use for spectacular effect that pantomimists made of entrances and exits through trap doors and from the flies. In *The Fall of Phaeton*, Neptune *'rises'*, presumably from the depths of the ocean, to complain to Jupiter about the effect of the Sun's heat on his domain; Terra also emerges from below with a similar complaint, and both deities *'sink'* after Phaeton's fall. Fielding travesties this device by having Neptune descend from the sky announcing that he is 'the mighty emperor of the sea'. Fustian observes that such an entrance would be more appropriate for 'the emperor of the air', but Machine, as always, is quick to provide a thoroughly inane rationalization that could satisfy no one but himself:

> Sir, he has been making a visit to Jupiter. Besides, sir, it is here introduced with great beauty: for we may very naturally suppose, that the Sun being drove by Phaeton so near the earth, had exhaled all the sea up into the air.

Fielding's burlesque of the harlequinades in pantomimes is, of necessity, almost entirely visual. The success of his mock harlequinades must therefore have depended largely on the skill with which the actors ridiculed the characteristic behaviour of Harlequin and the other *commedia dell 'arte* figures of pantomime, and on the way in which the burlesque scenic devices and stage effects were presented. Considering that the 'serious' in *Tumble-Down Dick* parodies *The Fall of Phaeton* so closely, one would expect Fielding's 'comic' (*Harlequin a Pick-Pocket*) to parody the harlequinade incorporated in Pritchard's pantomime (*Harlequin a Captive*) just as closely; but since the text of *The Fall of Phaeton* contains no account of the two comic interludes, it is impossible to be certain, even though the one piece of relevant evidence suggests that it does. In Pritchard's first comic interlude, Harlequin is addressed by 'a friendly Spright' called Genius, who has been enclosed in a tree by a wicked magician because he was 'Virtue's firm Friend, a Lover of Mankind'. Genius' speech, the only extant part of *Harlequin a Captive*, contains some strong words of advice about the wisdom of following the path of virtue:

> Let not your Mind to lawless Wishes stray,
> If virtuous, all things shall thy Will obey;
> Let *Colombine*, alone, your Passion move,
> And sure Success shall crown your faithful Love.

In Machine's first 'comic', a very different kind of 'spirit', the Genius of Gin, appears to Harlequin by rising out of a tub, and utters a travesty, but not a parody, of Genius' moral exhortation:

> Thou shalt make jests without a head,
> And judge of plays though canst not read.
> Whores and race-horses shall be thine,
> Champagne shall be thy only wine;
> Whilst the best poet, and best player,
> Shall both be forced to feed on air;
> Gin's genius all these things reveals,
> Thou shalt perform, by slight of heels.

There is a strong element of personal abuse in these lines because Fielding pokes fun at Rich's lack of education, extravagant tastes, and unintellectual pursuits. The various references to gin reflect on the so-called Gin Act of 1736, a widely resented excise measure designed to curb the ready availability of very cheap crude gin that had led to immoderate and sometimes fatal gin drinking by many lower-class Londoners.

The first 'comic' in *Tumble-Down Dick* is, like most harlequinades, a farcical chase in which Harlequin is pursued by the other characters, but Fielding's Harlequin is a thief and the villain of the piece, not the innocent victim as in orthodox pantomime. Even Thurmond's *Harlequin Sheppard* (1724), based on the robber Jack Sheppard's daring escape from the condemned cell in Newgate that made him legendary, is a tribute to Sheppard's courage and determination, not a condemnation of his criminal life; and in the Faust pantomimes, Harlequin is by no means villainous even though he meets the unpleasant end reserved for the Faust figure, as in Marlowe's tragedy. Fielding's Harlequin therefore has something in common with the burlesque Harlequin of *The English Stage Italianiz'd*, whose criminal activities include stealing the meat from Aeneas' plate and defrauding Dido's army. During the song in praise of gin at the opening of the mock harlequinade, Harlequin busily plies his trade by picking the pockets of the habitués of King's Coffee-House. By specifying that Harlequin steals a play from a poet, Fielding ingeniously dramatizes the accusation sometimes made against Rich that he plagiarized the work of contemporary playwrights for his pantomimes, especially plays he was offered for Covent Garden and turned down. Harlequin is caught, and is taken into custody by sleep-walking watchmen. It seems quite likely that this episode, with Harlequin as a prisoner, is based on an incident in *Harlequin a Captive*, if that title is a reliable guide to content. It is at this point that the Genius of Gin provides Harlequin with a magic wand. Harlequin's case is brought before an illiterate magistrate, who is seduced and bribed by Columbine into releasing Harlequin and imprisoning the poet. Columbine, like Harlequin, is therefore the antithesis of the naive and virtuous innocent of conventional pantomime.

The chase now begins. Instead of showing the magistrate gratitude for his miscarriage of justice, Harlequin gives him a violent blow and then runs away. Columbine tries to follow him but is prevented by the Justice's Clerk, who appears as the Pierrot of pantomime. In order to rescue Columbine, Harlequin returns to the magistrate's house inside a large china jar brought by two chairmen. The Justice is so pleased with the jar that he offers it to Columbine as a present, but Harlequin suddenly emerges from it and puts both the Justice and Pierrot to flight. Harlequin and Columbine are in turn pursued by the Justice and his Clerk. In one scene, Harlequin puts Columbine into a barber's chair and prepares to shave her. It is only by going to such bizarre extremes as this that Fielding is able to burlesque the fantastic world of pantomime at all. When their pursuers arrive, Harlequin blinds the Clerk with soap suds and magically transforms the Justice into a periwig block. Machine is delighted at what he calls the 'wit and humour' of this episode, and is puzzled when Fustian objects to transformations as 'odd'. To Machine, the transformation of a man into a periwig block is 'not odd at all' but very 'natural and easy'. By the standards of pantomime, this may indeed be so, but Fustian's interjection establishes just how unnatural those standards are. Machine's first 'comic' ends with more horseplay when Harlequin throws the Clerk into a trough in the barber's shop before setting off with Columbine.

The burlesque chase continues in Machine's other 'comic', with which *Tumble-Down Dick* ends, but it takes second place to Fielding's ridicule of the two licensed theatres for promoting pantomime at the expense of serious drama. As a result, the second 'comic' is not so much a satirical burlesque of harlequinades as an attack in pantomimic form on theatre managers. Covent Garden and Drury Lane are presented side by side on stage, together with their two Managers, representing Rich and Fleetwood respectively, and the Drury Lane Manager's right-hand man Pistol, who corresponds to Theophilus Cibber. Pistol was one of his favourite roles, and he had already been satirized under that name in *The Stage-Mutineers*, an anonymous play about the theatre war of 1733-34. Pistol's sack full of actors' contracts leads Fustian to complain about the poor pay of ordinary English actors compared with Continental performers, but as far as Machine is concerned pantomimists are infinitely more important than conventional actors, and this view is embodied in his entertainment. As soon as Harlequin and Columbine enter, both Managers court them assiduously, ignoring completely the Tragedy King and the Tragedy Queen who have approached them in the hope of employment. The Managers become even more excited when a dog dressed as Harlequin arrives, and after the burlesque element recurs with the entry of the Justice and his Clerk in pursuit of Harlequin and Columbine, the Covent Garden Manager picks up the dog before running off. The allusion to Rich's performance as a dog in *Perseus and Andromeda* reinforces the similar one in *Pasquin*.

In the final scene, the Justice threatens to commit a cartload of actors to prison as vagrants under an Act of 1713 that in real life was shortly to become the basis of Walpole's Licensing Act. Fielding is here referring to the increasing demand by many magistrates for more control of the theatres, especially the new, unpatented theatres like Fielding's own New Haymarket, which were claimed to be veritable hotbeds of immorality. In 1733 and again in 1735 parliamentary Bills were introduced to achieve this purpose, but both failed because of the strong opposition to any increase in Government censorship of the stage. However, when the Justice is offered two hundred pounds a year to become an actor, he accepts and is immediately transformed into a Harlequin, who joins the actors in the cart to sing the praises of Harlequin. In this profoundly satirical song, Fielding explains the popularity of 'Harlequin feats' by showing how closely 'the tricks of the stage' mirror the 'tricks' of real life – the widespread hypocrisy and corruption of 'court, country, and town', of both public and private life in Walpole's England. Fielding presents Harlequin as a perfect emblem of the merchant, the politician, and the courtier, all three being as slippery and chameleon-like as Harlequin. With its simultaneous ridicule of Harlequin and the Establishment, this concluding song cleverly ties together the various satirical strands that run through *Pasquin* and *Tumble-Down Dick*, and so helps to bind the two plays together into a single large-scale dramatic structure.

In *Tumble-Down Dick* social and political satire is incidental rather than central, but Fielding does not omit it altogether. The Justice, for example, takes his place in the rogues' gallery of ignorant and corrupt magistrates extending from Justice Squeezum in *The Coffee-House Politician* to Justice Thrasher in *Amelia*. On his first appearance in the mock harlequinade, he is being taught to spell; although 'a very ingenious man, and a very great scholar' according to Machine, he 'happened to have the misfortune in his youth never to learn to read'. The Justice subsequently succumbs to a bribe from Columbine for the release of Harlequin, and Machine's comment that Harlequin probably never 'escaped in a more natural manner' considerably enhances the satire. The distorted sexual values of high society also come under attack, as they do so often in Fielding's work from *The Modern Husband* to *Amelia*. When Old Phaeton angrily upbraids Clymene for cuckolding him by sleeping with Phoebus and for broadcasting her infidelity, she explains that he is really more at fault than she is. She argues that a truly modish husband in tune with the ways of the world would regard it as an honour rather than a disgrace for his wife to be the mistress of an important man; in the 'great cuckold's school' of London, every married man 'is glad to be the cuckold of his betters'. Clymene's earlier expression of this view in a passage parodying Pritchard's Clymene leads to an exposure of widespread moral anomalies in society in Air 11, 'Great courtiers palaces contain', on the theme, 'If you are rich, your vices men adore, / But hate and scorn your virtues, if you're poor'. The ironic play on the word 'great' throughout this song recalls *The Beggar's Opera*, especially as Walpole is obviously being alluded to; the closing lines about 'the great rogue' living 'in vogue' while 'small rogues are by dozens hanged' echo Air LVI in Gay's ballad opera (Lockit explains that if he and Peachum did not behave '*like the Great'* they would hang *'like poor petty rascals'*).[13]

Of all Fielding's plays, *Tumble-Down Dick* is the one that most closely corresponds to *The Rehearsal*. Like Buckingham, Fielding uses the rehearsal method to ridicule simultaneously a popular dramatic form and its principal exponent. Where Fielding differs from Buckingham is that he succeeds in mounting a three-pronged attack on Rich through the characters of Machine, Harlequin, and the Covent Garden Manager; Buckingham satirizes Dryden solely through the figure of Bayes. *Tumble-Down Dick* is also an ideal complement to *Pasquin*. As an afterpiece burlesquing pantomimic afterpieces, it dovetails perfectly into a full-length satirical play itself using the rehearsal method, and is therefore the antithesis of virtually all afterpieces, which were staged after the main play without any regard to their appropriateness. Produced together, *Pasquin* and *Tumble-Down Dick* conformed to the expected arrangement of an evening's entertainment at the theatre, but they provided a trenchant assault on such an evening's entertainment and on a host of other things as well.

NOTES

1. Quotations from *Pasquin* are taken from the edition of O. M. Brack, William Kupersmith, and Curt A. Zimansky (Iowa City, 1973).
2. See Emmett L. Avery, 'Foreign Performers in the London Theatres in the Early Eighteenth Century', *Philological Quarterly* 16 (1937) 105-23.
3. For further information on this point, see the second of my 'Three Notes on Fielding's Plays', *Notes and Queries* 21 (1974) 253-5.
4. In 'Some Notes on the Early Eighteenth-Century Pantomime', *Studies in Philology* 32 (1935) 598-607, Mitchell P. Wells establishes that in the eighteenth century the term 'pantomime' was reserved for productions such as Rich's and was not used to describe genuine *commedia dell'arte* performances by companies from France and Italy.
5. For a detailed study of Harlequin in England, see Cyril W. Beaumont, *The History of Harlequin* (London, 1926), especially chs 9-10. Leo Hughes gives an excellent account of the development of English pantomime in *A Century of English Farce*, 94-119. See also Emmett L. Avery, 'Dancing and Pantomime on the English Stage, 1700-1737', *Studies in Philology* 31 (1934) 417-52.
6. *A General View of the Stage* (London, 1759), 77-8.
7. *Ibid.*, 80.
8. *Ibid.*, 78.
9. 'The Defense and Criticism of Pantomimic Entertainments in the Early Eighteenth Century', *Journal of English Literary History* 5 (1938) 129.

10. For suggestions about the play's possible influence on Fielding, see the first of my 'Three Notes on Fielding's Plays'.
11. For a detailed examination of these two pantomimes, see Elvena M. Green, 'John Rich's Art of Pantomime as Seen in his *The Necromancer, or Harlequin Doctor Faustus*: A Comparison of the Two Faustus Pantomimes at Lincoln's-Inn-Fields and Drury Lane', *Restoration and 18th Century Theatre Research 4, 1* (1965) 47-60.
12. The only detailed comparison of the two plays is by Charles W. Nichols, 'Fielding's *Tumble-Down Dick*', *Modern Language Notes 38* (1923) 410-16.
13. In 'Political Allusion in Fielding's *Author's Farce, Mock Doctor*, and *Tumble-Down Dick*', 228-31, Sheridan Baker argues that the play contains extensive anti-Walpole satire, but some of his suggestions are over-ingenious and highly speculative.

Eurydice, The Historical Register for the Year 1736, and Eurydice Hiss'd

The 1736–37 season was Fielding's last as a dramatist and as a man of the theatre. His first new play of the season was a short satirical ballad farce called *Eurydice; or, The Devil Henpecked*, which was produced as an afterpiece to *Cato* at Drury Lane on 19 February 1737. Unfortunately there was a serious disturbance at the theatre that evening, sparked off by noisy footmen. The actors managed to complete *Cato* but abandoned *Eurydice* because of the uproar. The last straw seems to have been Fielding's presentation of Captain Weazel, a caricature of an army beau that was interpreted as an insult to the British army and therefore deeply resented. The outcome was that *Eurydice* suffered the same fate as *The Covent-Garden Tragedy* of being withdrawn immediately. When Fielding published the play in his *Miscellanies*, he provided the short and accurate description: 'As it was d-mned at the Theatre Royal in Drury Lane'. Even though the damning was due more to bad luck than to public distaste for the subject matter or to any dramatic defect, the play, like *The Covent-Garden Tragedy*, has often been regarded as an artistic failure because of its failure in the theatre. *Eurydice* is certainly slighter than a number of Fielding's plays, but simply as a farce it is lively and amusing, and there is more to it than his label of 'Farce' may suggest.

Although not a parodic or imitative satire of contemporary drama in the sense that *The Tragedy of Tragedies*, *The Covent-Garden Tragedy*, and *Tumble-Down Dick* are, *Eurydice* deserves to be considered as a dramatic burlesque for several reasons. Like *The Author's Farce*, *Pasquin*, and *Tumble-Down Dick*, it makes use of a rehearsal structure; like *Tumble-Down Dick*, it is a classical travesty; and like *The Author's Farce*, it ridicules Italian opera. Largely because the Author is not a Bayes-figure as Trapwit, Fustian, and Machine are in *Pasquin* and *Tumble-Down Dick*, Fielding does not develop the rehearsal framework to any great extent, but the dialogue between the Author and the Critic does help to emphasize the social and theatrical satire of the inner play. Towards the end of *Eurydice*, the Author justifies Orpheus' resort to recitative after losing Eurydice by arguing that it happened just as he lost his senses. I wish our opera composers could give as good a reason for their Recitativo.

CRITIC What, would you have them bring nothing but mad people together into their operas?

AUTHOR Sir, if they did not bring abundance of mad people together into their operas, they would not be able to subsist long at the extravagant prices they do, nor their singers to keep useless mistresses; which, by the bye, is a very ingenious burlesque on our taste.

CRITIC Ay, how so?

AUTHOR Why, sir, for an English people to support an extravagant Italian opera, of which they understand nor relish neither the sense nor the sound, is as heartily ridiculous and much of a piece with an eunuch's keeping a mistress: nor do I know whether this ability is more despised by his mistress, or our taste by our singers.

Fielding's use of the title *Eurydice*, rather than *Orpheus* or *Orpheus and Eurydice*, suggests that he intended the play to be, at least in part, a burlesque reply to an opera by Paolo Antonio Rolli called *Orpheus (Orfeo)*, which had been successfully produced at the Opera House towards the end of the previous season (March–June 1736). It is conceivable that Fielding also had in mind an anonymous pantomime called *Harlequin Orpheus; or, The Magical Pipe*, which had had a fairly good run at Drury Lane in 1735, or other pantomimes featuring some of the characters found in *Eurydice*. Nevertheless, *Eurydice* follows much more closely in the footsteps of two earlier classical travesties in prose, Gay's *Achilles* and Breval's *The Rape of Helen*, than it does in those of *Tumble-Down Dick*. Classical travesty and parodic burlesque, farce and satire, are inseparable in *Tumble-Down Dick*, whereas farce tends to predominate in *Eurydice*, in spite of its burlesque texture and the parallel to *Orpheus*. The reason for this is that *Eurydice* contains very little specific burlesque of Italian opera and does not parody Rolli's opera at all. Fielding's ridicule is implicit in his farcical treatment of characters and events accorded solemn treatment in *Orpheus*, but is not taken much beyond this, except for such non-burlesque passages as the Author's invective against opera. The only explicit reference to pantomime occurs immediately before the concluding chorus and dance, when Proserpine asks Pluto to provide dancers for the holiday celebration she is preparing: 'I desire you would wave your wand, and conjure back some of your devils that dance at the play-houses in the other world.'

The action of *Eurydice* is a farcical version of the classical story about Orpheus' descent to the underworld to retrieve his dead wife. In Rolli's opera, on the other hand, only three scenes are set in

Hades (I, i and III, ii-iii). The action of *Orpheus* encompasses the courtship of Orpheus and Eurydice, Eurydice's death, Orpheus' journey to the underworld to reclaim her, and their successful return to the real world. *Eurydice* deals only with the episode in Hades. The setting is therefore very similar to that of the Puppet Show in *The Author's Farce*, the land of the dead beyond the Styx, but the precise location of the Puppet Show is the Court of Nonsense whereas that of *Eurydice* is the Court of Pluto and Proserpine, which is the equivalent of hell. The henpecked devil of the alternative title turns out to be Pluto himself. Orpheus, who according to legend could charm anyone with the beauty of his voice, is appropriately transformed into an Italian singer and sometimes called Signior Orpheo. He almost certainly corresponds to the current male star of the Opera House in London, Farinelli, referred to in *Pasquin* as 'Faribelly'. Although comparable in some ways to Signior Opera in *The Author's Farce*, Orpheus differs from him in that he speaks far more than he sings, a feature of the play that is explained by the Author: 'I do not care to tire the audience with too much Recitativo; I observe they go to sleep at it at an opera.' Pluto and Proserpine are not the dignified deities and devoted couple of Rolli's *Orpheus*, but the stereotyped husband and wife of farce, constantly locked in marital combat like Lycomedes and Theaspe in *Achilles* and Menelaus and Helen in *The Rape of Helen*. Eurydice, too, is the antithesis of her namesake in *Orpheus*.

Fielding derives much of the humour of his play from the presentation of marriage as a state of war. The main joke is that Orpheus, having lost his wife, not only wants her back but actually makes the journey to Hades to recover her. Pluto observes that to grant Orpheus' request will not establish a dangerous precedent, 'for as he is the first man who ever desired to have his wife again, it is possible he may be the last'. Proserpine, on the other hand, while admitting that Orpheus' request is sufficiently amazing to be called a 'miracle', is determined that Eurydice shall not be delivered to Orpheus since she has already been 'confined within the fetters of matrimony' for more than a year and it would be another 'miracle' if she wanted to return to her husband. Despite Proserpine's threats, Pluto succumbs to the power of music when Orpheus sings, and grants his request. In her anger at her husband's decision, Proserpine lays down the condition that Eurydice must return to Hades if Orpheus looks at her during their journey to the other world. In Rolli's opera there is no mention of this condition; Proserpine is as much affected by Orpheus' singing as Pluto, and agrees with him that Eurydice should return with Orpheus. In spite of Orpheus' apparent devotion to his wife in *Eurydice*, their marriage is really no different from that of Pluto and Proserpine. As soon as they are left on their own, they indulge in squabbling and mutual recrimination. The last thing that Eurydice wants to do is to leave Hades for the real hell of married life, and she uses all her feminine wiles to invent reasons for not travelling with Orpheus. Eventually she outwits her husband by tricking him into looking at her during the journey, thus ensuring her return to the joys of hell.

The closest approach to genuine satirical burlesque in *Eurydice* is a passage of recitative shared by Orpheus and Eurydice when it seems that Pluto will not allow Eurydice to leave the underworld with her husband. The mock solemnity of their encounter is aimed at emotional scenes between parting lovers in Italian opera, as is the separation scene between Macheath and Polly in *The Beggar's Opera*; but the verbal repetitions at the end of this passage make it even more similar to Gay's burlesque of the forced separations of lovers in pathetic tragedy, the parting of Kitty and Filbert in *The What D'Ye Call It*:

> ORPHEUS Oh, my Eurydice! the cruel king,
>   Still obdurate, refuses to my arms
>   The repossession of my love.
> EURYDICE Unkind Fate,
>   So soon to put an end to all our joys!
>   And barbarous law of Erebus
>   That will not reinstate us in our bliss.
> ORPHEUS And must you stay?
> EURYDICE And must you go?
> ORPHEUS Oh no!
> EURYDICE 'Tis so.
> ORPHEUS Oh no!
> EURYDICE 'Tis so.

The other passages of recitative and the various airs sung by Orpheus and Eurydice are not without burlesque significance, but like most of Signior Opera's songs in *The Author's Farce* their ridicule of Italian opera is implied rather than satirically imitative, with the probable exception in performance of falsetto delivery by Orpheus. Orpheus' lament, 'Farewell, ye groves and mountains' (Air III), sung immediately after the above recitative, is the only song that seems to owe anything to the arias in *Orpheus*. In Rolli's opera Orpheus sings a not dissimilar aria, 'Mormorando pietosi o Ruscelletti' (I, v), in very different circumstances; he feels that his love for Eurydice is not requited.

Fielding makes at least as much fun of the cult of opera and of English audiences as he does of the form itself. Spindle, a court beau recently arrived in Hades, surmises that Signior Orpheo's most likely destination after leaving the underworld is England; and through Pluto's enraptured response to Orpheus' singing, Fielding mocks the modish devotees of Italian opera in London. After Orpheus' first grief-stricken recitative and air in which he pleads to have his wife restored to him, Pluto is so excited that he can hardly control himself: *'O caro, caro* – (What shall I do? If I hear another song I am vanquished.)' He is indeed 'vanquished' by Orpheus' next song, and this time he really does seem to take leave of his senses: 'I am conquered; by Styx, you shall have her back. Take my wife too; take every thing; another song, and take my crown.' Fielding also provides an interesting and amusing gloss on the popularity of Italian singers among fashionable English women. Both Captain Weazel and Spindle believe that the modern way to a woman's heart is through her ears and that Orpheus' voice is what tempts Eurydice to return to the world with him; but Eurydice, who patently does not believe that 'the merit of a man, like that of a nightingale, lies in his throat', dismisses these suggestions as the jejune psychologizing of beaux. The real reasons are sexual, because 'music puts softer and better things' in a woman's head than 'the signior that's singing', as she explains in Air 1:

> When a woman lies expiring
>   At fal, lal, lal, lal, la!
> Do you think her, sir, desiring
>   Nothing more than ha, ha, ha?

Finally, Fielding cannot resist a joke at the expense of the castrati. As a lover of Italian music, Charon deeply regrets that he has been unable to ferry a Signior Quaverino across the Styx to Hades, but the law specifies that no one can 'come into this country but men and women', and Signior Quaverino fails to qualify, being 'neither the one nor the other'.

Fielding's social and political satire is mainly directed against the beau monde, although lawyers and 'great men' do not escape unscathed. He presents Hades as indistinguishable from fashionable London except that, in Spindle's words, it is 'not quite so wicked'. Captain Weazel, who divides his time 'between cards, dice, music, taverns, wenches, masquerades', assures the newcomer Spindle that hell is 'the only place a fine gentleman ought to be in'. Spindle, who 'goes to the devil, not out of any inclination, but because it is the fashion', hopes to devote himself to 'one dear swing of raking, drinking, whoring, and playing the devil, as I have done in the other world'. Since the Court of Pluto and Proserpine is equated with upper-class London, it is possible that the henpecked ruler and his cunning, domineering wife correspond to George 11 and Queen Caroline, who did exert a strong influence on both her husband and Walpole, but Fielding never makes this explicit.

As a comic treatment of a classical myth, *Eurydice* is at least as successful as *Achilles* and *The Rape of Helen,* and it deserved a better fate in the theatre than it received. At the same time it is a comparatively lightweight work for Fielding at this time. Even though the social, political, and theatrical satire are cleverly integrated into the action and setting of *Eurydice*, they still seem rather peripheral to the farcical core of the play, the travesty of the Orpheus legend. The burlesque of Italian opera, while pervasive, is not developed at all fully. This does not mean that Fielding's satire and burlesque are ineffective; but they are decidedly not as intense as in *Pasquin* and *Tumble-Down Dick*, not to mention his next two plays, *The Historical Register for the Year 1736* and *Eurydice Hiss'd*. At times Fielding develops the farcical potential of his material purely for its own sake, without attempting to fuse farce with satirical burlesque as in *Tumble-Down Dick*, or with political satire as in *The Grub-Street Opera*. Consequently it is less inappropriate to call *Eurydice* a farce than any of his other burlesque and satirical plays.

It seems that after writing *Eurydice* Fielding began work on his third 'mythological' or 'classical' play but abandoned it after the disastrous reception of *Eurydice*. All that remains of this comedy, *Jupiter's Descent on Earth*, is an extended Introduction consisting of four short scenes, which Fielding published in *Miscellanies* under the title of *An Interlude between Jupiter, Juno, Apollo, and Mercury*. Had it been completed, *Jupiter's Descent on Earth* would have differed in purpose and method from both *Tumble-Down Dick* and *Eurydice*. It would certainly not have been a satirical burlesque of contemporary drama like *Tumble-Down Dick*, and it would have been more serious than *Eurydice*, essentially a dramatic satire like *Pasquin* rather than a farce; Fielding significantly uses the word 'Comedy' to describe it, not 'Farce' as in the case of *Eurydice*. Unlike the other two plays, it would not have travestied a classical story. As the title suggests and as *An Interlude* makes clear, the play would have dealt with a visit to the Earth by Jupiter in order to examine the state of human society. Because of his own honesty and integrity, Jupiter is hardly aware of the existence of lying, deception, hypocrisy, and flattery, and the core of the play would have been the collapse of his romantic illusions about mankind in the face of the widespread corruption, injustice, vice, and folly he discovers in human life. Although totally different in approach, *Jupiter's Descent on Earth* might well have resembled *Pasquin* in its profound satirical survey of contemporary society.[1]

When Fielding returned to London after spending the last few months of 1736 in Dorset, he immediately resumed his activities as 'Great Mogul' of the New Haymarket. As a theatre manager he had already shown himself to be extremely independent, specializing in new plays, especially satires and burlesques. He usually offered a very different kind of theatrical evening from Drury Lane, Covent Garden, and the Opera House, and by attracting good audiences demonstrated that the public could be entertained by more challenging plays than the standard fare of the older theatres. During his second and last season as a theatre manager, he became even more outspoken than he had been during his first, using the theatre quite literally as a platform from which to launch daring attacks on the Establishment and particularly on Walpole. The first of Fielding's two new plays for the New Haymarket, *The Historical Register*, opened on 21 March 1737 as an afterpiece to Lillo's tragedy, *Guilt Its Own Punishment; or, Fatal Curiosity* (1736), a play Fielding championed for its realism. According to the pro-Walpole newspaper *The Daily Gazetteer*, Fielding's new play was an attempt to overthrow the Ministry, and even if this accusation is somewhat exaggerated, it does make it clear that the New Haymarket had become a particularly sharp thorn in the side of the Government.

The Historical Register, like *Pasquin* in the previous season, was an immediate success, which is not surprising considering that it is in many ways a sequel to *Pasquin*. Both plays attempt an ambitious critical survey of English manners and morals; both expose the corruptness of political life, the self-seeking of men in public service, and the false values of the beau monde; both condemn aspects of the contemporary theatre; both hold well-known personalities up to scorn; and both employ a rehearsal framework. The most obvious differences are superficial; *The Historical Register* is shorter than *Pasquin* (three acts as opposed to five), even more episodic in structure, and its satire tends to be more direct and acerbic. Nevertheless, there are two significant differences of major relevance to the present study. In *Pasquin* Fielding includes a modicum of burlesque and uses the rehearsal method to ridicule contemporary dramatists, whereas in *The Historical Register* he does neither of these. Fielding's theatrical satire is aimed not at contemporary drama but almost exclusively at actors and theatre managers, notably Colley and Theophilus Cibber. Furthermore, Medley, the author of the inner play, is not a Bayes-figure, but the antithesis of a Bayes-figure, being Fielding's spokesman and possibly even a self-portrait:

> ... my design is to ridicule the vicious and foolish customs of the age, and that in a fair manner, without fear, favor, or ill-nature, and without scurrility, ill manners, or commonplace. I hope to expose the reigning follies in such a manner that men shall laugh themselves out of them before they feel that they are touched. (1)[2]

It is the two 'critics' to whom Medley presents his play who are the figures of fun; Sourwit, a sycophantic beau, and Lord Dapper, an inane and conceited aristocrat, are therefore the antitheses of Buckingham's Johnson and Smith. Dapper dislikes the New Haymarket not because it is difficult to see or hear the actors but because

> one can't see! One's self, I mean. Here are no looking glasses. I love Lincoln's Inn Fields, for that reason, better than any house in town. (1)

When Sourwit argues that Medley is breaking all the neoclassical rules by compressing the events of an entire year into a short play, it is the author and not the critic who comes out on top:

> Sir, I have several answers to make to your objection. In the first place, my piece is not of a nature confined to any rules, as being avowedly irregular, but if it was otherwise, I think I could quote you precedents of plays that neglect them. Besides, sir, if I comprise the whole actions of a year in half an hour, will you blame me or those who have done so little in that time? My register is not to be filled like those of vulgar news-writers with trash for want of news, and therefore if I say little or nothing, you may thank those who have done little or nothing. (1)

Fielding also departs from Buckingham's model in his treatment of the actors, who actually approve of the play they are about to rehearse, even though one of them feels that the satire should be 'a little stronger, a little plainer', something not easy to accomplish.

Fielding's total reversal of the orthodox rehearsal procedure allows him to hammer home the social and political satire of the inner play through the voice of Medley, and at the same time to ridicule in Sourwit and Dapper two characteristic figures of London high society. But this reversal does mean that Fielding completely abandons the purpose for which Buckingham originally developed the rehearsal technique; it is even more radical than his adaptation of Buckingham's method in *The Author's Farce* and *Pasquin*. What Fielding does is to take his transformation of the rehearsal method one stage further than he does in *Pasquin*, in which the discussion surrounding the inner plays ridicules the two dramatists in much the same way as in *The Rehearsal*, even though Trapwit's comedy and Fustian's tragedy are not burlesques like Bayes' heroic play. The result is that *The Historical Register* is a satire in the form of a rehearsal without a trace of imitative burlesque. It is easy to see how *The Historical Register* derives via *Pasquin* from the burlesque tradition rooted in *The Rehearsal*, but the play itself maintains only a tenuous connection with that tradition by means of its structure.[3]

The play takes its title from an annual publication of the same name, containing a supposedly impartial résumé of the major events of the past year and listing the births, deaths, marriages, and promotions of the social élite. Fielding's *Historical Register*, which travesties the official one, is anything but unbiased, and in his attempt to diagnose the ills of contemporary England he provides a caustic view of the 'major' social, political, and theatrical events of the year. In form, the play is a series of unrelated episodes, as befits an annual register, but it is given a measure of formal and thematic coherence by the rehearsal framework and the unwaveringly satirical standpoint. The first and last of the six episodes constituting the inner play are the most explicitly political, both the First Politician in the first episode and Quidam in the sixth episode being defamatory portraits of Walpole. Fielding's social satire is concentrated in the second and third episodes. In the first of these, he pours scorn on the affected women of high society whose obsessions with the *primo castrato* of Italian opera, Farinelli, and with modish trivia are symptomatic of the increasing 'luxury, effeminacy, and debauchery' of English life (II). The third episode is based on Christopher Cock's fashionable auction sales which were always well attended by the beau monde. The auctioneer in *The Historical Register* is Christopher Hen, who was played by a woman, and the auction is of 'such things as were never sold in any auction before, nor ever will again' (II). In satirizing Cock's auctions, Fielding exposes to ridicule the priorities of fashionable society and also provides a profoundly ironic commentary on such things as 'political honesty', 'patriotism', and 'modesty', showing in particular how words are abused by politicians.

Most of Fielding's satire relating to the theatre is directed against leading personalities. The theatrical target in the second episode, for example, is Farinelli, not Italian opera. Similarly, the passing references to pantomime are essentially hits at Rich. Lot 5 in Hen's auction is 'the wit lately belonging to Mr. Hugh Pantomime, composer of entertainments for the playhouses' (II), who could not be anyone but Rich. At the very end of the play there is a satirical jab at Rich under his stage name when Medley describes the cunning way in which Quidam regains his bribes as 'a very pretty pantomime trick, and an ingenious burlesque on all the *fourberies* which the great Lun has exhibited in all his entertainments' (III). Despite these remarks, the dance of the Patriots with holes in their pockets, so that they lose the bribes Quidam has given them, is not in fact presented as a burlesque of pantomime, but described as such in retrospect to link Walpole with Rich and so with Harlequin. Throughout the play Medley draws attention to the 'strict resemblance between the states political and theatrical' (II), claiming that both are in an equally deplorable condition, and the suggestion that Walpole is the harlequin of politics produces an interesting fusion of theatrical and political satire.

The most extended piece of theatrical satire, the fifth of the six episodes, is itself not devoid of political significance. The opening of this episode, with Apollo (i.e. Phoebus) *'in a great chair, surrounded by attendants'* (III), is similar to the scene in *Tumble-Down Dick* in which Phoebus sits *in a great chair in the Round-house, attended by Watchmen*. As in the earlier play Apollo is not the true Sun God but a mock-heroic substitute. Being the person responsible for 'the entire direction of all our playhouses and poetical performances', Apollo is identified with Charles Fleetwood, the patentee of Drury Lane, and less directly, by means of the metaphorical equation of 'the states political and theatrical', with Walpole. The Prompter, on whom Apollo relies very heavily for suggestions, is modelled on W. R. Chetwood, the experienced Drury Lane prompter who did exert a strong influence on Fleetwood. In casting Shakespeare's *King John*, Apollo and the Prompter give the parts to friends and relations, however unsuitable, and to 'actors who will mind their cues'; this is just as much a criticism of Walpole, for appointing his minions to positions in public life because they knew how to 'mind their cues', as it is of Fleetwood. The political level is made quite clear by the Prompter's derogatory remarks in reply to Apollo's question, 'What is this Robert?', when they come to the part of Robert Faulconbridge.

The 'Apollo' episode culminates in a brilliant caricature of Colley Cibber under the damning name of Ground-Ivy, an indigenous British creeper. One of Cibber's most misguided endeavours in the field of playwriting was to 'tailor' *King John*, as the Marplays in *The Author's Farce* would have put it, turning it into a piece of anti-Catholic propaganda called *Papal Tyranny in the Reign of King John*. Although Cibber himself was convinced that this was a decided improvement on the original, nobody else seems to have shared his opinion. The Drury Lane company planned a production in 1736 but abandoned it when it was in rehearsal because they believed it would be a disaster. Fielding seized on this fiasco to attack Cibber in a way closely resembling his treatment of Marplay Senior in *The Author's Farce*. When Ground-Ivy arrives during the casting of *King John*, he surprises Apollo by telling him that the play 'as now writ will not do'. To Ground-Ivy, Shakespeare is not 'one of the greatest geniuses that ever lived', but 'a pretty fellow' who 'said some things which only want a little of my licking to do well enough'. Ground-Ivy's 'licking' is identical to Marplay Senior's 'tailoring'; he will improve Shakespeare by 'alteration':

> It was a maxim of mine, when I was at the head of theatrical affairs, that no play, though ever so good, would do without alteration. For instance, in the play before us the Bastard *Faulconbridge* is a most effeminate character, for which reason I would cut him out and put all his sentiments in the mouth of *Constance*, who is so much properer to speak them. (III)

Colley Cibber actually made this and equally drastic changes, partly out of misplaced neoclassical zeal for what Ground-Ivy calls 'propriety of character, dignity of diction, and emphasis of sentiment'. At a time when a more purist attitude towards Shakespeare was emerging, thanks to his recent editors, Rowe, Pope, and Theobald, Medley's ironic observations on Cibber's mutilation of Shakespeare would have met with approval:

> ... as Shakespeare is already good enough for people of taste, he must be altered to the palates of those who have none; and if you will grant that, who can be properer to alter him for the worse? (III)

Fielding also ridicules Colley Cibber's poetic efforts as Poet Laureate. In *Pasquin* he had made fun of Cibber's laughably bad odes, but in *The Historical Register* he actually burlesques them. In place of the customary prologue, Medley begins his play with an 'Ode to the New Year', which he claims to be 'the very quintessence and cream of all the odes I have seen for several years last past' and therefore totally lacking in 'wit'. The opening of this mock ode recalls some lines from Doodle's and Noodle's speeches at the beginning of *The Tragedy of Tragedies*:

> This is a day in days of yore,
> Our fathers never saw before:
> This is a day, 'tis one to ten,
> Our sons will never see again.
>   Then sing the day,
>   And sing the song,
>   And thus be merry
>   All day long. (I)

This probably does surpass Cibber's annual New Year's Day odes in inanity, but Fielding's inanity is the deliberate nonsense of burlesque whereas Cibber's is the imaginative bankruptcy of a bad poet.

Like his father, Theophilus Cibber comes in for his share of Fielding's unloving attention. As in *Tumble-Down Dick*, he appears as Pistol, an 'insignificant fellow in town who fancies himself of great consequence and is of none' (III). Medley's intention is 'to exhibit' Pistol not as an actor but as a theatre manager, but the mention of Pistol's 'ministerial' function suggests that Walpole is again an indirect target of the satire. The brief 'Pistol' episode, the fourth of the six, derives from one of the most celebrated quarrels in English theatrical history. At the end of 1736 Fleetwood planned a production of *The Beggar's Opera* at Drury Lane, but an unexpected difficulty arose over casting. Fleetwood initially selected Susannah Cibber (Theophilus' wife) to play Polly, but changed his mind when Kitty Clive, the leading lady of the company, objected to being given the lesser role of Lucy. Throughout November and

December the newspapers fanned the flames of this controversy, and a satirical afterpiece about it, Henry Woodward's *The Beggar's Pantomime; or, The Contending Colombines,* was produced at Lincoln's Inn Fields in December. Before the end of the month, Woodward extended his satire of the affair by incorporating into his play a brief sequel called *Pistol in Mourning.* In this revised version, Pistol feels insulted when Mrs Roberts (Kitty Clive) rather than Mrs Hamilton (Susannah Cibber), whom he has intervened to support, is given the leading role. In *The Historical Register* too, Pistol, who regards himself as 'Prime Minister theatrical' and consequently employs a high style, is mortified 'that we should with an upstart of the stage / Contend successless on our consort's side'. Pistol appeals to the crowd, who have assembled to see him 'run mad' in the streets of London, to side with him:

> Say then, O town, is it your royal will
> That my great consort represent the part
> Of Polly Peachum in *The Beggar's Opera*? [*Mob hiss* (11)

Because he has been brought up to interpret a hiss as a mark of approval, Pistol is delighted by this response and recalls the similar honour accorded to two of his father's plays, *Caesar in Egypt* (1724) and *Love in a Riddle* (1729), both of which were poorly received, and deserved by a third, the recent *Papal Tyranny in the Reign of King John*:

> Thanks to the town – that hiss speaks their assent.
> Such was the hiss that spoke the great applause
> Our mighty father met with when he brought
> His *Riddle* on the stage. Such was the hiss
> Welcomed his *Caesar* to the Egyptian shore;
> Such was the hiss in which great *John* should have expired.
> But wherefore do I try in vain to number
> Those glorious hisses which from age to age
> Our family has borne triumphant from the stage? (11)

There is a further reference to the quarrel over *The Beggar's Opera* between the fifth and sixth episodes when Sourwit asks Medley, 'What's become of your two Pollys?', to be told that 'they were damned at my first rehearsal, for which reason I have cut them out; and to tell you the truth, I think the town has honored 'em enough with talking of 'em for a whole month' (III).

Ridicule of theatrical personalities, especially playwrights, is a feature of rehearsal plays that stems from Buckingham's presentation of Dryden as Bayes, but it is almost always closely linked with burlesque and satire of particular plays and dramatic genres. *Tumble-Down Dick* is eminently orthodox in this respect, and even in *The Author's Farce* Fielding's attack on theatre managers is thematically, though not formally, connected with the satire in the Puppet Show.

What is so different about *The Historical Register* is that the personal abuse of theatrical figures is an end in itself. Fielding concentrates his satire on the two theatrical events of 1736 that caused serious embarrassment to the Cibber family, the damning of *Papal Tyranny in the Reign of King John* in rehearsal and the dispute over the casting of Polly Peachum. It is true that in the 'Apollo' episode Medley defends Shakespeare from all writers who have attempted to 'improve' his plays: 'I have too great an honor for Shakespeare to think of burlesquing him, and to be sure of not burlesquing him I will never attempt to alter him, for fear of burlesquing him by accident, as perhaps some others have done' (III). But there is no doubt that Fielding's principal intention in dealing with the rewriting of Shakespeare was to make Colley Cibber a laughing stock. Fielding's inclusion of these two choice pieces of theatrical gossip in his *Register* of the most important events of 1736 admirably suits his purpose of castigating Walpole's England, but it also demonstrates just how far removed from the burlesque tradition the play is.

On 13 April 1737 *The Historical Register* was presented for the first time as a mainpiece and was followed by a new afterpiece, *Eurydice Hiss'd; or, A Word to the Wise,* also a rehearsal play. The relationship between these two plays is similar to that between *Pasquin* and *Tumble-Down Dick.* The rehearsal of a tragedy by Spatter in *Eurydice Hiss'd* follows the rehearsal of Medley's play in *The Historical Register* in much the same way as Machine's pantomime follows Fustian's tragedy in the earlier pair of plays. Lord Dapper and Sourwit are again the 'critics' and behave exactly as they do in *The Historical Register.* Lord Dapper, for example, is very anxious for the rehearsal to begin, otherwise 'I sha'nt get my hair powdered before dinner, for I am always four hours about it'. Like *Tumble-Down Dick, Eurydice Hiss'd* can stand on its own, but because it is grafted onto an existing play it is also part of a dramatic structure subsuming both plays; when *The Historical Register* and *Eurydice Hiss'd* were published in May 1737 they appeared together. Again like *Tumble-Down Dick, Eurydice Hiss'd* is more truly a dramatic burlesque than the play it follows, but considering the extreme unorthodoxy of *The Historical Register* as a rehearsal play this does not mean that *Eurydice Hiss'd* actually resembles *Tumble-Down Dick.* Even *Pasquin* is more orthodox than *Eurydice Hiss'd* in some ways.

Technically *Eurydice Hiss'd* is a most curious and intricate work. All rehearsal plays are plays about plays, but *Eurydice Hiss'd* goes one better, being a play about a play about a play. Furthermore, the innermost play is one of Fielding's; the rehearsed play, Spatter's *The Damnation of Eurydice,* deals with the failure of *Eurydice* at Drury Lane. Spatter, who is presented as the author of *Eurydice* as well as of *The Damnation of Eurydice,* is not a Bayes-figure, but a semi-ironic self-portrait, rather like Medley in *The Historical Register*. When asked about his tragedy, Spatter explains that after being condemned for *Eurydice* he is offering his new play as an act of 'atonement', and that in writing about one of his dramatic flops he has hit on a clever way of achieving theatrical success: 'for as the town have damned my play for their own sakes, they will not damn the damnation of it.' Yet he does not regard his play as a tragic masterpiece, as a Bayes-figure would have done, and willingly admits that his tragedy is 'ten times as ridiculous' as Medley's comedy. For Spatter, as for Fielding, it is better to be 'ridiculous than dull', better to make an audience laugh than to send them to sleep. In *The Damnation of Eurydice*, the author of *Eurydice* is presented as Pillage, the 'hero' of Spatter's tragedy, but he is much more Bayes-like than Spatter. *Eurydice Hiss'd* therefore contains not just one but two self-portraits of Fielding, the more important of which, Pillage, is really a self-caricature. Considered as the Bayes-figure in *Eurydice Hiss'd*, Pillage is unique. He is not the author of the inner play but its principal character; and although he is one of Fielding's targets, he is also equated with Fielding in some respects. The rehearsal method could hardly become more involuted than this.

Not surprisingly, the inner play also departs from Buckingham's model, but not quite to the extent that Trapwit's and Fustian's plays in *Pasquin* do. *The Damnation of Eurydice* is more obviously a mock tragedy than Fustian's *The Life and Death of Common-Sense*, but even so it is not primarily an imitative satire of contemporary tragedy and, despite certain resemblances, is not really comparable to Bayes' play in *The Rehearsal* or to *The Tragedy of Tragedies* and *The Covent-Garden Tragedy*. *The Damnation of Eurydice* is a mock tragedy more in the way that *The Rape of the Lock* is a mock epic. Pope uses the discrepancy between style and content to criticize the beau monde, not classical epic. The main victim of the mock-heroic incongruity resulting from a non-tragic subject being given a tragic treatment in *The Damnation of Eurydice* is not eighteenth-century tragedy but Pillage. Fielding employs the same technique as in some of his burlesque attacks on drama, but his purpose is different.[4]

Since Pillage corresponds to Fielding himself to some extent, it may seem odd that he should be the main satirical butt of *Eurydice Hiss'd*, but Fielding is by no means indulging in self-flagellation. Throughout *Eurydice Hiss'd* the stage is a metaphor for politics, so that there is the same 'strict resemblance between the states political and theatrical' as in *The Historical Register*. By continuing the parallel drawn between the theatre and politics in the earlier play, Fielding integrates the two plays much more closely than he does *Pasquin* and *Tumble-Down Dick*, or even *The Election* and *The Life and Death of Common-Sense* in *Pasquin*. At the literal level, Pillage is a highly successful playwright and theatre manager like Fielding himself;

but at the metaphorical and more important level, he is the most influential and important politician in the land, Walpole. As Sourwit points out, Pillage is 'a very odd name for an author' and is not particularly meaningful at the literal level, but as a satirically descriptive name for Walpole it is very apt. The failure of *Eurydice* on the stage has its most obvious political counterpart in the failure of Walpole's Excise Bill in 1733, one of his few serious parliamentary setbacks.[5] Fielding's simultaneous presentation of himself and Walpole as Pillage is certainly unexpected and may seem puzzling at first sight, but it is also ingenious. By pretending to treat the damnation of *Eurydice* as a tragic calamity, Fielding invites his audience to laugh at him; but it is he, paradoxically, who has the last laugh. His friends and political allies would have admired his ability to laugh at himself in public, and they would also have appreciated the extreme impertinence of his identification of himself with Walpole and of the parallel he draws between the fates of *Eurydice* and the Excise Bill. Fielding's enemies and political opponents would have enjoyed the opportunity of laughing at him, especially as he himself provided it, but he cleverly turned the tables on them. By making them laugh at him, he trapped them into laughing at Walpole as well.

Even in Spatter's description of *The Damnation of Eurydice* to Sourwit, there are hints that the inner play is not really about what it appears to be about. The comic tragedy is

> of a most instructive kind and conveys to us a beautiful image of the instability of human greatness and the uncertainty of friends. You see here the author of a mighty farce at the very top and pinnacle of poetical or rather farcical greatness, followed, flattered and adored by a crowd of dependents. On a sudden, Fortune changing the scene, and his farce being damned, you see him become the scorn of his admirers and deserted and abandoned by all those who courted his favor and appeared the foremost to uphold and protect him.

If 'policy' is substituted for 'farce', and 'political greatness' for 'poetical or rather farcical greatness', the resemblance of Pillage to Walpole is clear. Pillage's first speech, with its startling suggestion that Cardinal Wolsey was a dramatist, makes the connection between politics and the theatre even more explicit:

> Who'd wish to be the author of a farce,
> Surrounded daily by a crowd of actors,
> Gaping for parts and never to be satisfied;
> Yet, say the wise, in loftier seats of life,
> Solicitation is the chief reward,
> And Wolsey's self, that mighty minister,

> In the full height and zenith of his power,
> Amid a crowd of sycophants and slaves,
> Was but perhaps the author of a farce,
> Perhaps a damned one too. 'Tis all a cheat,
> Some men play little farces and some great.

The reference to Wolsey is meant to bring to mind his fall and consequently to prefigure the fate of Pillage. It is therefore a prediction of Walpole's fall, which Fielding probably believed to be imminent but which did not occur for another five years.

The action of *The Damnation of Eurydice* obeys the neoclassical rules by being limited to the day on which Pillage's new farce is produced. At the literal level, the first episode, one of Pillage's levees, is a comic presentation of the successful Fielding being beseiged by 'actors soliciting for parts, printers for copies, boxkeepers, scene-men, fiddlers and candle-snuffers', although it would be wrong to make a simple equation between Pillage and Fielding even at this level. Since levees were receptions held by aristocrats, politicians, and other important figures in public life, which provided an opportunity for people to seek favours from men of greater influence than themselves, the idea of a 'poet's levee' strikes Sourwit as a contradiction in terms, but Spatter explains that his 'poet is a very Great Man'. At the political level, the levee is one of Walpole's in which he tries to ensure the support of his sycophants by promising to find them employment in the future. To guard against any adverse reaction to his new play, Pillage instructs his friends to attend the theatre and to applaud at the least sign of criticism. This recalls Bayes' similar reliance on his friends in *The Rehearsal*, but whereas Buckingham is simply ridiculing Dryden, Fielding's satire is not really theatrical at all. He is accusing Walpole of attempting to dupe the general public and to silence attacks on his policies and style of government, as Pillage's final speech establishes:

> Then I defy the town, if by my friends,
> Against their liking, I support my farce,
> And fill my loaded pockets with their pence,
> Let after-ages damn me if they please.

The next episode, Pillage's confrontation with his friend Honestus, is a complete contrast to the levee. Honestus is a just and impartial critic at the literal level, and the voice of moral integrity and incorruptibility at the political level. Pillage is eager to have under his wing 'one honest man' whom he can rely on for support, but Honestus cannot be bought and refuses Pillage's bribes:

> Faith, sir, my voice shall never be corrupt.
> If I approve your farce, I will applaud it:
> If not, I'll hiss it, though I hiss alone.

Honestus' extended denunciation of the ways in which playwrights, theatre managers, and biased critics try to predetermine the reception of new productions, regardless of their dramatic worth, is also an attack on corruption and injustice in politics:

> I rather hope to see the time when none
> Shall come prepared to censure or applaud,
> But merit always bear away the prize,
> If you have merit, take your merit's due;
> If not, why should a bungler in his art
> Keep off some better genius from the stage?

His subsequent complaint about the rising prices and declining standards of the theatre is also double-edged. It is certainly aimed at Fleetwood's management of Drury Lane, where admission prices had recently been put up, and probably at Rich's management of Covent Garden as well, but it is just as much a criticism of Walpole's financial policies and excise measures and of the quality of his Government. Pillage's defence is that there are new expenses to be met, but Honestus points out that, if this is so, the public have a right to expect value for money, an improvement in standards rather than the reverse:

> Then give us a good tragedy for our money,
> And let not Harlequin still pick our pockets
> With his low paltry tricks and juggling cheats
> Which any schoolboy, was he on the stage,
> Could do as well as he.

The combined ridicule of pantomime and Walpole recalls the 'Quidam' episode in *The Historical Register* where Walpole is also referred to as the harlequin of politics and accused of indulging in trickery for financial gain.

There is virtually no resemblance between Fielding and Pillage in the 'Honestus' episode, but the next episode, in which Pillage is visited by his Muse, is as much concerned with the writing of *Eurydice* as with politics. Pillage's Muse accuses him of being unfaithful to her by producing *Eurydice* with the help of some other muse. She speaks with the indignation and self-righteousness of a devoted wife who has just discovered that her husband has not only been sleeping with another woman but has had a child by her as well:

> PILLAGE Why wears my gentle Muse so stern a brow?
>   Why awful thus affects she to appear,
>   Where she delighted to be so serene?
> MUSE And dost thou ask, thou traitor, dost thou ask?
>   Art not thou conscious of the wrongs I bear,

> Neglected, slighted for a fresher Muse?
> I, whose fond heart too easily did yield
> My virgin joys and honor to thy arms
> And bore thee *Pasquin*.
> PILLAGE Where will this fury end?
> MUSE Ask thy base heart whose is *Eurydice*?

Fielding's splendid mock-heroic writing is directed against himself, but because the situation is not without parallels in contemporary drama, it also burlesques those passionate outbursts of jealousy almost invariably expressed in stilted rhetoric in tragedy. Indeed, this passage is strongly reminiscent of the burlesque quarrel between Bilkum and Stormandra in *The Covent-Garden Tragedy*, with its catalogue of questions, its repetitions of 'dost thou', and Stormandra's denunciatory 'base wretch'. Pillage convinces his Muse that her anger is unjustified because he alone is responsible for *Eurydice*, a 'trifling offspring of an idle hour' not worthy of her concern. Although this altercation seems to be devoid of political significance, Fielding may be alluding to Walpole's private life, in which his mistress took priority over his wife. It is after the reconciliation of Pillage and his Muse that political considerations come to the fore. Pillage's mention of 'scribblers who for hire / Would write away their country's liberties' provokes the Muse into a powerful piece of invective against such pro-Walpole hack writers for vindicating an oppressive régime. She would much rather 'indite the annual verse' required of the Poet Laureate, Colley Cibber, which is mercilessly parodied in *The Historical Register*, than have anything to do with 'wretches so below the muse'. The episode concludes with further burlesque of dramatic poetry, this time declarations of undying love. Pillage's ludicrous address to his Muse is couched in the high-flown figurative language usually reserved for those perfections of womanhood, sentimental heroines:

> Come to my arms, thou masterpiece of nature.
> The fairest rose first opening to the sun
> Bears not thy beauty, nor sends forth thy sweets,
> But that once gathered loses all its pride,
> Fades to the sight, and sickens to the smell.
> Thou, gathered, charmest every sense the more,
> Canst flourish and be gathered o'er and o'er.

Eurydice Hiss'd ends with the damnation of *Eurydice* and its effects on Pillage. Because the catastrophe of his tragedy is 'a thing of too horrible a nature', Spatter does not present it on stage but provides a description of it in true neoclassical manner. A member of the audience (the Third Gentleman) leaves the theatre to tell his friends about the disaster he has observed. Although the 'conscience' metaphor is the only explicit reference to corrupt politics, the description implicitly applies to the failure of the Excise Bill on its second reading as well as to the reception of *Eurydice*:

> 'Tis true. At first the pit seemed greatly pleased,
> And loud applauses through the benches rung,
> But as the plot began to open more,
> (A shallow plot) the claps less frequent grew
> Till by degrees a gentle hiss arose;
> This by a catcall from the gallery
> Was quickly seconded. Then followed claps,
> And long 'twixt claps and hisses did succeed
> A stern contention: victory hung dubious.
> So hangs the conscience, doubtful to determine,
> When honesty pleads here and there a bribe.
> At length from some ill-fated actor's mouth
> Sudden there issued forth a horrid dram,
> And from another rushed two gallons forth.
> The audience, as it were contagious air,
> All caught it, hallooed, catcalled, hissed and groaned.

The superbly controlled tone and sustained solemnity of this passage make it the finest example of mock-heroic writing in the play. There is no trace of parody, but with its parentheses and inversions it does burlesque the portentous and bombastic epic style so common in eighteenth-century tragedy, especially at moments of crisis.

Even Pillage's so-called friends have turned against him. As soon as the doom of the play was certain, his sycophants, who had cheered and applauded at first, not only abandoned their allegiance to him but led the hissing and booing. Honestus alone proves to be a true friend. Faced with disaster and disgrace, Pillage does not kill himself as a tragic hero would, but drinks himself into insensibility, as befits the 'hero' of a mock tragedy. At the political level, Fielding is alluding to Walpole's fondness for alcohol:

> PILLAGE Already I have drunk two bottles off
>   Of this fell potion and it now begins
>   To work its deadly purpose on my brain.
>   I'm giddy. Ha! My head begins to swim,
>   And see Eurydice all pale before me.
>   Why dost thou haunt me thus? I did not damn thee.
>   By Jove, there never was a better farce.
>   She beckons me – say – whether – blame the town
>   And not thy Pillage. – Now my brain's on fire!
>   My staggering senses dance and I am –
> HONESTUS   Drunk.
>   That word he should have said that ends the verse.

Pillage's failure to complete his speech resembles Queen Common-Sense's similar failure in Fustian's tragedy in *Pasquin*, both burlesquing tragic speeches curtailed by death. In fact, the whole of his drunk speech is a burlesque of the disjointed lines spoken by distraught and dying characters in Restoration and Augustan tragedy, such as Belvidera's last speeches in *Venice Preserv'd*, which are burlesqued in *The What d'Ye Call It*. Fielding may even have remembered Kitty's mad speech in Gay's play; its opening, 'Hah! – I am turn'd a stream' (II, viii), is half-echoed in Pillage's 'Ha! My head begins to swim', and both characters think they see a ghost. It is left to Honestus to sum up, and he does with a mock-sententious 'message' that ridicules the didactic final speeches with which many contemporary tragedies end:

> May men grow wiser, writers grow more scarce,
> And no man dare to make a simple farce.

This couplet recalls Lovegirlo's equally 'tragic' and 'moralistic' conclusion to *The Covent-Garden Tragedy*.

Whether or not Pillage is speaking for Fielding when he claims to have written 'nine scenes with spirit in one day', Fielding certainly did write some of his plays, including *Eurydice Hiss'd*, at great speed. Nevertheless, there is nothing careless or clumsy about this play, which stands out as one of his most brilliant and inventive. As a rehearsal play it is highly original, and the mock-heroic writing in the inner play is witty and accomplished. Yet despite its obvious links with the burlesque tradition, *Eurydice Hiss'd* is essentially a political allegory, not a satirical burlesque of contemporary drama. In themselves the passages of genuine burlesque are excellent, especially in the 'tragic' dénouement, but they are incidental to the real core of the play, the attack on Walpole. There can be no doubt that the real driving force behind the play was Fielding's desire to enlarge on his ridicule of Walpole in *The Historical Register*. Perhaps what is most impressive about the play is the sheer cleverness of its satirical method. Fielding obviously could not attack Walpole directly, but by treating the failure of *Eurydice* as a major personal disaster deserving 'tragic' handling and so making himself the apparent victim of his play, he found a particularly ingenious way of satirizing Walpole without incurring a Government ban. The amusing self-depreciation is at the same time a much more serious indictment of Walpole. Virtually the entire action of *The Damnation of Eurydice* is imbued with political significance, and Fielding sustains with considerable subtlety the connection between the theatrical narrative and the political meaning it carries.

Since taking over the New Haymarket, Fielding had become progressively more daring in his assaults on Walpole, and these culminated in Pillage's fall with its implied assumption that Walpole was about to follow suit. Fielding must have realized that he was on a collision course with Walpole, but it is unlikely that he was trying to see how far he could go without provoking the Government to take measures against him, and it is even more unlikely that he was actually goading the Government into action. The degree of confidence with which he steered his course in 1737 suggests that he genuinely shared the Opposition belief that Walpole's days of power were numbered. Furthermore, he probably believed that Walpole would not risk regulating the theatres for fear of provoking severe repercussions, especially from those who shared Fielding's view that any curtailment of free speech was a threat to liberty itself. Fielding was wrong. Walpole survived to turn the tables on Fielding with the Licensing Act. The supreme irony is that Fielding had unwittingly forecast his own fate, not that of Walpole. Fielding's ingenuity rebounded against himself; it was Pillage as Fielding who really 'fell', not Pillage as Walpole.[6]

NOTES
1. See William Peterson, 'Satire in Fielding's *An Interlude between Jupiter, Juno, Apollo, and Mercury*', *Modern Language Notes* 65 (1950) 200-2.
2. Quotations from *The Historical Register* and *Eurydice Hiss'd* are taken from William W. Appleton's combined edition of the two plays (London, 1968). Although *The Historical Register* is not included in Trussler's *Burlesque Plays of the Eighteenth Century*, it is included in a parallel anthology, *Eighteenth Century Drama: Afterpieces*, ed. Richard W. Bevis (London, 1970).
3. In addition to the discussions of the play in Appleton's edition and in Cross, *The History of Henry Fielding*, I, 200-16, and Dudden, *Henry Fielding*, I, 194-201, see Charles W. Nichols, 'Fielding and the Cibbers', *Philological Quarterly 1* (1922) 278-89, and his 'Social Satire in Fielding's *Pasquin* and *The Historical Register*', *Philological Quarterly 3* (1924) 309-17.
4. Two short mock tragedies published in 1736 about the new Gin Act, which Fielding refers to in *Tumble-Down Dick* and *Eurydice*, also exploit the methods of burlesque for largely non-burlesque ends. *The Deposing and Death of Queen Gin* by 'Jack Juniper' and *The Fall of Bob; or, The Oracle of Gin* by 'Timothy Scrubb' (John Kelly) treat the Gin Act, which was intended to reduce substantially the consumption of the spirit, in a mock-heroic way as a national disaster of tragic proportions. Although the use of a high style for an undignified subject does create some burlesque of the rhetoric of contemporary tragedy, this is secondary to the topical anti-Government satire, especially in the more complex *The Fall of Bob*. With its survey of moral corruption in Walpole's England, this social and political satire follows in the footsteps of *Pasquin*. As the main title of the play indicates, the controversy surrounding the Gin Act provided an excellent opportunity for

pillorying Walpole and for blaming his Ministry for the ills of society.
5. See Charles B. Woods, 'Notes on Three of Fielding's Plays', *Publications of the Modern Language Association of America* 52 (1937) 368-73.
6. Three plays produced during the same months as *Eurydice, The Historical Register,* and *Eurydice Hiss'd* (February-April 1736) contain satire of the theatre similar to that in several of Fielding's plays of the 1730s, and the author of one of these, Robert Baker, acknowledges his debt to Fielding by describing his rehearsal play, *The Mad-House,* as being 'After the Manner of Pasquin'. Baker's afterpiece is not a burlesque but is notable for its jibes at pantomime and rope dancing. At the end, the critical commentator, Satyre, suggests that the inner play would be more fashionable and successful if the author Friendly 'had work'd up these Characters into a Pantomime, and introduced it under the Character of *Harlequin Mad-doctor'* (II, xii) instead of sticking to ballad opera. Francis Lynch's *The Independent Patriot; or, Musical Folly* is neither a rehearsal play nor a burlesque afterpiece but a satirical comedy attacking the modish affectations of fashionable society, especially the cult of all things Italian and French. 'The reigning Taste's all *Italian*', complains Medium, thinking particularly of opera: 'Musick has ingross'd the Attention of the whole People: The Dutchess and her Woman, the Duke and his Postilion, are equally infected – The Contagion first took Root in the shallow Noddles of such of our itinerant Coxcombs as were incapable of more virtuous Impressions' (I, i). As in the cases of *The Mad-House* and *The Independent Patriot,* there is no burlesque in the anonymous afterpiece *The Author's Triumph; or, The Manager Manag'd,* but it resembles *The Author's Farce, Pasquin,* and *The Historical Register* in its criticisms of Colley Cibber, theatre managers, and audiences. According to Tatter, the theatre has become so degraded that the public prefer performing animals to serious plays, an accusation repeated when the Manager and the actors are shown to be antagonistic to dramatists. The Manager, who is more interested in acrobats, dancers, and animals than in plays, tells the playwright Dramatick: 'If you cou'd bark, Friend, or dance the Ladder-dance, I might talk with you.' Cibber is ridiculed in his role of Poet Laureate by Tatter: 'No, no – the Laureat isn't dead – but the Poet is – Why we have had no Poet Laureat these many Years, Sir – We have, indeed, a Prose Laureat – A Bombast Laureat – A Laureat that rhymes, as School-Boys ring, without Harmony, or Order.'

Conclusion

If *The Historical Register* and *Eurydice Hiss'd* had not been so successful, the Government could have ignored them; but the popularity of the plays, containing the most audacious political satire that had ever appeared on the English stage, forced the Government to reply. An article in *The Daily Gazetteer* on 7 May 1737, possibly by a senior member of Walpole's administration, severely censured Fielding for misrepresenting the Government and for damaging the reputation of England in the eyes of the world. It also warned him that his vitriolic personal and political satire could not be allowed to continue. This article made it clear that the Government now regarded Fielding as an intolerable nuisance. Five days later Fielding published the two plays with a preliminary essay called 'Dedication to the Public'. In this he mischievously claims that it is he who has been misrepresented and misunderstood; his plays, he argues, were meant to be pro-Walpole propaganda, not the opposite. Writing in a profoundly ironic vein, he continues the exposure made in the plays themselves of the corruption to be found in the theatrical and political life of the time. On 21 May the Opposition newspaper *Common Sense* published a properly argued reply by 'Pasquin' (presumably Fielding) to the article in *The Daily Gazetteer*, but by then Walpole was taking steps to silence Fielding by legislating against the non-patent theatres.

The specific pretext for the Licensing Act was an anonymous play called *The Golden Rump*, which was neither published nor performed. This was based on 'The Vision of the Golden Rump', a particularly outrageous piece of anti-Walpole journalism which appeared in *Common Sense* in March. In May the play was offered to Henry Giffard for production at Lincoln's Inn Fields, but he showed it to Walpole who paid him generously for the manuscript. Walpole could not have acquired this supposedly obscene, libellous, and seditious play at a more opportune moment. The controversy over *The Historical Register* and *Eurydice Hiss'd* was at its height, and the Government may well have been looking for an excuse to put an end to political satire on the stage. Walpole's handling of events after purchasing the text of *The Golden Rump* reveals his tactical cleverness as a politician. On 24 May, when the parliamentary session was drawing to a close, he introduced a Bill to amend the Vagrancy Act of 1713 and steered it through both Houses in a couple of weeks. The main proposals of the Bill were to close the non-patent theatres in London and to ensure that in future all plays intended for production were licensed beforehand by the Lord Chamberlain. The ostensible reason for the Bill was to protect public morality from abuse in the theatre, but the real reason was to put an end to ridicule of Walpole and his Government on the stage. The Bill became law on 21 June, and three days later the three unlicensed theatres, including the New Haymarket, were closed. Fielding's career as a dramatist and theatre manager was over.

The severity and suddenness of Walpole's measures almost certainly took Fielding by surprise; he was shot down in full flight as a man of the theatre. Although Fielding had done more than anyone else to provoke the Licensing Act, he made no public pronouncement about it and seems to have accepted it with resignation as a *fait accompli*. He could have continued to write for the stage, but with the new regulations in force he would have had to work under restrictions obviously unacceptable to him. Rather than turn out innocuous comedies, farces, ballad operas, or even orthodox burlesques, he wisely decided to abandon the theatre altogether. Whereas in the first half of his career as a playwright he was particularly interested in burlesquing contemporary drama and attacking the condition of the theatre, in the last two years of that career he concentrated on dramatic satires, adapting the rehearsal form for non-burlesque ends so as to widen the scope of his critical scrutiny. But it was precisely that wider scrutiny, especially of politics, that the Licensing Act was designed to prohibit. Three previously unperformed plays of his, *Miss Lucy in Town*, *The Wedding-Day*, and *The Good-Natured Man*, were staged after the Licensing Act, but these were largely written before 1737.

After the Licensing Act, Fielding temporarily suppressed his literary aspirations, and for two years devoted himself wholeheartedly to studying law at the Middle Temple. Then in November 1739 he launched his own periodical, *The Champion; or, British Mercury*, and ran it for eighteen months before handing over the editorship to his old friend James Ralph. A year later, in November 1740, Samuel Richardson's *Pamela; or, Virtue Rewarded* was published anonymously. This novel was an immediate success, but despite its immense popularity a few critics protested that Richardson's heroine was not the embodiment of virtue she was intended to be, but an arch-hypocrite and the embodiment of pretence to virtue. Fielding shared this view, and in *An Apology for the Life of Mrs Shamela Andrews*, which appeared in April 1741 as the work of 'Conny Keyber', wrote a devastating burlesque of Richardson's novel in which he set out to reveal the true nature of Pamela. Fielding applied the technique of satirical burlesque he had previously used against contemporary drama to a contemporary novel, but his purpose was rather different in that his principal target in *Shamela* was Richardson's morality, not the novel form as such, nor the epistolary method, nor even Richardson's style. *Shamela* is one of the finest prose burlesques in the language, but it evidently satisfied only Fielding's immediate desire to ridicule the sentimentality and spurious values he found in *Pamela*. After completing *Shamela* he began work on a totally different and much more complete reply to *Pamela*, one which not only satirized Richardson's novel but also presented an alternative ethical code. This time, Fielding did not answer Richardson with a skit but with his own kind of novel, the comic epic in prose, *Joseph Andrews*. Thanks to Richardson, oddly enough, Fielding had found his literary forte.

Although the Licensing Act brought an end to political satire on the stage, it had no effect on non-political rehearsal and burlesque plays. These continued to be written and produced, but in the fifty years after the Licensing Act only Sheridan's *The Critic* can be classed with the work of Buckingham, Gay, and Fielding. By 1737 the great period of English satiric writing that had begun in the middle of the preceding century was drawing to a close; Pope died in 1744 and Swift in 1745. Not surprisingly, most of the masterpieces of English burlesque drama belong to this period. Broadly speaking, there is a softening of dramatic burlesque in the second half of the eighteenth century so that it loses its satirical bite and pales into light-hearted, farcical entertainment. The extravaganza, which is burlesque or even nonsense for its own sake rather than for the sake of exposing contemporary dramatic weaknesses and absurdities, is usually associated with the nineteenth century, but its development from satirical burlesque can be traced in the eighteenth century. As has been pointed out in the chapter on *The Tragedy of Tragedies*, Fielding's burlesque displays an extreme exuberance and exaggeration that is amusing in itself, although it is of course parodic and satiric. If *The Tragedy of Tragedies* points forward to the extravaganza, a play it influenced considerably, Carey's *Chrononhotonthologos* (first produced as an afterpiece in February 1734), does so even more. Carey's play, 'The Most Tragical Tragedy, That ever was Tragediz'd by any Company of Tragedians', is the outstanding burlesque of the 1730s not by Fielding, but is more extravagant and nonsensical than *The Tragedy of Tragedies*, as well as being much less closely related to the heroic tragedies it burlesques. If the names of some of Fielding's characters seem absurd, those of Carey's characters are doubly so. The eponymous hero's name is more than a mouthful but at least it does not occupy an entire decasyllabic line like the name of the courtier Aldiborontiphoscophornio. Carey actually published his 'tragedy' as the work of 'Benjamin Bounce', an altogether more flippant pseudonym than Fielding's 'Scriblerus Secundus', and incorporated almost surreal acrobatics by having the King of the Antipodeans walk on his hands and wear his crown on his feet. Typical of Carey's burlesque bombast is General Bombardinion's greeting when he is visited by King Chrononhotonthologos:

> This Honour, Royal Sir! so Royalizes
> The Royalty of your most Royal Actions,
> The Dumb can only utter forth your praise;
> For we, who speak, want Words to tell our meaning.

Carey indulges himself to the full in the comic possibilities of his super-inflated idiom, but because heroic tragedy was still a living form and because Carey keeps one eye on it even at his most farcical, his play does possess a satirical backbone that prevents it from degenerating into a trivial farce. Without that backbone, Carey's flamboyant method would result in uncritical extravaganzas, and this is precisely what happened. *Chrononhotonthologos* remained popular for a long time, outliving heroic tragedy on the stage, and it therefore exerted a strong influence on the subsequent development of burlesque drama, especially its debilitated nineteenth-century form.[1]

With Fielding, the significance of Restoration and Augustan dramatic burlesque becomes clear. The satirical burlesques of Buckingham, Gay, Fielding, and their lesser contemporaries amount to a critical analysis of most of the developments in drama after 1660 by writers concerned about the current state of the theatre. In general the burlesquers upheld the neoclassical principle that the purpose of drama was to instruct and divert, indeed to instruct by diverting. Consequently they deplored the attitudes of playgoers who treated the theatres merely as places of fashionable entertainment and of theatre managers and playwrights who were content to satisfy the taste of the town regardless of standards. Dramatic forms that seemed to offer nothing but mindless and escapist spectacle, such as pantomime and Italian opera, were obvious targets for the defenders of Reason, Nature, and Good Sense, but the more intellectually respectable forms of tragedy and comedy also came under fire, and this is more interesting because it points to a decline in the principal genres themselves. Buckingham exposed the essential artificiality of the Restoration heroic play, and Gay and Fielding burlesqued most subsequent developments in tragic drama because they recognized their essential artificiality. With the exception of Lillo's bourgeois tragedy in the 1730s, which escaped ridicule, much Augustan tragedy was not in touch with reality and did not present credible human emotions. Even in the more domestic and sentimental plays, there is often the same straining after sublimity that epitomizes pseudo-classical and heroic tragedies, and as Pope demonstrates in *Peri Bathous* his contemporaries frequently mistook the bathetic for the sublime. It is significant that Fielding, though a very prolific dramatist, never attempted tragedy, not even the bourgeois tragedy he approved of and defended.

One of the parodoxes of English literary history is that the period when neoclassicism exerted its strongest influence and when writers felt an obligation to rise to the two highest literary forms in the neoclassical classification of genres, epic and tragedy, proved to be largely inimical to the successful realization of either. If they are to succeed, epic and tragedy, like other art forms, cannot be created by an act of will regardless of cultural context. They become genuine artistic possibilities only when the cultural environment is propitious for their development, and the demythologizing and rationalistic intellectual milieu of Restoration and Augustan England, influenced by Royal Society empiricism and Lockeian 'enlightenment', was not favourable to the creation of orthodox epic or tragedy. Consequently, and again paradoxically, the greatest Augustan 'epic' poem is Pope's gloomily satirical mock epic or inverted epic *The Dunciad,* and two of the other major 'epic' achievements of the period are realistic novels, Fielding's 'comic epic-poem in prose' *Tom Jones* and Richardson's 'domestic epic' *Clarissa.* Mock epic, like the burgeoning novel, corresponded to the Augustan emphasis on society and on man's position within and obligations to society. The transformation of epic into mock epic and of tragedy into mock tragedy was almost inevitable in an age deeply concerned with these forms though much less attuned to their creation than to the development of satire. The tragic vision of life could no longer be adequately transmitted through the direct medium of tragic drama, as had been possible in Elizabethan and Jacobean England. It had to be recreated in new forms such as mock epic (*The Dunciad*) and prose fiction, whether novelistic (*Clarissa*) or fabulistic (*Gulliver's Travels*).

It has sometimes been argued that neoclassicism was responsible for the decline in tragedy after 1660, but the establishment of neoclassical standards and the consequent increase in literary polish, decorum, and propriety during the later seventeenth century cannot alone explain why Dryden's eloquent rewriting of *Antony and Cleopatra* in accordance with the 'unities' as *All for Love* (1677) should be so lacking in tragic feeling when compared with Shakespeare. *All for Love,* often regarded as the best Restoration tragedy, is a much tidier play than Shakespeare's, and although artistic tidiness is not in itself a fault, it does in this case (as in so many contemporary tragedies) go hand-in-hand with a rather simple opposition of love and honour that is totally different from the complexities and ambiguities of Shakespeare's play. And it is precisely the absence of these complexities and ambiguities, not the neoclassical structure as such, that is indicative of the lack of genuinely tragic vision in *All for Love* and in numerous lesser tragedies of the period. Otway's *Venice Preserv'd*, which is less rigidly neoclassical and more Elizabethan in tone than *All for Love*, and Rowe's *Jane Shore*, consciously 'Written in Imitation of Shakespear's Style', are two of the most powerful tragedies of the Restoration and Augustan theatre, but these too pale beside the early seventeenth-century masterpieces they are so obviously trying to emulate. It is symptomatic that the most self-conscious attempt to write great and sublime drama after the Restoration heroic play, Augustan pseudo-classical tragedy, which set out to recapture the power and grandeur of Greek tragedy by drawing on classical history and mythology, should be so static and stillborn. Plays such as Addison's *Cato*, Philips' *The Distrest Mother*, and Thomson's *Agamemnon* may aspire to an exalted purity of tragic experience and a timeless universality, but the familiar accusation that pseudo-classical tragedy is coldly intellectual rather than imaginative in conception and activated by didacticism rather than tragic emotion is largely valid. Gay's extremely topical *The Beggar's Opera* has proved to be much more universal than the would-be universal pseudo-classical tragedies of the time, partly because it is so ambiguous and multi-layered. John Loftis is undoubtedly right when he argues that

> Augustan tragedy is at best declamatory . . . We note and are repelled by an assurance of statement in Augustan tragedy, a positiveness that leaves little room for the uncertainties that are so prominent in human experience and hence in the greatest tragedies . . . The Enlightenment was notoriously an age of intellectual self-confidence; and the Lockeian political system that controlled tragedy after 1688 was a tidy system, encouraging an intellectual tidiness in the plays.[2]

The most exciting and certainly the most 'novelistic' development in tragic drama during this period is the bourgeois tragedy of George Lillo and his successors, such as Edward Moore. To some extent this is a development of pathetic tragedy, which became popular during the last two decades of the seventeenth century and itself looked back to Elizabethan domestic tragedy. In *The Orphan* (1680), the first of Otway's two important tragedies, the central theme is neither heroism nor the conflict between love and honour but disastrous love, and the main character, Monimia, is a woman, the first of many distressed heroines to appeal directly to the pity of audiences and readers. As the word 'pathetic' suggests, there is a fatal imbalance in such plays – fatal for tragedy – in that the emphasis is put on only one of the essential ingredients of tragedy so that pathos virtually becomes an end in itself. This represents the sentimentalizing of tragedy, and therefore its impoverishment, but pathetic tragedy also marks a domesticating and democratizing of the genre, a process Lillo continued in a more radical way. What, with the benefit of hindsight, can be called the 'novelistic' tendencies in pathetic tragedy are most obvious in some of Rowe's 'she-tragedies' in the early eighteenth century, in which there is a sense of strain between form and content. Rowe adheres to orthodox neoclassical structuring, with its great compression and heightening of effect, but in some ways his aims seem to be those of 'novelistic' psychological realism: a detailed realistic examination of individuals under domestic, social, and moral stress. It is interesting to note that Richardson's *Clarissa* resembles Rowe's 'she-tragedies' in several ways. The pathos surrounding Clarissa herself and Rowe's heroines is similar, and Lovelace in the novel was partly modelled on Lothario in *The Fair Penitent*, but Richardson's convincing study is an artistic triumph because he found in the epistolary novel an excellent literary vehicle for minutely exploring human behaviour and psychology in its everyday context.

The tension between tragic form and 'novelistic' subject matter is even more striking in the subsequent development of domestic tragedy, Lillo's bourgeois tragedy itself. Obvious as the many weaknesses of his seminal *The London Merchant* (1731) are today, Lillo's work was in its way revolutionary, which is why it exerted so powerful an influence. By making a middle-class apprentice, George Barnwell, its hero, Lillo was the first dramatist since the Restoration to violate the neoclassical dogma that only high-born characters could be tragic protagonists. For Lillo, the merchant class, now rapidly increasing in economic power and social prestige, was worthy of the highest literary forms. But were the highest literary forms of the Augustans the most appropriate vehicles for Lillo's purposes? Plays like *The London Merchant* do try to investigate seriously the actualities of bourgeois life, the moral problems affecting the rising middle classes, and the psychology and behaviour of individuals, but they do so within a framework of tragic drama inherited from the preceding century and suited to other aims. Lillo's themes really required the spacious, unhurried, and analytical treatment which the emerging novel was able to provide; or, if not that, a radically new dramatic form to match the newness of the subject. Lillo's artistic radicalism did not extend that far, and admirable as his pioneering attempt to expand tragedy was, his adherence to tragic conventions was constricting and inhibiting rather than liberating.

If Augustan domestic tragedy was moving towards the *drame* or problem play and, even more significantly, towards the novel, so was the more serious variety of contemporary comedy. Lillo's *The London Merchant* and Steele's equally influential sentimental comedy

The Conscious Lovers (1722) can be linked without incongruity. By the time Fielding was active in the theatre, one important strand of comedy was abandoning the satirical tradition of seventeenth-century comedy, deriving from Jonson, and radically transforming the nature of the genre. Throughout the period 1660–1737, comedy rarely attracted the attention of burlesquers, but the decline of the Jonsonian tradition into farcical intrigue comedy (burlesqued in *Three Hours after Marriage*) ran side-by-side with the development of the Restoration comedy of 'wit' or 'manners'. Indeed, the establishment of farce as an independent form on the English stage dates from the end of the seventeenth century, especially with the advent of the afterpiece as a standard theatrical offering; farce was the principal form of afterpiece for many years and subsequently continued to hold the stage alongside pantomime.

The emergence of sentimental comedy was one of the most important dramatic developments of the period and a symptom of far-reaching changes in society as a whole, just as the emergence of bourgeois tragedy was. As John Loftis argues, 'comedy could not record the society of the late seventeenth and early eighteenth centuries without itself undergoing changes so pronounced as to constitute the extinction of the Restoration tradition, if we think of that tradition as concentrating upon wittily ironic social criticism and the interactions of a group of traditional characters, character relationships, and plot situations'.[3] The emphasis in comedy gradually moved away from the exposure and ridicule of folly to the presentation of exemplary characters. After 1688, the theatre was subjected to moralistic criticism because of its reputed immorality, and although playwrights answered these criticisms, comedy was in transition towards moral propriety and decency even in the 1690s. The traditional moral function of comedy, of bringing people to an awareness of their foibles, follies, and vanities by making them laugh at those of others, was gradually giving way to an attempt to inculcate moral values and induce high standards of behaviour by appealing to the emotions with examples of admirable conduct. Plays like that quintessence of sentimental comedy, *The Conscious Lovers*, therefore embody the ethical core of sentimentalism, its ideas about the fundamental goodness and benevolence of the human heart (as opposed to head).

If *The London Merchant* is revolutionary, so is Steele's play. Like Lillo, Steele deals seriously with current social issues, especially those concerning the merchant class, so that *The Conscious Lovers* 'is in a special sense a comedy of ideas, of ideas that in dramatic form were in 1722 fresh and new', as John Loftis claims.[4] But by manipulating the medium of comedy for the sake of moral doctrine and middle-class propaganda, however high-minded, Steele and his followers throughout the eighteenth century paralysed themselves artistically. In his attempt to be true to the best in contemporary bourgeois life, Steele was aiming at a greater emotional and psychological realism than the stylization of orthodox comedy permits. Yet to take an obvious example, the famous recognition scene at the end of *The Conscious Lovers*, in which Sealand and his long-lost daughter Indiana are reunited with histrionic outbursts of paternal and filial devotion, is so manifestly sentimental that it lacks conviction, even though Steele tries to render their meeting credible by prolonged treatment. The credibility he obtains, like that of the scenes of contrition and reformation discussed by Arthur Sherbo, 'is not the credibility of real life; it is rather a concocted credibility that belongs in the fundamentally artificial world of sentimental drama'.[5] It is not altogether surprising that Steele's recognition scene soon attracted the attention of burlesque writers, including Fielding in *The Author's Farce*. Nevertheless, beneath the sententiousness, emotionalism, and didacticism of sentimental comedy can be found a genuine endeavour to trace the psychological processes of the individual consciousness and to analyse social and familial relationships. As in bourgeois tragedy, the subject matter is 'novelistic', but once again there is a clash between form and content. John Loftis' observation that in the early eighteenth century 'there appears in drama what we may in retrospect call a novelistic drift, a movement away from formalization in plots, characterization, and dialogue'[6] is shrewd, but even though sentimental comedy may have been struggling against the dramatic conventions it derived from seventeenth-century comedy, it was still severely hampered by them.

To illustrate this, it is worth returning to a play by Fielding himself, his social-problem comedy, *The Modern Husband*, which is very different from his earlier Restoration-style comedies and which in 1732 he regarded as by far his most important work to date. In this essentially serious play, Fielding deals very realistically with fashionable society in London in order to expose what he thought to be the widespread vice of selling one's wife's favours to wealthy men for considerable financial reward. Although unlike *The Conscious Lovers* in a number of ways, *The Modern Husband* has much more in common with it than with conventional comedy. What makes Fielding's play so interesting is that it anticipates both the London scenes in the final part of *Tom Jones* and more particularly his last novel, *Amelia*; but in terms of artistic success there is no comparison, and it is not enough to assert that Fielding was much more mature and skilful by the time he wrote his novels. As Fielding's two major critical biographers, Wilbur L. Cross and F. Homes Dudden, and other commentators, including Laura Brown,[7] have pointed out, the novel is a much more satisfactory vehicle for his purposes. Although consciously departing from traditional conceptions of comedy, Fielding's adoption of the framework of comic drama acted as a straitjacket on his material and aims, which required the more leisurely and discursive treatment possible in prose fiction. As a result there is a tension between the demands of dramatic convention and Fielding's desire to examine his characters in some depth and to present a convincing picture of the activities and behaviour of contemporary high society. The play falls between two stools. It is indicative that the names of the characters, such as Lord Richly, Mr Bellamant, Mr Modern, and Lady Gaywit, are exactly what one would expect in an orthodox comedy, although Fielding is endeavouring to portray accurately the psychology of individuals. The outcome of the play is happy, as the conventions of comedy as well as the sentimental ethic demand, with the characters receiving their just deserts; but such an ending seems arbitrary, too easy a resolution of the moral dilemmas presented in the play. Dudden rightly observes that 'with a few small alterations, this strangely sombre comedy might easily be converted into a tragedy'.[8] The conventional dénouement is false to the substance of the play because it virtually obliterates the sense of potential tragedy present throughout. Dramatic form itself necessitates a high degree of compression and selection that suits traditional comedy, but drives Fielding and writers of sentimental comedy into sententious melodrama. The need for strong dramatic situations conflicts with the attempt to present personal relations and social conduct realistically. *The Modern Husband* epitomizes the way in which sentimental comedy really is, as that oxymoronic term suggests, an artistic contradiction. Sentimental comedy is an expression of the bourgeois culture emerging in the late seventeenth and early eighteenth centuries, but, as Lionel Stevenson asserts, it is the novel that is, *par excellence,* 'the literary medium of a bourgeois culture'.[9] Fielding was very fortunate in that the publication of *Pamela* following so closely on his expulsion from the theatre helped him to find the vehicle that he needed to fulfil his serious literary aspirations, the novel.

Yet this is inevitably a retrospective judgment. It is at least possible to speculate about what might have happened if the Licensing Act had not been passed. There can be no doubt that this Act had a stifling effect on the development of English drama, since its censorship provisions ensured that the two patent theatres would take an even more cautious and conservative line in future than they had done in the past. Before the passing of the Act, the 1730s had proved to be a relatively exciting, innovatory, and experimental decade in the theatre, and as playwright and theatre manager Fielding was more responsible than any other single person for this revitalization. In tragedy there was the advent of middle-class domestic tragedy with Lillo's *The London Merchant* and *Fatal Curiosity,* and in comedy there was the appearance of the serious, quasi-Shavian problem play with Fielding's own *The Modern Husband* and *The Universal Gallant*; while dramatic satire, deriving from the burlesque tradition and *The Beggar's Opera* in particular, and again mainly associated with Fielding, came into its own for a very brief period. It is tempting to think that but for the Licensing Act this new dramatic vitality would have attracted all sorts of talent, in the way that happened in England in the late 1950s. Perhaps gifted writers would have developed domestic tragedy and the social-problem play in Ibsenite and Shavian directions, and perhaps Fielding or someone else would have produced a dramatic equivalent of *Gulliver's Travels* or *The Dunciad*.

There has certainly been a tendency in recent scholarship to see the Licensing Act as a kind of execution of fruitful developments in drama just when they were likely to mature. Without the Licensing Act the history of English drama and literature might have been substantially different, with drama becoming more realistic and novelistic, and the novel not maturing nearly as quickly as it did. The Licensing Act undoubtedly had the effect of channelling literary talent towards the new form of the novel and away from the theatre. Fielding is the outstanding and trend-setting example, but other major prose writers might have developed differently in different circumstances. Smollett was a playwright as well as a novelist, but his great creative effort went into his novels, while Goldsmith, who eventually revealed himself to be a born dramatist, did not write for the stage until the last few years of his life. On the other hand, the cultural situation in the middle of the century, with a rapidly increasing reading public, was ripe for the flowering of the novel, as Ian Watt has shown in *The Rise of the Novel*. The novel had the great advantage of being new and therefore free from the inhibiting conventions that traditional dramatic forms, especially tragedy and comedy, were unable to slough off. Whenever promise is cut short, there is a natural human tendency to exaggerate the promise as though to compensate for the loss; and because the Licensing Act did deal a blow to promising dramatic developments, it is possible to imagine that these might have led to dramatic works of the stature of *Tom Jones, Clarissa, Peregrine Pickle,* and *Tristram Shandy*.

Nevertheless, the kind of artistic radicalism needed to present adequately 'novelistic' material was almost inseparable from the burgeoning novel, whereas even writers as gifted as Lillo and Fielding were finding it hard to adapt the structures of tragedy and comedy, which they inevitably employed, to suit their subjects. Without the Licensing Act, the novel would have flourished, although the drama of the middle of the century would probably have been much more interesting than it is. Without the Licensing Act, Fielding's career would have been different, but not necessarily all that different. *Pamela* might still have spurred him into prose replies rather than dramatic ones. As several scholars, notably J. Paul Hunter, have argued, there is a sense of strain in Fielding's later plays indicating his dissatisfaction with the nature of the genre in which he was working. The use of a rehearsal framework in his last five plays, involving an intermediary or intermediaries between action and audience, suggests that Fielding was developing a narrative as opposed to a dramatic form of art:

> He seems to be resisting the dramatic mode and moving toward forms that could more readily accommodate extreme degrees of artistic self-consciousness in its two main thrusts – concern with the process of creation and with the nature of response. Fielding's separation from the theater was a forced one, but the expulsion was fortunate, freeing him from a relationship and commitment that had always been in some sense against the grain.[10]

Deplorable as its effects were on drama, the Licensing Act occurred at an opportune moment as far as Fielding's own artistic development was concerned, precipitating a change that might otherwise have been much more protracted and painful.

NOTES

1. For a more detailed discussion of the play, see my 'Henry Carey's *Chrononhotonthologos*', *Yearbook of English Studies* 4 (1974) 129-39.
2. *The Politics of Drama in Augustan England*, 160.
3. *Comedy and Society from Congreve to Fielding* (Stanford, 1959) 3.
4. *Ibid.*, 83.
5. *English Sentimental Drama* (East Lansing, Mich., 1957) 35.
6. *The Politics of Drama in Augustan England*, 152.
7. In her essay in generic history, *English Dramatic Form, 1660-1760* (New Haven and London, 1981), Laura Brown develops a thesis about the decline of drama and the rise of the novel that is particularly relevant to the present study, although she does not discuss burlesque drama, even in the chapters concerning Fielding.
8. *Henry Fielding*, I, 103.
9. *The English Novel, A Panorama* (London, 1960) 9.
10. J. Paul Hunter, *Occasional Form*, 69.

Index

Addison, Joseph, 113
   opera as threat to English art, 24, 61-2
   Cato, 38, 48, 112, 181, 208
afterpieces, 7-9, 156
   masques, 25
Amelia, 178, 211
Apology for the Life of Mrs Shamela Andrews, An, 204-5
Arrowsmith, Joseph, 12
Aubert, Mrs, *Harlequin-Hydaspes*, 33, 62
audience preferred entertainment to improvement, 4, 8, 161-4
   deplored by serious writers, 61-2, 131-3, 202n6, 206; 'puppet show' description used by Fielding, 94
Author's Farce, The, 6, 86-110, 211

ballad operas, 8, 73, 107
   form created by Gay, 60-2
Banks, John, *The Unhappy Favourite*, 46-8, 123; *The Albion Queens*, 50; *Vertue Betray'd*, 123
Bayes, 12, 19-20
   figure used as model, 12; Fustian, 154-5; Machine, 159; Marplay Junior, 91; Marsilia, 24; Medley, 187; Semibreve, 25; Spatter, 193-4; Trapwit, 152-3
Beaumont, Francis, 2
Bentley, Richard, 113, 114, 116
booksellers, attacked by Fielding, 87, 97
   see also Curll, Edmund
Breval, John Durant, 5, 54
   The Rape of Helen, 6, 82; compared with *Eurydice*, 182-3
British Stage, The (anon), 163-4, Pl.16
Buckingham, George Villiers, Second Duke of, *The Rehearsal*, 6, 9, 11-23, 171
   compared to *Tumble-Down Dick*, 179
   compared to *The What D'Ye Call It* (Gay), 40-1, 43
   title used in pamphlet war, 23n1
   The Tragedy of Tragedies as direct heir, 112
   see also intermediaries
burlesque, situational, 55, 102, 120-21
   in *The Rehearsal* (Buckingham), 16-18
burlesque, verbal, 16, 98, 117, 120, 149
   bombast, 124-6, 131, 140-42, 170-71, 197-9
   brevity suits, 8-9, 28-9
   Fielding's use of simile, 122-4, 129-30, 140, 147-8
   mock-heroic, 32, 40, 138
   questions, 138
   significant absence, 54-5
   see also death-, farewell-, love-scenes, parodied; simile arias
burlesque, visual, *see* stage presentation
burlesques, 2-9, 10n3, 201-2n4
   ballad opera as vehicle, 61-62
   good, definition, 14-15
   origins, 11-12, 24-5
   real characters, created by irony, 42, 65
   twentieth century classification, 33-4
Butler, Samuel, 3

career in theatre, Fielding's
   concluded, 181, 203-4
   see also New Haymarket Theatre
Carey, Henry, 82-3
   Chrononhotonthologos, 6, 205-6, Pl.21

Index

caricatures, 55, 111, 188
  as dramatic technique, 11
  British Army, 181
  in Fielding's Puppet Show, 96
  of dramatists, 19, 25
  of Royal Family, 128, 185
  see also Cibber, Colley and Walpole, Sir Robert
Champion, The, 204
children, introduced at critical moment, 49
Cibber, Colley, 83-4, 89-93, 111
  actor, 57
  attacked by Fielding, 96-7, 109n6, 152, 202n6; in *The Historical Register*, 190-3
  bad English, 99
  plays, 25, 35, 46
  The Rival Queans, 31-2, 53
Cibber, Theophilus, 31, 90-3, 150, 191
  'Pistol' his favourite role, 177, Pl.17
classical tragedy, 207
classical stories travestied, 4-5, 36; in *Achilles* (Gay), 76-82; in *Eurydice*, 181-3; in *Jupiter's Descent on Earth*, 186
Cock, Christopher, 189
Coffee-House Politician, The, 104, 177
Collier, Jeremy, 34
comedy, burlesqued, 7, 33-5, 206
  by Fielding, 1, 88
  in *Three Hours after Marriage* (Gay), 54, 57-60
  see also sentimentalism
commedia dell'arte, 179n4
  drawn on, 8, 33, 54, 161
Congreve, William, 38, 52, 57
Cooke, Thomas
  The Battle of the Poets, 111
  Penelope (with Mottley), 75-6, 167
Cotton, Charles, 3-4
Covent Garden Theatre, see Rich, John
Covent-Garden Tragedy, The, 32, 38, 135-49, 198
  poetic style, 6
critical studies of Fielding's drama, 9n1
Curll, Edmund, 93, 114

Daily Gazetteer, The, 187, 203
dances, intrusive, ridiculed, 18, 27, 97, 173-4
ballet, 69
Davenant, Sir William
  Macbeth, parodied by Duffett, 28
  The Playhouse To Be Let, 4, 9, 11, 26
death-scenes, parodied, 115, 122
  in *The Covent-Garden Tragedy*, 144-6
  in *Eurydice Hiss'd*, 199-200
  in *Pasquin*, 157
  in *The What D'Ye Call It* (Gay), 50-2
Dennis, John, 36-7, 55, 90
  treatment in *The Tragedy of Tragedies*, 111, 113, 114, 116
deus ex machina, 8, 17, 18, 34, 71
Don Quixote in England, 89, 151
Dorset Garden Theatre, 25-6, 30
dramatists, contemporary, satirized, 7, 19, 152, 192-3
  in *The Female Wits* (W.M.), 24
  in *The Welsh Opera*, 128-9
Drury Lane Theatre, 89-90, 156, 177, 197
Dryden, John, 38, 114
  and heroic plays, 13
  arranged supportive audience, 20, 196
  identified as Bayes, 11, 19-20, 179, 192
  All for Love, 44, 49, 51, 120, 207-8
  Cleomenes, 122-3
  The Conquest of Granada, 20-1, 171; Almanzor parodied, 15, 121
  Marriage A-la-Mode, 17
  Tyrannick Love imitated, 18, 37
Duffett, Thomas, 26-33
D'Urfey, Thomas, 12, 24, 165

emotional appeal, burlesqued, 44-7, 64, 69, 102
English Stage Italianiz'd, The (D'Urfey?), 165, 176
epilogues satirized, 104, 154
Estcourt, Richard, *Prunella*, 33, 61-2, 71
Eurydice, 181-5, 193-4
Eurydice Hiss'd, 193-200
extravaganzas, 117-19, 205

farce, 57, 121-1, 210
  in *Three Hours after Marriage* (Gay), 60
  mistaken identity, 77
  see also *Eurydice*

Index

farewell-scenes, parodied, 46-7, 184
Farquhar, George, *Love and a Bottle*, 33-4
Female Wits, The (W.M.), 12, 24, 35n1
Fleetwood, Charles, *see* Drury Lane Theatre
framing device, *see* play within a play

Gay, John, 36-85, 86,
    influence on Fielding, 136-41, 143, 145
    Achilles, 5, 75-82, 167, 182-3
    The Beggar's Opera, 60-75, 85n20-1, 178, 208, Pl.4, Pl.5; burlesque of Italian opera, 8-9, 100; dispute over roles, 191-3; resemblances to *The Author's Farce*, 95, 101-2; source for *The Grub-Street Opera*, 128-8
    The Mohocks, 36-8, 168
    Polly, 73-5, 78-9, 83
    The Rehearsal at Goatham, 82-3
    The Shepherd's Week, 41-2, 47, 51
    Three Hours after Marriage (with Pope and Arbuthnot), 54-60, 91, 102, 210
    The What D'Ye Call It, 6, 25, 38-54, 100
ghost scenes, 53, 112, 142-3
    in *Pasquin*, 154, 157-8
Gildon, Charles, 12, 25, 38
Gin Act (1736), 175-6, 201-2n4
Gods, mythological, satirized, 75, 82, 167-75, 186
Golden Rump, The (anon), 203, Pl.20
Grub Street, 87, 104, 108, 109n2, 128
Grub-Street Journal, The, 87, 148-9
Grub-Street Opera, The, 128-31

Handel, George Frederick, 61, 62, 67-70
Harlequin/Harlequinade, 98, 156, 179n5
    for extensive treatment, *see Tumble-Down Dick*
    see also commedia dell'arte
Heidegger, John, 61, 101, Pl.8
heroic drama, 13, 206-6
    attacked, in *The Rehearsal* (Buckingham), 13-14; in *The Tragedy of Tragedies*, 112-13, 118-19, 122-6; burlesqued, 7, 16-17, 20-2, 32; heroes, 66, 70-1, 74, 146

    see also Achilles (Gay)
Historical Register for the Year 1736, The, 187-92
Hogarth, William, 135, Pl.11
honour, 16, 79-81, 146-7
    in *The Tragedy of Tragedies*, 120-21
Howard, Sir Robert, 13

Idaspe (Mancini), 24-5, 32-3
intermediaries, 214
    in *The Author's Farce*, 95
    in *Euridice*, 181
    in *Eurydice Hiss'd*, 193
    in *The Historical Register*, 187-8
    in *Tumble-Down Dick*, 159, 167
    Johnson and Smith, dramatic function, 6, 14, 17, 21-2; figures copied, 25, 107-8
irony
    in *The Ballad Opera* (Gay), 64-6
    in *The Tragedy of Tragedies*, 113, 114, 116
    in *The What D'Ye Call It* (Gay), 38, 40, 42-4

Jack the Gyant-Killer (anon), 105, 107
Johnson, Samuel, of Cheshire, 89, 100, Pl.7
Joseph Andrews, 205
Jupiter's Descent on Earth, 186

King's Company, 10, 26, 31

Lee, Nathaniel, 38
    The Rival Queens, 31-2, 44, 53
letters, as dramatic technique, 57-8
Letter Writers, The, 112
Leveridge, Richard, 25
Licensing Act (1737), 7, 177, 203-4, 212
Lillo, George, 1, 206, 208
    Guilt Its Own Punishment, 187
    The London Merchant, 209-10, 212
    Silvia, travestied by Fielding, 130
lion character, 24, 25, 33
literary terms, 10n3,n4
Lottery, The, 131
love/honour conflict, *see* honour
Love in Several Masks, 86, 89
love-scenes, parodied
    in *The Author's Farce*, 88, 100
    in *The Beggar's Opera* (Gay), 60, 78
    in *The Covent-Garden Tragedy*, 139-44

Index

love-scenes, parodied – *contd.*
　in *Eurydice Hiss'd*, 198
　in *Pasquin*, 153
　in *The Tragedy of Tragedies*, 118-20
　parental devotion, 138

Manley, Mrs, 24
Marvell, Andrew, 23n1
mask, author's, 21, 39-40, 63-4
Milton, John, parodied by Gay, 37
Mock Doctor, The, 135
mock opera, 82-3
mock plays, *see* play within a play
Modern Husband, The, 1, 131-3, 178, 211-13
Mottley, John, and Cooke, Thomas, *Penelope*, 75-6, 167

neoclassicism, 3, 206-9
　conventions, 8, 36; nature, 22, 41-2, 64; time, 188, 196
New Haymarket Theatre, 150, 177, 186-7, Pl.6
novel, more suitable for theme than drama, 205, 207-9, 211-14, 214n7

Odingsells, Gabriel, *Bays's Opera*, 105-7
Old Debauchees, The, 135
Opera of Operas, The (Arne) (Lampe), 116
operas, Italian, 8, 32-3, 107, 206
　detail of burlesque by Gay, 60, 62-77
　English success, 61-2
　masques, 25
　prison scenes, 68, 69
　satirized, 5-6, 7, 24, 94; in *The Author's Farce*, 99-101; in *Eurydice*, 181-6
opera singers, 73, 99, 185, Pl.3
　Farinelli, 183, 189, Pl.18
　prima donnas, 98, 191-3; Cuzzoni and Bordoni rivalry, 61, 64, 68-9
　Senesino, Francesco, 61, 96
Otway, Thomas, 124, 208
　Venice Preserv'd, 38, 47, 49, 51; ghosts, 53

pantomime 8, 121, 179n4,n5, Pl.15
　Fielding's use of underworld, 95
　genre criticized, 98, 206; in *Bays's Opera* (Odingsells), 105
　for extensive treatment, see Tumble-Down Dick
Pasquin, 105, 150-59, 202n6, Pl.12, Pl.13
　relationship with *The Historical Register*, 187, 193
pedantry, ridiculed in *The Tragedy of Tragedies*, 111-16, 127
personal satire, 35, 187-8, 203
　see also caricatures
Philips, Ambrose
　The Distrest Mother, 45, 49, 208; victim of *The Covent-Garden Tragedy*, 38, 135-48
　Pastorals, 41-2, 51
Phillips, Katherine, 4
play within a play/rehearsal techniques, 5, 24-6, 214
　in *The Author's Farce*, 87, 93-103
　in *Bays's Opera* (Odingsells), 105-7
　in *Eurydice*, 181
　in *Eurydice Hiss'd*, 193-4
　in *The Fashionable Lady* (Ralph), 105-8
　in *The Historical Register*, 187-8
　in *Pasquin*, 151-2, 157
　in *The Tragedy of Tragedies*, 114
　in *Tumble-Down Dick*, 159, 167-9
　in *The What D'Ye Call It* (Gay), 40-4, 112
　for extensive treatment, see Buckingham, *The Rehearsal*
poetry
　burlesque methods, 3, 6, 56
　dramatic, 13-14, 115
　mock-heroic, 36-7, 98-9
politics
　Fielding's, 87
　satirized, ended by Licensing Act, 203-4; electoral malpractices, 151; in *The Author's Farce*, 98, 109-10n14; in *The Beggar's Opera* (Gay), 60, 65-6; in *Eurydice Hiss'd*, 194-201; in *The Historical Register*, 188-90; in *Pasquin*, 150, 159; in *The Rehearsal* (Buckingham), 13; in *The Tragedy of Tragedies*, 111, 127-8
　see also Walpole, Sir Robert
Pope, Alexander
　backed by *The Grub Street Journal*, 148
　caricatured, 25
　Scriblerus Club, 54, 55, 86-7

Pope, Alexander – *contd.*
  The Dunciad, 108, 136, 207; criticism of pantomime, 163; dramatised in *Pasquin,* 155; Fielding's influence, 87; his on Fielding, 95; possible 'heroes', 92, 96; society's decline, 89, 97, 159
  Peri Bathous, 86, 90, 207; Cibber's Preface guyed, 111; Fielding's bathos, 115
  The Rape of the Lock, 40, 194
Porter, Thomas, 17
Pritchard, William, *The Fall of Phaeton,* 166-75

Ralph, James, 111, 204
  Rape upon Rape, see The Coffee-House Politician
  The Fashionable Lady, 105-8
rehearsal techniques, *see* play with a play
reversal, sudden, 16-17, 50, 153
  in *The Author's Farce,* 101-2
  in *The Beggar's Opera* (Gay), 68, 69, 71-2
  in *The Covent-Garden Tragedy,* 146
  in *The Welsh Opera,* 130-1
  modified in *Pasquin,* 149
  see also deus ex machina
Rich, John, 159-66, 197, Pl.14
  as actor, 173; 'dog', 104, 156, 177, Pl.9
  mocked by Fielding, 96, 175, 179, 189
  plagiary, 176
Richardson, Samuel, 204-4
  Clarissa, 207, 209, 213
  Pamela, 212, 214
Rolli, Paolo Antonio, *Orpheus,* 182-4
Roving Husband Reclaim'd, The (anon), 33-4
Rowe, Nicholas,
  caricatured, 25
  his 'she-tragedies', in particular *The Fair Penitent,* and *Jane Shore,* drawn on, 209; in *The Covent-Garden Tragedy,* 144, 146; in *Three Hours after Marriage,* 58; in *The What D'Ye Call It* (Gay), 38, 44-9, 51
Royal Academy of Music, 61, 62

Scarron, Paul, 3-4

Scriblerus Club, 54, 55, 86-7, 101
self-portrait of Fielding, 187, 193-4
sentimentalism, 7, 47
  comedy, 34, 153, 209-12; dénouements, 101-4;
  tragedy, 32, 38; virtuous rejection parodied, 34; in *Achilles,* 77-8
  see also love
Settle, Elkanah, *The Empress of Morocco,* 26-8, Pl.2
sex reversal, 24, 27, 30
Shadwell, Thomas, plays, burlesqued by Duffett, 29-31
Shakespeare, William, 2, 126-7, 190-1
  plays drawn on: *Antony and Cleopatra,* 207; *Hamlet,* 2, 38, 126-7; *Julius Caesar,* 68; *King Henry VI,* parts II and III, 91; *King John,* 190; *King Lear,* 46; *Macbeth,* 53, 141; *Midsummer Night's Dream, A,* 2, 25, 43
Shaw, George Bernard, 1, 131
Sheridan, Richard Brinsley, *The Critic,* 12, 25, 43, 205
simile arias, 64, 67, 73
Smollett, Tobias, 213
society, satirized, 50, 210
  in *The Beggar's Opera* (Gay), 60, 65-7
  in *The Covent-Garden Tragedy,* 137-8
  in *Eurydice,* 185-6
  in *The Historical Register,* 188-90
  in Pasquin, 150, 151-2, 159
  in *Tumble-Down Dick,* 178
song
  Duffett's parody songs, 28
  in *The Beggar's Opera* (Gay), 63-4, 67, 69-70
  in *Polly,* 73-4
  irrelevance ridiculed, 18, 97
Southerne, Thomas, 38, 46-7
stage presentation, 53, 55, 119
  activity, gratuitous, 154
  battle scenes burlesqued, 158-9
  criticized in *The Rehearsal* (Buckingham), 17-19
  in *The Author's Farce,* 98
  in pantomime, 161-2, 174-5
  satirized by Duffett, 26-32
standards, fight against decline of traditional literary values, *see* the references under Pope, Alexander
Steele, Sir Richard, 32

Index

Steele, Sir Richard – *contd.*
   The Conscious Lovers, 101, 103, 209-11
Swift, Jonathan, 86, 113-14
   Gulliver's Travels, 55, 119, 207
   A Tale of a Tub, 18, 39, 40

Temple Beau, The, 86, 89
theatre, satirized, 107-8, 164, 179, 202n6
   in *The Author's Farce*, 87-8, 94, 97, 104
   in *The Historical Register*, 189-90
   in *Pasquin*, 156-9
theatre managers, 150
   attacked, 7, 187, 192-3; in *The Author's Farce*, 87-94, 104
Theobald, Lewis, 156, 173
Thurmond, John, 163-4, 176
Tom Thumb, see *The Tragedy of Tragedies*
Tom Jones, 211, 213
tragedy, 7, 34, 108-9, 206-9
   burlesqued, first by Gay, 38, 60; in *The Covent-Garden Tragedy*, 135, 149; in *The Tragedy of Tragedies*, 111-34
   form not attempted by Fielding, 1
   see also classical tragedy, death-scenes, farewell-scenes
Tragedy of Tragedies, The, 6, 111-34, 205, Pl.10
   origins, 11, 107, 108-9
Tumble-Down Dick, 5, 6, 25, 32, 159-80

Universal Gallant, The, 150, 213

Villiers, George, Second Duke of Buckingham, *see* Buckingham, George Villiers, Second Duke of

Walpole, Sir Robert, 150, 151, 178, 180n13, 201-2n4
   acted against Fielding, 203-4
   attacked, as Pillage in *Eurydice Hiss'd*, 195, 201; in *The Author's Farce*, 90, 98; in *The Historical Register*, 187-93
   caricatured, 83, 127-8
   Excise Bill, 195, Pl.19
   liaison with Maria Skerrett, 129-30, 198
   parallel with Macheath, 72
Weaver, John, 160-1
Welsh Opera, The, see *Grub-Street Opera, The*
Wilks, Robert, 89-90
Woodward, Henry, 192
Woodward, John, caricatured, 55
Wright, John, *Mock-Thyestes*, 4, 6, 26